Enchanting Bellamy

by

Cyril Hughes Hartmann

The smile of peace—the wildness of despair—
The soft'ning sigh—the soul-dissolving tear;
Each magic charm the boasted Oldfield knew
Enchanting Bellamy! revives in you.

CUNNINGHAM

WILLIAM HEINEMANN LTD
MELBOURNE :: LONDON :: TORONTO

FIRST PUBLISHED 1956

PRINTED IN GREAT BRITAIN
AT THE WINDMILL PRESS
KINGSWOOD, SURREY

To

MARGARET

ILLUSTRATIONS

The endpapers are from Hogarth's caricature of Rich's Triumphant Entry into Covent Garden Theatre

Introduction

In the Introductions to my recent books I have ventured to give my reasons for writing them. The explanation on this occasion may seem a trifle bizarre. The epithets most commonly bestowed on my former work by critics and reviewers have been 'accurate' and 'scholarly', usually in juxtaposition. I am far from ungrateful for these compliments, but there have been moments when I have felt some slight resentment at the, perhaps unintentional, implication of plodding industry with some admixture of weightiness, and I have longed to kick over the traces for once and write a book to which neither of these adjectives could properly be applied. Here it is.

Even now, it will, perhaps be wiser for me to give an 'accurate and scholarly' explanation why the book is both inaccurate and unscholarly. George Anne Bellamy, upon whose *Apology* any account of her life must be chiefly founded, is often wildly inaccurate, and it is not always possible to detect and correct her inaccuracies. And the book is unscholarly because I frankly admit that I have repeated, if with reservations, many of her tall stories, which I myself do not for a moment believe. It is true that the cloven hoof of the historian as *advocatus diaboli* may appear here and there, for I have felt impelled to try always to check her statements and have done my best to see that all the material I myself have introduced is authentic.

I would like to anticipate a possible criticism, already hinted at by a friend who asked me, in effect: "Why write the life of a woman who has already done it so admirably herself?" Apart from the fact that Mrs. Bellamy's *Apology* is, as I have pointed

ix   A*

out, extremely unreliable, it is also very long—six volumes—and not very easy to obtain. Students and scholars can, of course, find copies in such libraries as the British Museum, the Bodleian, the London Library, and the Garrick Club; but where is a member of the general reading public to find it? I myself had the greatest difficulty in procuring a copy. It is singular, by the way, that a book which speedily went through several editions should now be so rare.

An alternative would have been to produce a new edition of the *Apology*, but this would have entailed an elaborate paraphernalia of notes which would have over-weighted a book already too long. The modern reader needs explanations about many persons, places, things, and incidents, with which Mrs. Bellamy could, or, at any rate, did, assume that her readers at the time were familiar.

My book, then, is substantially Mrs. Bellamy's own story, selected and re-assembled from the dismantled sections of her *Apology* and re-written in the light of information derived from many other sources. I must ask such readers as are already acquainted with the *Apology* or are curious enough to have recourse to it to accept my version of the facts rather than Mrs. Bellamy's own where they differ, not necessarily because I may, perhaps, be more truthful and accurate than she was and have, moreover, no axe to grind, but simply because I have been able to consult many books of reference and sources of information that were not available to her. No doubt a great many of her mistakes, distortions, exaggerations, diminutions, and even deliberate inventions and mendacities still remain in my version, and the most I can claim is that I have tried to eradicate them and that I have frankly admitted it when I have been quite unable to resolve discrepancies between her narrative and known facts. I give due warning that the book as a whole should not be taken too seriously. It has diverted me to write it, and I hope it will divert others to read it.

The title is a quotation from a poem addressed to Mrs. Bellamy by the Scottish poet, John Cunningham. Whatever may have been his sentiments, the epithet is intended by me to apply only to her appearance, her personality, and her acting, which I truly believe to have been enchanting when she was in the bloom of her youth.

For their kind permission to reproduce portraits in their possession I have to thank Major Ryder (John Calcraft and Henry Fox), the Garrick Club (the Lindo portrait of Mrs. Bellamy), Mr. Ralph Brown (Garrick and Mrs. Bellamy in *Romeo and Juliet*), the National Gallery of Ireland (James Quin), and the National Portrait Gallery (Woodward). The other engravings come from my own collection. I very much regret that I have been unable to locate the present whereabouts of the portrait of Mrs. Bellamy by Francis Cotes, which belonged to Sir George Metham. I would also have wished to include pictures of Metham and West Digges, but I have failed to discover any portrait of the former, while the only likenesses available of Digges are a very poor little drawing of him as an old man in *Cato* by Roberts and a small engraving as , neither of which were worth reproducing.

Research for a book of this kind often leads one into unfamiliar by-ways, where one needs local guidance or special information, and in this connection I must acknowledge the valuable help I have received from Major Ryder of Rempstone, Colonel W. H. Carver, J.P., of North Cave, Captain Lindsay-Smith, of East Donyland Hall, Colonel Robert Gore-Browne, and several reverend gentlemen, both Anglican and Roman Catholic, whom I think I should not mention by name, but to whom I would like to record my gratitude.

CYRIL HUGHES HARTMANN.

Chapter One

AT THE AGE OF FOURTEEN little Miss Seal ran away from school
and placed herself under what was euphemistically known as
the 'protection' of the middle-aged Lord Tyrawley. The
young lady was the only child of a prosperous Quaker farmer
of Maidstone, who had made a fortune from his hop gardens
and invested the proceeds in real property, including the fine
estate of Mount Sion, in the neighbourhood of Tunbridge
Wells. Several years later he had died rather suddenly as the
result of a chill, and, as he had made no will, his entire property
had passed to his widow, who sold the farm at Maidstone and
settled at Tunbridge Wells, where she augmented her already
ample income by letting lodgings to people of quality during
the season. Being still young and good-looking, she did not
lack for suitors and presently gave her hand to an apparently
flourishing builder named Busby, whom she imprudently
married without giving a thought to securing any part of her
fortune for herself or making any provision for her four-year-
old daughter.

Among the persons of high rank who frequently occupied
Mrs. Busby's lodgings at Tunbridge Wells was Mrs. Godfrey,
sister of the great Duke of Marlborough. In her youth, as
Arabella Churchill, she had been the mistress of James, Duke
of York, afterwards King James II, and was the mother of the
famous Marshal-Duke of Berwick and three other children by
her royal lover. Later she had married Colonel Godfrey and
had two legitimate daughters by him. Since Mrs. Godfrey's
waiting-woman and trusted personal attendant was Busby's
daughter by his former marriage, for her sake she took an

I

interest in her landlady's family and, having conceived a fancy for Mrs. Busby's pretty little daughter, who was then about ten or twelve years old, offered to bring her up and have her well educated. In the belief that she herself could provide suitably for her child, Mrs. Busby at first declined this generous offer; but she did appreciate the social advantages of having Mrs. Godfrey as a patron and consented to her taking the little girl back to London with her for a few months. This must have been in 1722, for shortly after her arrival the Duke of Marlborough died, and she was taken by her step-sister to see the dead hero lying in state.

Meanwhile Mr. Busby had been getting into serious financial trouble, and his wife discovered that he had dissipated all her property. Now, therefore, she was only too pleased to accept Mrs. Godfrey's offer of help, and her daughter was placed in a fashionable boarding-school for young ladies in Queen Square, Westminster. Somehow or other, while she was there, she made the acquaintance of Lord Tyrawley, who became enamoured of her youthful charms. It was no difficult task for this brilliant and experienced man of the world to turn the little girl's head, and he soon persuaded her to elope with him.

James O'Hara, second Lord Tyrawley, was a man of some eminence in society. The only son of Charles O'Hara, first Lord Tyrawley, a distinguished soldier, he, too, had adopted the military profession. Entering the Royal Fusiliers as a lieutenant in 1703, he had fought all through the Spanish campaign; he was present at the siege of Barcelona and was wounded at the battle of Almanza, where his father commanded the left wing under Galway. Later he had fought in Flanders under Marlborough, and was again wounded at the battle of Malplaquet in 1709. In 1714 he followed his father as Colonel of the Royal Fusiliers. He was created Baron Kilmaine in the peerage of Ireland in 1722, and two years later succeeded to the English peerage of Tyrawley on his father's death.

His association with Miss Seal probably began about 1724

and seems to have lasted several years, during which time she bore him a son. He settled her in his apartments at Somerset House and openly lived with her there. It seems possible that he seduced her under promise of marriage, and he appears for a time at least to have allowed her to be known as Lady Tyrawley. But about 1727 he went over to Ireland, and, finding his affairs there in a very parlous state, came to the conclusion that the only possible way of straightening them out was to make an advantageous marriage. He fixed his choice on the Honourable Mary Stewart, daughter of Viscount Mountjoy. She was by no means handsome, but she had made no secret of her partiality for him, and Tyrawley believed that she would have a fortune of some £30,000 from her mother, the daughter and sole heiress of the wealthy Viscount Blessington.

Lord Mountjoy naturally made enquiries about his pro-spective son-in-law, and, having heard rumours about the existence at Somerset House of a lady who called herself Lady Tyrawley, wrote a polite letter to her asking her about the exact nature of her connexion with Lord Tyrawley and giving his reason for doing so. His letter arrived shortly after the birth of her son "when she was not quite recovered from the weakness attendant on a lying-in". Overcome with surprise and fury, Miss Seal incontinently sent Lord Mountjoy all the loving letters Tyrawley had been writing to her since he went o Ireland, including one she had received by the same post and had not even opened. In this her lover informed her of the distressed situation of his affairs and the consequent necessity for him to make a rich marriage. He swore that he would stay with his wife no longer than was necessary to secure her fortune and would then hasten back to his true love, who alone possessed his heart. He added that he had deliberately chosen Miss Stewart, who was both ugly and foolish, so that there would be no danger of his falling in love with her.

On receiving Miss Seal's revealing packet, Lord Mountjoy instantly forbade the marriage, but it was too late, for the couple had already married secretly, and his only consolation was to deny his daughter any dowry, in order that Tyrawley's one and only object in marrying her should at least be frustrated. Baulked of the fortune which had been his wife's sole attraction for him, Tyrawley had no intention of living with her, and he sought a diplomatic post abroad in order to escape from her. In January, 1728, he was appointed Ambassador in Lisbon. He left his wife behind, giving her an allowance of £800 a year, and she took up residence in the apartments at Somerset House vacated by his indignant mistress.

Miss Seal had taken refuge with her mother, who now lived in London and occupied a house in Great Queen Street, Lincoln's Inn Fields, recently left to her by a relative. She had not seen her daughter since her elopement, with which she professed to have been much displeased, but she could not well refuse to take her in in her distress.

Deprived of Tyrawley's protection, Miss Seal now had to discover some means of supporting herself, and she sought the advice of a Mrs. Butler, an actress at Drury Lane, with whom she had lately become friendly. Mrs. Butler opined that she could do no better than follow her own profession. Miss Seal was tall and handsome and possessed a good figure; but since she had had no experience of the stage and her capacities were unknown, Mrs. Butler was afraid she might have some difficulty in securing an engagement at one of the London theatres and suggested that she should try her luck in Dublin. Miss Seal thought this excellent advice, and, leaving her little son under her mother's care in London, made her way over to Ireland. Although she proved to have very little talent as an actress, her good looks helped her, and for a time she played small parts. But she was by no means so indispensable as she imagined in her conceit, and when she was foolish enough to quarrel with her employers, she found herself obliged to seek some other means of earning her living.

When she had first parted from him, Lord Tyrawley had plied her with letters begging her to return, but, on receiving

4

no reply from her, had at length desisted from his entreaties. But now, though not invited to do so, she formed the extraordinary resolution of going to him in Lisbon "in order to renew her affectionate intimacy with him", and somehow or other found means to undertake the journey out to Portugal. She was not quite so welcome as she would have been earlier, for Lord Tyrawley, who could not do without female companionship, had by now formed a permanent connexion with a Portuguese girl known as Donna Anna, whom he had seduced from the household of the Countess de Olivarez. But, being well able to cope with more than one lady at a time, he expressed himself delighted to see his former mistress and placed her in the family of an English merchant resident in Lisbon, where he would often visit her. Knowing her temper of old, he did not think it necessary to tell her of the existence of his new mistress, and she fondly imagined that she was still the only object of his affections.

There now appeared upon the scene a certain Captain Bellamy, master of a trading vessel, who fell in love with his fair compatriot and asked her to marry him. Piqued by her reiterated refusals, he came to the conclusion that her affections must be engaged elsewhere and soon decided that his rival could be none other than Lord Tyrawley, though he does not seem to have suspected the true nature of the connexion, possibly because "his lordship's visits were neither long nor frequent". But he taxed Miss Seal with being enamoured of the Ambassador and suggested to her that she was wasting her time, since his liaison with his Portuguese mistress had long been notorious, and she was now, in fact, expecting her second child by him.

Miss Seal, who seems to have had no previous suspicions, was quite as furious as she had been on the first occasion when her lover's deceit had been revealed to her, so furious, indeed, that she impetuously took Captain Bellamy on the rebound. She consented to marry him forthwith and went off with him in his ship to Ireland. Lord Tyrawley knew nothing of what had happened until after they had sailed.

Rather too soon after her arrival in Ireland Mrs. Bellamy gave birth to a daughter, to her husband's "inexpressible astonishment and dissatisfaction". His wife had been amazingly successful in concealing her condition from him to the last, but she had not known him long enough to have any chance of being able to persuade him that the child could possibly be his. The captain was so disgusted that he left her at once and never afterwards either saw her or corresponded with her.

Such is the romantic story of her birth and origin as given by George Anne Bellamy herself in her *Apology*. Unfortunately, it is quite impossible to reconcile certain elements in it with the facts. Her difficulty was that, though she knew that Lord Tyrawley was her father, she believed herself to have been born in 1730 or 1731, several years after his departure on his embassy to Lisbon. For this reason Miss Seal's unlikely visit to Lisbon had to be invented to make the parentage credible. The truth undoubtedly was that, when Tyrawley went off to Lisbon, deserting both his mistress and his wife, Miss Seal was already expecting her second baby, and that she then married Captain Bellamy and went with him to Ireland without revealing this inconvenient fact. Her first appearance on the stage in Ireland must have taken place *after*, and not before, her marriage to Bellamy and the birth of her daughter.

The child was born at Finglas, near Dublin, on April 23rd, and in honour of the saint whose day it was Mrs. Bellamy decided to have her christened Georgiane. It was by that name that she was known for more than thirty years, until she discovered that a mistake had been made and that she had really been given the names of George Anne. The strange error made by a deaf, inattentive, or ignorant parson or clerk appealed to her fancy, and for the rest of her career she elected to be known as George Anne. In her *Apology* she gave the year of her birth as 1731. Later she altered it to 1730. It was almost certainly 1728.

Lord Tyrawley was well aware that Miss Seal was pregnant

when he abandoned her and was certain that he was the father of her child. Now, one of the things Tyrawley always prided himself upon was his readiness to acknowledge his bastard children, whoever their mothers might be; and so, on discovering that the Bellamies had gone to Ireland, he wrote to the adjutant of his regiment, Captain Pye, who happened to live near Finglas, requesting him, if a child were born to Mrs. Bellamy in time for it to be his, to take it away from its mother and to assume charge of it. His lordship would, of course, be responsible for all the expense. He seems to have taken it for granted that it would be easy to gain possession of the child, either because there was really no marriage with Captain Bellamy, or because, if there was, Bellamy would act as he, in fact, did, and take himself off when he discovered how he had been deceived. Mrs. Bellamy seems to have offered no objection to giving up the child, which for the first few years of its life was reared by a nurse engaged by Captain Pye.

Thus freed of all encumbrances and responsibilities, Mrs. Bellamy returned to the stage—if, indeed, she had ever been on it before. She never rose to any great height as an actress and played mostly secondary parts, but in March, 1734, she is recorded as having undertaken the leading part of Sylvia in the *Recruiting Officer* at the Aungier Street Theatre in Dublin.

As soon as Georgiane was old enough, Lord Tyrawley instructed Captain Pye to send her to France to be educated at a convent. She was to be accompanied by an older girl, Maria Frazer, the penniless orphan daughter of an officer in the army, whom Tyrawley had adopted out of friendship for her dead father. Mrs. Pye went with the two children to London to provide them with suitable clothes and make enquiries about suitable convents.

By this time Mrs. Bellamy had succeeded in obtaining a theatrical engagement in England, and she was now playing at Covent Garden. Seeing her name on the theatre play-bills, the maid-servant in charge of little Georgiane conceived the sentimental idea of taking the child to visit her mother,

7

unbeknown to Mrs. Pye, who certainly would not have permitted this contravention of Lord Tyrawley's direct orders. When they were shown up to Mrs. Bellamy's lodging, the child, delighted by her mother's attractive appearance, eagerly ran towards her, only to be rebuffed with the exclamation: "My God, what have you brought me here? This goggle-eyed, splatter-faced, gabbart-mouthed wretch is not my child! Take her away!" During her sojourn in Dublin Mrs. Bellamy had picked up some useful and expressive terms from boatmen on the Liffey. But it is not surprising that little Georgiane, accustomed to being petted and made much of, resented this reception, and, as she says, "went away as much disgusted with my mother as she could be with me."

Mrs. Pye was able to arrange for the children to be escorted over to France by a Mrs. Dunbar, an Irish lady who lived in Boulogne and happened to be on a visit to London. At Boulogne they were to be under the tutelage of Mr. Smith, a wine merchant of that town, who was to pay their fees at the convent and generally keep an eye on their welfare. Lord Tyrawley had given instructions that, if they were not happy where they were placed, they were to be moved at once, and they did not remain long at their first convent, that of the Nunciats in the lower part of the town. According to Georgiane herself, they became terrified because, shortly after their arrival, a nun was immured between the walls, "the punishment usually inflicted on those of the sisters who unfortunately break their vows of chastity." Even if this barbarous custom may have obtained in mediæval times, it is quite incredible that it could have been practiced in enlightened eighteenth-century France; but old legends die hard, and it is possible that the children, having heard sinister tales from ignorant people, gave full rein to their imaginations when one of the sisters was, quite properly, interred within the walls of the convent after dying a perfectly natural death through illness or old age. The dirtiness of the convent and the nuns themselves, which Georgiane gives as a subsidiary reason for their removal, is much more credible and is more likely to have influenced Mr. Smith, whose wife came at once on receiving their appeal and took them to the convent of the Ursulines in the upper town.

Here they were blissfully happy, so happy, indeed, that they were almost heart-broken when they had to leave. But Lord Tyrawley, who was about to conclude his mission and return to England, had ordered them to be sent for to await his arrival in London. Although neither of her parents was of that faith, it was as a Roman Catholic that Georgiane returned to England. The nuns had evidently placed their own interpretation on the solemn duty of education entrusted to them.

The two young ladies were met at Dover by one Du Vall, formerly a servant of Lord Tyrawley's and now a peruke-maker in St. James's Street. With him they were to lodge until the Ambassador's return from Portugal. Du Vall's wife was a lively and agreeable Frenchwoman, "much younger than her husband, and of rather too gay a disposition for his tranquillity," and she introduced the girls to her neighbour and great friend, Mrs. Jones, who had persuaded her husband to give up his humdrum business as a cutler and open a china and bijou shop in fashionable St. James's Street.

Mrs. Jones, who was the daughter of a well-to-do Westminster apothecary, had received what was known as a 'genteel education', and she had speedily made the shop a rendezvous for people of rank and fashion. The two girls, who were in and out of the shop all day, naturally became known to many of the ladies of fashion who were customers there, and it was now that Georgiane first met and made friends with three young ladies only a few years older than herself, Lady Caroline Fitzroy, daughter of the Duke of Grafton, the Honourable Miss Conway, and Miss Elizabeth St. Leger. Long afterwards she was to lose favour with Lady Caroline, who married the Earl of Harrington in 1746, but, according to her, the two other ladies honoured her with their friendship all their lives. And it is quite likely that this was

9

true, even though there may have been an element of condescension in their feelings for her, especially after she went on
the stage.

When her *Apology* was published at the end of her life, many
critics scornfully derided the claims of a mere actress to have
been on intimate terms with so many ladies in high society—
though they were far from denying that she might have
known the gentlemen and have been on even excessively
intimate terms with them. But it is more than probable that
Mrs. Jones and Mrs. Du Vall were not silent about Georgiane's
origin and that many people accepted her as a daughter of Lord
Tyrawley, who was always quite open about his illegitimate
progeny and expected his friends to recognise his connection
with them. Whatever may have been the degree of her
intimacy with them—and it is likely that her arrant snobbish-
ness may have led her to exaggerate it—there can be no doubt
whatever that George Anne Bellamy really did know all these
fashionable and aristocratic people she claimed to be acquainted with. And, with her social ambitions, she always took
particular pains to try to ingratiate herself with the feminine
members of the circle in which she aspired to move. The men
she could secure easily enough.

Whether in ignorance of Lord Tyrawley's prohibition or in
defiance of it, Georgiane seems somehow to have got in touch
with her mother, who was still a member of the Covent
Garden Company, acting such secondary parts as Mrs. Page in
the *Merry Wives of Windsor*, Lady Truman in the *Drummer*, and
Narcissa in *Love's Last Shift*. On March 27th, 1742, the part of
the precocious hoyden, Miss Prue, in Congreve's *Love for
Love* was played at Covent Garden by "Miss Georgiane
Bellamy, who never appeared on any stage before". Georgiane
had forgotten—or affected to have forgotten—this appearance
when she published her *Apology* in 1785, but was able to recollect it when it was pointed out to her by an unknown
correspondent. In her additional volume she pleaded that it
had made so slight an impression on her mind that it had

slipped her memory. But she now recalled that Mr. Bridgwater had entreated her mother to let her play the comic character of Miss Prue for him at his benefit, which she accordingly did. Although it is true that the part was one which could conceivably be played by an inexperienced child, especially at a benefit performance when the audience would be in exceptionally indulgent mood, the circumstance is a little difficult to reconcile both with her alleged age—according to her own reckoning she would have been only eleven at the time—and with the rest of the account of her early life as she herself gives it.

A still slighter impression—for she never recollected it at all—must have been made on her mind by an even earlier appearance in the very minor part of 'Servant to Columbine' in the pantomime, *Harlequin Barber*, performed at Covent Garden for the benefit of the dancers, Monsieur and Madame Mechel, on April 20th, 1741. But this was a mute part which might well have been played by the little daughter of one of the members of the company. That she did make these isolated early appearances is incontrovertible, and it must be in the rest of her account that the errors are to be sought. But it remains true that she did not make her professional début on the stage until November, 1744.

At last Lord Tyrawley arrived from Lisbon. His embassy had been a great success; he had made himself very popular with the Portuguese; and their King, who had wished him to stay in Portugal and had even offered to make him Commander-in-Chief of his army if he would remain,* had marked his esteem by presenting him with fourteen bars of gold on his departure. According to Horace Walpole, he had also brought three wives and fourteen children back to England with him; but, in spite of his well-known propensities, this may be a slight exaggeration.

* This is not so extraordinary as it may seem. In the seventeenth and eighteenth centuries the highest commands in the Portuguese army were often held by foreigners.

As soon as he arrived he sent for Georgiane and Maria Frazer to join his heterogeneous household in Stratton Street. He himself treated them with great kindness, but his chief Sultana, the Portuguese mistress, Donna Anna, who rendered herself conspicuous by wearing her long black hair plaited down to her posterior, was displeased and alarmed by the advent of a little rival to her own daughter. But, for fear of angering Lord Tyrawley, she was clever enough not to show her jealousy and dislike of Georgiane herself and took the subtler course of upsetting the child by venting her spleen on her unfortunate companion, Maria Frazer. And this expedient proved most successful. Georgiane's sympathy for her persecuted friend made her unhappy too, and, in addition, she found it difficult to get used to her father's strange manner of living, "for though my lord lived in all the splendour a person of his rank is entitled to, and indeed much beyond his income; yet his house had much more the appearance of a Turkish seraglio than the mansion of an English nobleman." She entreated him to allow her and Maria to live elsewhere and prevailed upon him to let them lodge with their friend Mrs. Jones in St. James's Street. Lord Tyrawley was quite agreeable to this arrangement; he could still see the girls as often as he wished, for he was wont to spend much of his time at White's Chocolate-house, and he would stroll round to Mrs. Jones's shop two or three times a day if he felt so inclined.

For a time this happy state of affairs continued, then unfortunately Maria Frazer caught the measles and died after a very brief illness. Georgiane was so distressed by the loss of her dearest friend that she too became ill, and her father decided that she needed country air and carried her off to a small house he had rented in Bushey Park. He had decreased the inordinate number of his household in residence by sending the younger boys to the celebrated academy for young gentlemen kept by a clergyman called Fountayne in Marylebone, while Georgiane's own brother, whom he had also recognised, had been placed in the Royal Navy and was already at sea. But

Georgiane had to renew her uncongenial association with the female members of the family, which, besides herself, consisted of three more daughters, all by different mothers. And there was always Donna Anna. But, luckily for Georgiane, shortly after her arrival the Portuguese mistress incurred her lord's dire displeasure by arrogating to herself the title of Lady Tyrawley at a party to which she had taken the three other girls. Tyrawley was so incensed at this piece of presumption that he packed them all back to London, keeping only Georgiane with him.

The ensuing months at Bushey Park were very happy ones for the little girl, whom her father affectionately called 'Pop', a pet name which endured and was afterwards used by many of her intimate friends. Lord Tyrawley remained with her all the week, but left her on Saturdays, when he was always of the King's private party at Richmond. From there he usually went on to London for the night, presumably to visit Donna Anna at his seraglio in Stratton Street, and he would return to Bushey Park on the Sunday. Georgiane got on quite well with her formidable father. Horace Walpole describes him as a brutal man, though he had "a great deal of humour and occasional good breeding, but not to the prejudice of his natural temper, which was imperiously blunt, haughty, and contemptuous with an undaunted portion of spirit". He possessed a cynical and caustic wit; when asked if he had found much alteration in England after his long absence in Portugal, he said he saw none at all; he found nothing but a fog, whisk,* and the House of Commons, and my Lord Grantham walking on tiptoe as if he was still afraid of waking the Queen—who had died some five years before.

There was little or nothing in Lord Tyrawley's library calculated to appeal to the tastes of a very young girl. He possessed only one romance, La Calprenède's *Cassandra*, which he forbade her to read as being unsuitable for her at her age. She had to have recourse to reading Pope's celebrated trans-

* The card game then known indifferently as 'whisk' or 'whist'.

13

lation of Homer. But in this she had an ulterior motive. She was aware that the illustrious poet lived in the neighbourhood and that her father was well acquainted with him, and she determined to learn some of his lines by heart and then dazzle him with a display of her taste and knowledge. And so, when she had mastered a selection of what she considered appropriate passages from the great work, she badgered her father until he at last consented to take her over to Twickenham and present her to the poet. But, alas! as soon as she was introduced to her host on entering his villa and before she could even open her mouth, Pope rang for his housekeeper and directed her to take 'Miss' and show her the gardens and give her as much fruit as she chose to eat. Georgiane was so mortified at being treated as a child that there and then she resolved to transfer her attentions from Pope's *Iliad* to Dryden's *Æneid*. Perhaps she was unaware that Dryden was long dead and blissfully beyond the reach of juvenile recitations. But the day was not to be so disappointing after all, for, upon being told that the carriage was waiting and gladly hastening to make her escape from the scene of her discomfiture, she found Lord Chesterfield with her father. He too had called to visit Pope and had accepted Tyrawley's invitation to return with him to Bushey Park. This great wit and accomplished man of the world knew exactly how young ladies in their teens should be treated and was as courtly and flattering as Pope had been cold and distant.

Pope and Chesterfield were by no means the only celebrities Georgiane encountered during her stay in Bushey Park. Lord Tyrawley was a man of catholic tastes and many interests and loved the company of the witty and the gay. She attributed the excessive vanity, which she acknowledged to be one of her besetting weaknesses, to the spoiling she then received from her father's fashionable and famous friends, who, to pay court to him, were too lavish in their praises of his pretty little daughter with her dark hair and huge blue eyes. Because she was so often referred to as 'the fair Bellamy', it seems to have been generally assumed that she was blonde, and the engraving of her prefixed to the later editions of her *Apology* might certainly give this impression, but she herself clearly implies that she was dark-haired, and this is borne out by Lindo's portrait of her.*

In the autumn of 1743 Lord Tyrawley was appointed Ambassador to Russia. Although ready to beget illegitimate children in any country, he did not think it tactful to arrive with any he had already had elsewhere, so he decided that suitable arrangements must be made for Georgiane during his absence. On hearing of his problem, one of the ladies of quality whose acquaintance Georgiane had made at Mrs. Jones's shop —she does not say who it was—sent a message to Lord Tyrawley intimating that she would be delighted to have the girl to stay with her while he was abroad. Tyrawley was greatly relieved by this easy solution of his difficulty and himself called upon the lady to convey his grateful acceptance of her offer. The only stipulation he made was that Georgiane was on no account to consort with her disreputable mother.

---

* In her *Apology* (Vol. IV, pp. 22–23) she makes mention of "a little black woman", whose description, she says, answered in every particular to her own. Elsewhere she reveals that her eyes were blue. See *postea*, p. 165.

Chapter Two

WHILE GEORGIANE HAD BEEN LIVING IN LUXURY with her aristocratic father, her mother had fallen on rather evil days. She had been ill-advised enough to marry—or, perhaps, not quite marry, a son of Sir George Walter, a dissipated boy in the army young enough to be her own son. This young man had soon tired of her, and, one evening, while she was at the theatre, he had left to join his regiment at Gibraltar, taking with him not only most of her worldly possessions, but even her clothes, to adorn another lady he had selected as a companion for the voyage. It now occurred to Mrs. Bellamy (or Walter) that it might be a good idea if she could persuade Georgiane to come and live with her, especially as Lord Tyrawley had arranged to give his daughter an allowance of a hundred pounds a year to pay for her clothes and her maid, during his absence in Russia. Georgiane herself alleges that she complied with her mother's request out of humanity and a sense of duty, but she showed that she was well aware that her action would not meet with approval by removing to her mother's lodging without taking leave of the lady in whose care she had been placed.

The small sum of money she was able to take with her did not last the two of them very long, so Mrs. Bellamy borrowed on the security of a valuable watch and a few trinkets belonging to her daughter in the hope that the amount thus raised would tide them over until the next instalment of Georgiane's allowance became due. Fortunately, too, at this rather awkward moment they made the acquaintance of a Mrs. Jackson, the well-to-do invalid wife of an East India Company official, who had recently arrived in England for her own health and the education of her two daughters, who were much of Georgiane's age. This generous woman invited the Bellamies to stay with her in a house she had taken for the summer, and accordingly, at the end of the theatrical season, Georgiane and her mother removed to Montpelier Row, Twickenham.

One evening, when they were out for a walk, they chanced to meet the popular and well-known Irish actress, Peg Woffington, with whom Mrs. Bellamy had often played both in Dublin and at Covent Garden. Peg told them that she was living in a villa at Teddington and invited them forthwith to come and stay with her for a few days. Since Mrs. Jackson had already hinted to them that she was expecting other guests, it happened to be extremely convenient for them to do so.

Although Georgiane must already have met plenty of her mother's theatrical friends at Covent Garden, it was at Peg Woffington's home that she first became immersed in the world of the theatre. Most of Peg's friends and acquaintances were connected with the stage in one way or another, and at the Teddington villa nothing but the theatre was talked of from morning till night. Moreover, Peg herself and some of her friends were already making names for themselves in their profession. Among her intimates was the young Irish actor, Thomas Sheridan. Born in 1719, the son of a distinguished classical scholar, Dr. Thomas Sheridan, and godson of his father's great friend, Dean Swift, he had been educated at Westminster and Trinity College, Dublin, with a view to his becoming a schoolmaster or a clergyman. But he had preferred a theatrical career and had scored so great a success in the part of Richard III in Dublin in 1743 that he had been invited to appear at Drury Lane in the following season and was already installed in apartments at Kingston, where with lavish generosity he entertained all comers, including more often than not a crowd of admiring but impecunious compatriots from his old university. His rooms were also haunted by the rising young actor, David Garrick, who came there in the hope of persuading the lovely Peggy to renew her liaison with him, which had been broken off owing to his persistent reluctance to sanctify it by marriage.

Peg Woffington was eager at this time to launch her younger sister, Polly, on a theatrical career, and had arranged for some informal performances to be given in a barn at Kingston in order to test her abilities. The play chosen was Ambrose Philip's *The Distressed Mother*, an adaptation into English of Racine's famous tragedy, *Andromaque*. Polly Woffington played the principal part of Andromache, and the other little less exacting role of Hermione was given to Georgiane Bellamy. Peg herself and Mrs. Bellamy watched over their respective fledglings as attendants. David Garrick himself consented to appear as Orestes, while the part of Pyrrhus was played by a friend of Sheridan's, Mr. Sullivan, a Fellow of Trinity College, Dublin. The local gentry were invited to form the audience. But it was Georgiane's performance which aroused most admiration and seemed to designate her as a more promising candidate for the stage than the intended heroine of this little experiment. And, in truth, Polly, who possessed much of her elder sister's charm and wit but little of her talent for acting, soon abandoned all idea of a theatrical career in favour of a marriage with the Hon. Robert Cholmondeley and the more congenial role of a lady of fashion, which she filled to admiration.

On their return to Twickenham the Bellamies found Mrs. Jackson very ill, but Mrs. Bellamy nursed her with such devotion and skill that, on her return to London in the autumn, she invited her and Georgiane to continue to live with her at the house she had taken in Henrietta Street, Covent Garden. It was fortunate for them that they were thereby certain of having a roof over their heads, for Du Vall now informed them that Georgiane's allowance from her father would no longer be paid. Lord Tyrawley had written to tell him that, since his daughter had chosen to disregard his strict injunction to have nothing to do with her mother, he himself would have nothing to do with her.

Although she had not been re-engaged for the forthcoming season at Covent Garden, Mrs. Bellamy still sometimes had occasion to call at the house of John Rich, the patentee of the theatre, and, possibly with an eye to the main chance, she usually took Georgiane with her. At this time Rich was undoubtedly the most powerful figure in the world of the theatre. The son of Christopher Rich, the celebrated autocratic manager who had controlled the three chief playhouses, dominated the theatrical scene, and oppressed all the actors at the close of the seventeenth century, he had been born and bred in the theatre and had known no other education and upbringing. It might have been expected, therefore, that if he excelled in anything it would be in the departments of speech and manners which are so essential for actors, but it was just in these respects that he was most deficient, though he himself never seems to have realised it. In spite of his failure as an actor owing to the vulgarity of his enunciation, he always imagined not only that his speech was impeccable, but also that he was peculiarly qualified to instruct others in the difficult art of elocution. The truth was that his own great gifts lay in quite other directions. As a manager, he had made a considerable fortune from John Gay's *Beggar's Opera*, which he had produced in 1728 at his theatre in Lincoln's Inn Fields on the insistence of the Duchess of Queensberry, who had offered to pay his losses if the piece should fail. In 1732 he had removed with his company to the new theatre in Covent Garden, where besides continuing to produce tragedies and comedies, he had developed and expanded the newly revived art of pantomime. Under the name of Lun he had gained a tremendous reputation for himself in the silent part of Harlequin, and his pantomimes drew great crowds to Covent Garden by reason of the lavishness of their scenery and costumes and the ingenuity of the mechanical devices by which he obtained his effects. He became a pastmaster in the art of spectacle, which he later extended to his other productions. Every comedy, every tragedy, must have its procession or its scene of pageantry. His predilection

19

for elaborate spectacle became a joke, which he himself was the first to relish. Though quick-tempered and occasionally obstinate and unreasonable, he was far too good-natured ever to become as dictatorial as his father; John Rich's kind heart and generosity made him as popular as Christopher had been unpopular for his bullying and avarice.

Georgiane soon became very friendly with Rich's young daughters, and they used to amuse themselves by acting plays together. On one occasion when they were rehearsing *Othello*, in which Georgiane was playing the Moor, Rich himself happened to pass by the door and stopped to listen. He was so much impressed by Georgiane's rendering of her lines that he came in and congratulated her, adding that, if she wanted to go on the stage, he would offer her an engagement at Covent Garden. Thrilled and flattered by his approval, Georgiane hastened home to her mother and told her of the offer and of her own eagerness to accept it. Mrs. Bellamy, who had herself experienced "all the disadvantages attendant on a theatrical life," at first hesitated—or affected to do so; but Mrs. Jackson added her persuasions to Georgiane's and eventually she consented, "but only on condition that the manager would assure her of his supporting her daughter in a capital line." Her reluctance may, indeed, have been wisely feigned just in order that she might insist upon this condition. Rich readily agreed to it, since the ladies in his company were not, as Georgiane elegantly puts it, "altogether suited either for the characters of young heroines in tragedy or of sprightly girls in genteel comedy." There was more than an element of truth in this. The lovely Mrs. Horton, though still retaining her great beauty, had been on the stage for some thirty years and was no longer in her first youth; there was nothing either tragic or genteel about that robust and vivacious comedienne Kitty Clive; while the great Mrs. Pritchard, the most famous Lady Macbeth of her time, carried too much weight in both senses of the word to play the part of a very young girl. There was room in the Covent Garden company for an *ingénue*.

Georgiane learnt two parts that Rich considered to be suitable for her, and he decided that she should make her first appearance in that of Monimia, the tragic heroine of Otway's *The Orphan*. Monimia, ward of Lord Acasto, secretly marries his son, Castalio. But Castalio's twin brother, Polydore, is also in love with her, and assuming Castalio's passion for her to be as dishonourable in intention as his own, by subterfuge gains admission to her chamber and spends what should have been her bridal night with her, she supposing him to be her husband. On realising the truth next day she poisons herself, and Polydore, discovering too late that Monimia was really Castalio's wife, provokes a quarrel with him and deliberately runs on his sword that he may be slain. Castalio thereupon stabs himself to death.

The ladies of the Covent Garden company may have been willing to acquiesce in this young girl's introduction amongst them, but there was a formidable obstacle to be encountered in the leading man, James Quin, then still accounted the greatest actor of the time in spite of the growing rivalry of the youthful David Garrick, whose natural style was eventually to oust his outworn conventional school of acting from the boards. But in 1744 Quin ruled Covent Garden with a rod of iron, and even the manager was more than a little afraid of him. It was, therefore, with some diffidence that he took Georgiane to be introduced to the great man in his dressing-room and to acquaint him that she was to play Monimia. Quin gazed in amazement at the dark-haired, blue-eyed child, who looked even younger than she was.

"It will not do so, sir," he said firmly.

"It shall do, sir," replied Rich as firmly, and probably as much to his own surprise as Quin's.

Quin, who hitherto had ignored Georgiane herself, now turned and fixed his eye on her. "Child," he said, "I would advise you to play Serina before you think of Monimia."

This was sound advice; but the part of Serina in *The Orphan* was a very small one and not all commensurate with

Georgiane's ambitions, so she rather pertly replied that, if she did, she would never live to play the Orphan.

Quin continued to insist upon the impropriety of a mere child's attempting to play a part of so much importance. He was, of course, quite right, though it is to be suspected that his real objection to Georgiane's playing the part was that her extremely youthful appearance would emphasise still more his own increasing unfitness to play his accustomed part of Monimia's youthful brother, Chamont, the proud, censorious, suspicious soldier, who is the most interesting character in the play and provides great acting opportunities. Quin was now over fifty and inclined to be corpulent, and he was probably well aware that his other favourite part of Falstaff was really more suited to his years and figure. Finally he announced that, if Rich persisted in his absurd resolution, he would publicly declare his sentiments on the subject and would decline to attend any rehearsals of the play. His attitude put the manager's back up; Rich was on the whole an easy-going man, but he now swore that he would show everyone that he would be the master when he chose to be at the trouble. He instructed the prompter to call a rehearsal of *The Orphan* for next morning. But it could not take place, for neither Quin nor Hall and Ryan, who were to play Castalio and Polydore, deigned to appear. Rich promptly imposed heavier fines than usual upon them for non-attendance. All his pride and obstinacy were aroused, but he realised that this tussle with his company must be an embarrassing ordeal for Georgiane, and, in a kindly effort to keep up her spirits, he carried her off to his own mercer and allowed her to choose a new costume for Monimia instead of the shabby old dress from the stock wardrobe with which she would normally have been fobbed off. It was usually only for new productions that new dresses and new scenery were provided.

The fines imposed by Rich were effective in so far as Hall and Ryan were concerned, for they did attend the rehearsal next morning, though Quin did not. But the two actors did not trouble to exert themselves. Georgiane says that Hall mumbled over the part of Castalio, while Ryan whistled through that of Polydore. She admitted later, however, that perhaps she was doing Ryan some injustice, for he had had this odd tremor in his voice ever since he had been shot in the jaw by a robber in Queen Street as he was going home after the theatre one evening some ten years before. This defect in his voice became less disagreeable when the ear was used to it, and the London audiences had long become accustomed to it, and, being aware of its origin, readily extended their indulgence towards a good and popular player. Ryan, indeed, was talented and versatile, and there were some parts in which he nearly achieved greatness. Garrick acknowledged that he admired Ryan's conception of Richard III so much that he founded his own rendering of the part on it. In private life Ryan was the kindliest of men, and if he failed in courtesy and consideration towards a young girl on this occasion, it must have been because he had weakly allowed himself to be persuaded thereto by his great friend, Quin. Possibly, too, he shared Quin's apprehensions about the contrast between her youthfulness and his own advancing years. Like Quin, he was over fifty.

Rehearsals of this kind cannot have been of much service to Georgiane, but luckily she was able to see a performance at Drury Lane some nights before that arranged for her own first appearance, and this, she says, made her better acquainted with the play than twenty rehearsals would have done.

At last the fateful evening of November 22nd arrived. Rumours of the dispute between the manager and his leading man over the engagement of a new and untried actress had got abroad, and Quin had not been reticent in expressing his views of her incapability. Rich, on the other hand, had been lavish in his praises of his latest discovery, and, as the true story of her origin was not yet generally known, suggestions were not wanting that the manager's interest in this young actress were due to the fact that he was really her father. But this apparent solicitude for her was principally due to irritation at Quin's attempt to dictate to him and a desire to show that he was master in his own theatre. Having pledged himself for Georgiane's success, he endeavoured to ensure it by planting trustworthy friends and supporters in all parts of the house.

Georgiane's name was not mentioned in the play-bills; it was simply stated that Monimia was to be played by "a young Gentlewoman, being her first appearance on any stage". This was almost, but not quite true. But it was her first appearance as a serious actress, and she was very nervous.

Though greeted with warm and sympathetic applause on her first appearance, she was so dazzled by the lights and stunned by the applause that she was deprived of both memory and voice and could not proceed. A Mr. Chitty, an assiduous play-goer who had become regarded as the dictator of the pit, inspired by compassion for the actress's extreme youth and probably also by some prepossession for her figure, loudly called for the curtain to be lowered till she had recovered from her confusion. This was done, and in the interval before it was raised again the anxious Rich entreated and exhorted the terrified girl to pull herself together. But she was still so nervous that she could scarcely raise her voice and could only stumble haltingly through her part. At every opportunity, when she was off the stage, Rich came to her and tried to comfort and encourage her, while Quin maliciously chortled over her failure. But not until the approach of her great scene in the fourth act did she regain her confidence. Then suddenly, to the astonishment of the audience, the surprise and relief of the other performers, and the exultation of the manager, she felt inspired and acted with such power and pathos that before the play ended the audience had taken her to its heart. So had Quin. Fascinated by her performance, he had waited behind the scenes until the end of the act, and then lifted her in his arms and cried: "Thou art a divine creature, and the true spirit is in thee." Disaster had changed into triumph, and London was so eager to see the new Monimia that Rich took the unusual course of keeping the play on for another night.

Quin had not merely succumbed to the emotion of the moment on the night of November 22nd; his conversion was complete and lasting. The natural benevolence of his heart had asserted itself, and from now onwards he took a paternal interest in Georgiane and constituted himself her mentor, protector, and adviser. One of his first acts was to enquire into the circumstances in which she lived. His position and prestige at this time were so great that at the theatre he lived a life apart, rarely associating off the stage with any member of the company except his old friend, Ryan, and never entering the Green Room. Consequently he knew nothing of the private life of Mrs. Bellamy, even though she had been a minor member of the same company for some years. But now, being apprised of the slenderness of her resources, he sent her a bank-bill for a handsome sum so that she and her daughter might not want for anything. Upon Georgiane herself he conferred the signal honour of a general invitation to the suppers he held four times a week after the theatre at his lodging in Bow Street. But he laughingly warned her never to come alone, because, as he said, he was not too old to be censured. Mrs. Bellamy had lately developed an interest in religion, which now absorbed all her time, attention, and energies, and it was Mrs. Jackson who usually chaperoned Georgiane at these gay assemblies, where she met many of the most distinguished actors, dramatists, and literary figures of the time. Mrs. Jackson herself was delighted to encounter there a kinsman of her own, the celebrated poet and dramatist, James Thomson, author of *The Seasons* and of the words of the song, 'Rule Britannia', set to music by the equally celebrated Dr. Arne.

Georgiane continued to meet with success, playing the parts of tragic young heroines and sprightly young girls in genteel comedies. She was never to become a really great actress, but she had talent enough to be able at this time and for some years to come to carry off such parts, since her inexperience was offset by her radiant youth, freshness, prettiness, and gaiety. And the public, ever susceptible to these qualities which are the gifts of God and not the result of thought or hard work, was indulgent towards her even when she had to attempt roles as yet beyond her capacity, as when she took the exacting part of Eudocia in Hughes's *Siege of Damascus* at very short notice on the sudden indisposition of Mrs. Pritchard. Other parts she played during this season were Lucia in Addison's *Cato*, Celia in *Volpone*, Anne Boleyn in *Henry VIII*, Arsinoe in *Mariamne*, and the forsaken, forlorn Aspasia to Quin's Melantius and Mrs. Pritchard's Evadne in Beaumont and Fletcher's *Maid's Tragedy*.

Dramatic writing in England was at this time at a very low ebb. Playwrights, it is true, were numerous and prolific, but their work was so mediocre that before about 1760 very few new plays were produced at either of the great theatres, Drury Lane and Covent Garden, and most of the plays dated from the Restoration period or, at latest, from the days of Queen Anne. Dryden, Lee, Rowe, Otway, Etherege, Wycherley, Congreve, Farquhar, and Vanbrugh were still the favourite dramatists. Certainly many of Shakespeare's plays were revived, and some of Beaumont and Fletcher's, with Ben Jonson's *Alchemist* and *Volpone*, but mostly in almost unrecognisable versions dating from the early eighteenth century. Buckingham's *Rehearsal* still held the boards, and Gay's *Beggar's Opera*, which was still regarded almost as a new play, was as popular as ever.

The criterion of a play's success was not then its consecutive run, but the number of performances during the whole season. Sometimes a play, if very well received, would be kept on for as many as nine or ten consecutive nights, but it was more usual for it to be played for two or three, then on alternate evenings for a week or so, and thereafter in the same way from time to time throughout the season, which started in September and continued until the end of May or the beginning of June at the latest. For the first few weeks of the season both companies would put on plays for three nights a week, but from about the second week in October they would play all six nights. There were no plays on Sundays, Christmas Eve, Christmas Day, January 30th, the anniversary of the execution of King Charles I—this tribute to the martyred monarch dated from the revival of the theatre at the Restoration—and Wednesdays and Fridays in Lent. And the Bishops a few years later persuaded the Lord Chamberlain to order the theatres to be closed for the whole of Holy Week.

At the beginning of the season it was usual to stage those plays from the previous season's repertory which had been most successful. New plays and fresh revivals of old ones were reserved for later on, especially at the height of the season in January and February. At the benefits, which began towards the end of March, the performers, who selected their own plays, would naturally tend to choose those in which they believed they had scored their greatest triumph, either in their own opinions or in that of the audience.

Tragedies alternated with comedies, so that each of the principal players would appear on an average three or four times a week. The tragedy or comedy in five acts came first in the bill and was almost invariably followed by an afterpiece, which consisted of a short farce or light comedy, an opera, burlesque, ballet, or pantomime. And sometimes, to give extra good measure, there would be entertainments of singing, dancing, or recitations between the acts of the main piece.

The companies at Covent Garden and Drury Lane were repertory companies in the full and true sense of the word, and all the performers had to be able to retain a great number of parts in their memories and be able to play them even at a day's notice. The staging of the plays presented little difficulty, for new scenery and dresses were provided only for new productions, and the sets were for the most part conventional and could be adapted for almost any play. Elaborate scenic effects were confined almost entirely to pantomime and to the masques and processions which Rich, especially, loved to introduce without much regard for their suitability. The performers wore the costume of their own day. Certain conventions were observed. Tragedy queens and empresses usually appeared in black velvet robes and young heroines in satin as white and pure as stock costumes could be expected to be. A large proportion of the dresses in the theatrical wardrobes consisted of the cast-offs of people of rank and fashion, purchased by the managements from their former owners, though ever since the time of that great patron of the theatre, King Charles II, the greatest in the land and even members of the royal family had deigned to present some of their more magnificent clothes to the theatres when they had served their purpose and the gold or silver of their embroideries had become rather too tarnished to be worn at Court.

On February 15th, 1745, Georgiane appeared for the first time as Blanch in the veteran Colley Cibber's egregious *Papal Tyranny in the Reign of King John*, a much botched and mangled version of Shakespeare's *King John*. This play had been compiled some nine years before and had actually been put into rehearsal then, but Cibber, annoyed by criticisms directed against him for his persistence in meddling with Shakespeare, had withdrawn it before it was performed. He now consented to disinter it for patriotic reasons, its violent strictures on papal pretensions being considered timely and salutary in view of the possibility of a Jacobite rising on behalf of the Catholic Stuarts. Quin played King John, Mrs. Pritchard was Constance, and Cibber himself, though quite inaudible in the large auditorium of Covent Garden owing to a total lack of teeth, took the part of the papal legate, Pandulph. Perhaps because of its appropriateness to the hour, it proved popular enough to be given ten performances. But Drury Lane took some of the wind out of Cibber's sails by maliciously staging a revival of Shakespeare's play, or, at any rate, of something more nearly approximating to it, and the public did not altogether endorse Cibber's claim that he had made it more like a play than he found it in Shakespeare. Fielding, indeed, had said that no man was better calculated to alter Shakespeare for the worse, and had dubbed him 'Ground-Ivy'.

For this occasion only, and in deference to the wishes of the conservative Cibber, Georgiane's name figured on the play-bills as 'Mrs. Bellamy'. Because of her youth she was usually billed as 'Miss Bellamy'. The old custom of calling all actresses 'Mrs.' had begun to die out, and girls in their teens were now designated 'Miss', a term which had lost the entirely un-complimentary significance that had attached to it in the seventeenth century. Married women like Mrs. Pritchard and Mrs. Cibber assumed their husband's surnames on the stage as well as in private life, but those, like Kitty Clive and Peg Woffington, who did not marry, still adopted the appellation of 'Mrs.' as soon as they attained maturity and a measure of fame. Georgiane Bellamy was to cling to the implication of virginity rather longer than most and certainly longer than she had any right to do.

As an inexperienced newcomer to the stage Georgiane was at first paid a very small salary, but the kindly Rich sought to make amends for this by giving her a benefit free of all charge on one of his own nights. This was an exceptional concession, for though the principal members of the company always performed without salary at one another's benefits, the production expenses of the night and the salaries of such minor players as could not be expected to give their services free were usually deducted from the proceeds before the profits were handed to the beneficiary. The accepted custom was that only the principal players received the gross proceeds of a benefit performance free of all expenses, and only they received a benefit entirely to themselves; lesser members of the company would share one between them. But popular though she already was with her audiences and grateful though she was to the manager for his generous gesture, Georgiane did not expect to gain very much from her first benefit. It was true that a benefit could be very lucrative if the beneficiary pos-sessed wealthy and influential friends, for the prices of all the

B*

seats in the house were raised for the occasion, and what were known as 'gold tickets' were issued for the boxes and the extra seating which was often built for the night on the stage itself. And some wealthy admirers would make a direct and very substantial contribution in addition to the payment for their gold tickets. From such sources as these she did not yet expect to receive much, even though she had been fortunate enough to attract the favourable attention of two very great ladies, the Duchess of Queensberry and the Countess of Cardigan.

The eccentric Duchess of Queensberry was the daughter of Henry Hyde, Earl of Clarendon and Rochester, and a granddaughter of Charles II's famous Chancellor. She had married the 3rd Duke of Queensberry in 1720. Kitty Queensberry— "Kitty ever bright and gay", as Pope called her—was a beautiful and brilliant woman who had ever been a good friend to drama and literature and their exponents and interpreters. She had been John Gay's patroness, and the friend of Swift, Pope, Congreve, Prior, and Thomson. But though the most loyal and generous of friends, she was nothing if not uncompromising and fearless with her tongue and her pen, and spared nobody the lash of either if she thought they deserved it. At the time of the dispute over the production of Gay's *Polly* in 1729, when the court had taken sides against the poet, she had written the King himself a letter which must be among the rudest communications ever addressed to a sovereign by a subject. Even her messenger had remonstrated with her, and had besought her to reconsider it and produce a modified version. But her modifications had proved to be so much ruder that he had preferred to take the original to the King. As a result the Duchess had been forbidden the Court and had not reappeared there since. But royal disapproval vexed her not a whit; she was still the Duchess of Queensberry, and as good as a sovereign herself in the society she infinitely preferred.

Georgiane's other patroness also belonged by both birth and marriage to the highest families of the land. The youngest daughter and heiress of the 2nd Duke of Montagu, she was married to the 4th Earl of Cardigan, head of the Brudenell family. She was at this time in her early thirties.

A few days before Georgiane's benefit was due to take place she received a message at the theatre from the Duchess desiring her to be at Queensberry House next day before twelve o'clock. Since she proposed also to wait upon Lady Cardigan that morning in order to solicit her patronage, she dressed herself in her very best clothes and hired a sedan-chair to take her first to Montagu House, which was situated in the Privy Garden at Whitehall. Having been very graciously received there by Lady Cardigan, who promised to patronise her benefit, she ordered the chairmen to proceed to Queensberry House, the stately mansion the Italian architect Leoni had built for the Duke on the north side of Burlington Gardens between Savile Row and Old Burlington Street. Emerging from the chair, Georgiane knocked at the door and gave her name to the porter. Presently the Groom of the Chambers appeared, and she asked him to acquaint Her Grace that she had arrived. But great was her consternation when he returned and informed her that Her Grace said that she knew no such person. And when Georgiane protested that it was by the Duchess's own direction that she had taken the liberty to wait upon her, he mere'y shrugged his shoulders and said that there must have been some mistake in the delivery of it. The humiliated girl had no alternative but to beat an ignominious retreat.

To add to her mortification, her mother happened to have staying with her a female relative from Ireland, who disliked Georgiane and never lost an opportunity of disparaging and maligning her. Georgiane returned her dislike and said of her that "her deformed body was a fit receptacle for her depraved mind". This woman represented to Mrs. Bellamy that the much-vaunted invitation from the Duchess was nothing more than a chimera of Georgiane's own brain, generated by her insupportable vanity. Nettled by her insinuations and sarcasms, Georgiane betook herself off to the theatre on the plea of having business there, though she was not playing that evening.

On entering the theatre she was immediately accosted by the Austrian minister, Prince Lobkowitz, who told her that he had come on behalf of the *corps diplomatique* to request a box at her benefit. She thanked him for the honour and said she was sure they might be accommodated with a stage-box. But when she sent for the housekeeper and asked him to make the appropriate entry in his book, he informed her to her utter astonishment that there was not a single box left in the house, all, except those engaged for the Countess of Cardigan, the Dowager Duchess of Leeds, and Lady Shaftesbury, having been engaged by the Duchess of Queensberry. Georgiane thought that the man must be joking, especially as it was he who had given her the alleged message from the Duchess the night before; but he assured her solemnly that it was true and that, in addition, the Duchess had sent for two hundred and fifty tickets. In the circumstances Prince Lobkowitz obligingly agreed to be content with a balcony for himself and his diplomatic friends.

Georgiane hastened home to tell her mother of this unexpected good fortune and found awaiting her a note from the Duchess herself asking her to wait on her next morning. There was no doubt that this note was genuine, and Georgiane felt reassured by it; but she was determined all the same not to risk another rebuff in the presence of sniggering chairmen and flunkeys, and so she decided to go to Queensberry House quietly dressed and on foot so that there might be no witnesses to her discomfiture if some malicious practical joke were being played upon her. But she was by no means free from perturbation when she knocked once again on the door of the ducal mansion. This time, however, there had been no mistake, and she was immediately ushered into the Duchess's private apartment, where she found Her Grace engaged in cleaning a picture.

"Well, young woman," was the Duchess's greeting. "What business had you in a chair yesterday? It was a fine morning, and you might have walked." Then, glancing with approval at Georgiane's modest linen gown, she continued: "You look as you ought to do now. Nothing is so vulgar as wearing silk in a morning. Simplicity best becomes youth. And you do not stand in need of ornaments. Therefore dress always plain, except when you are upon the stage."

Eager to atone and to ingratiate herself after this reproof, Georgiane offered to take over the cleaning of the picture, only to be thoroughly snubbed for her pains. "Don't you think I have domestics enough if I did not choose to do it myself?" the Duchess rapped out.

Georgiane hastened to apologise for her apparent presumption, explaining that she had only made the offer because she had learnt how to clean pictures at Mrs. Jones's shop in St. James's Street and really believed she had attained a tolerable proficiency in the art.

"Are you the girl I have heard Chesterfield speak of?" exclaimed the Duchess.

Georgiane replied that she had the honour of being known to his Lordship.

The Duchess thereupon ordered a canvas bag to be brought from her cabinet. "No Queensberry can give a person less than gold," she said in explanation. "There are two hundred and fifty guineas, and twenty for the Duke's tickets and mine, but I must give you something for Tyrawley's sake." And she gave the astonished and delighted girl a bank-bill from her pocket-book.

Although it had been quite right for little Miss Bellamy to come to Queensberry House on foot the situation was now entirely altered. With all this money about her she must risk no accident, and the Duchess insisted upon sending her home in her own coach.

The benefit was a great success, and the receipts surpassed Georgiane's most hopeful expectations, but she herself always maintained that, though the Duchess's munificence on this occasion was much greater than Lady Cardigan's, she was far better pleased with the reception she met with from the latter, who indeed continued to honour her with her patronage and protection while she remained on the stage.

Being well aware of the pitfalls and temptations that surrounded a young girl embarking upon a theatrical career, especially if she were quite as young and as pretty and prepossessing as Georgiane, Quin continued to keep a watchful eye on her, and from time to time took it upon himself to offer her paternal advice. One day, after a rehearsal of Beaumont and Fletcher's *The Maid's Tragedy*, he called her into his dressing-room. She followed him with some trepidation, fully expecting to receive a severe reprimand for deficiencies in her acting. But it was for a different reason that Quin wanted to see her. "My dear girl," he said, "you are vastly followed, I hear. Do not let the love of finery, or any other inducement, prevail upon you to commit an indiscretion. Men in general are rascals. You are young and engaging, and therefore ought to be doubly cautious. If you want any thing in my power, which money can purchase, come to me and say, 'James Quin, give me such a thing,' and my purse shall always be at your service."

The generous old actor's counsel was tactful and well-timed, if wasted. Georgiane was, indeed, already surrounded with admirers, in the minds of most of whom the thought of marriage was far from uppermost, and who were, therefore, likely to offer other inducements,. But Georgiane herself, at this time at any rate, very prudently made it quite clear to them all that she would not be willing to listen to any proposals but marriage and a coach.

Two of her admirers were especially pressing in their attentions. One was William, fifth Lord Byron, a young man of twenty-two or three "who had little to boast of but a title and an agreeable face", and the other a Mr. George Montgomery, a gentleman of her own faith who would eventually inherit a considerable estate in the East Riding of Yorkshire. He was descended in the female line from an ancient Roman Catholic family, the Methams of Metham, whose seat, North

Cave, was situated between Howden and Beverley. When Philip Metham, the last of the male line and a bachelor, had died in 1732, the estate had passed to his two sisters, Dorothy and Barbara, the younger of whom had married a Mr. Hugh Montgomery. George was the son of this marriage. He was born in 1716 and was therefore twenty-eight at the time when he met Georgiane.

George Montgomery was frank enough to tell her that he could not comply with either of the conditions she had laid down for the disposal of her heart. He was entirely dependent on his family, whose consent to a marriage with an actress he could not hope to obtain. And, as for a coach, he simply could not afford one. For these reasons he thought it best to bid her a reluctant farewell and retire into his native Yorkshire. Georgiane confessed that she liked him for his candour: "The generous conduct of this gentleman (whose passion I was well convinced was sincere) in not attempting to deceive me, made an impression upon my mind greatly in his favour."

No notion of marrying little Miss Bellamy ever entered Lord Byron's head; his intentions from the first were wholly dishonourable. And he pursued them with assiduity. But Georgiane's own account of the whole episode must be viewed with extreme caution. According to her, Lord Byron was so piqued by her obdurate refusal to listen to his unworthy proposals that he arranged with a friend of his, a certain elderly Earl—whose name Georgiane does not divulge "through tenderness to his family", as she claims, or, possibly, because he never existed—to enter into a conspiracy to abduct her. Byron's reason for enlisting his services was because he had some acquaintance with Georgiane's mother. He had known her when she was on the stage, and, having placed her under some trifling obligations to him, was a constant visitor to Mrs. Jackson's house. And he himself professed to be in love with a young lady, who was one of Georgiane's most intimate friends, though his intentions towards her were no better than Lord Byron's towards Georgiane.

One Sunday evening in the late spring this nobleman called at Mrs. Jackson's house and told Georgiane that her friend was in a coach at the end of Southampton Street and desired to speak with her. Without staying to put on her hat or gloves, Georgiane ran down to the coach, but "to her unspeakable surprise" found herself hoisted into it by his Lordship and driven off at a gallop. To her passionate remonstrances he replied that she had better consent to make his friend, Lord Byron, happy and be happy herself than oppose her good fortune. And he cynically added that Lord Byron was shortly to be married to a rich heiress and would then be in a position to provide handsomely for her. When the coach arrived at his own house at the top of North Audley Street, then on the confines of the town, her abductor took her within, and, having told her that he was going to inspect a suitable lodging which had already been engaged for her, he left her.

When he returned not long after, he was accompanied, says Georgiane, by the very last person in the world she expected to see—her own brother. Naturally assuming that he had come to her rescue, she flew to his arms, but to her great astonishment was roughly repulsed by him. The shock and disappointment caused her to faint, and, when she came to, she found herself alone with an old woman servant, who told her that she had had orders to convey her to the lodgings that had been taken for her. She asked eagerly what had happened to her brother, and the old woman told her that he had assaulted her master and had threatened both him and Lord Byron with a prosecution for abduction. But as he believed that Georgiane had consented to the elopement, he had declared that he would never see her more but would abandon her to her fate.

Georgiane says that she afterwards heard the explanation of her brother's peculiar conduct, which certainly needs some explanation, but which the explanation she gives certainly does not explain. Having returned from sea, he had been on his way to visit his mother and sister and had just reached the top of Southampton Street when he witnessed the abduction of

Georgiane, though he did not then know that it was his own sister who was being carried off. With true chivalry he had run to the rescue of the distressed lady, but the coach had been driven so fast that it was soon out of sight and he had had to give up the chase. But on entering Mrs. Jackson's house and enquiring for his sister, he had been greeted by that lady with the cry: "Oh fly, sir, to her relief, Lord — has this moment run away with her."

Furious with rage and anxiety, the young naval officer had hastened off to the Earl's house, and, being told that his Lordship was out, had waited outside the door until he returned and then seized hold of him and forcibly exacted an explanation from him. He had then gone on to see Lord Byron at his house in Marlborough Street. Byron had declared upon his honour that he knew nothing whatever about the affair and had not even seen Miss Bellamy that evening, which last at any rate was perfectly true. Young O'Hara believed him, and, apparently without making any further enquiries, concluded that his young sister was "depraved enough to enter into an illicit connection with an old unprincipled married man and was a lost abandoned girl". Overcome with grief and disgust, he had decided to leave London forthwith and rejoin his ship at Portsmouth.

It is rather difficult to credit this story, and especially the part played in it by a presumably intelligent naval officer. How, for instance, could O'Hara have believed so readily that his sister had been a willing party to an elopement if with his own eyes he had witnessed the abduction and thought it his duty to try and rescue the unfortunate lady who was being forcibly carried off? And is it likely that, even if he had believed Georgiane to be guilty, he would have abandoned so young a girl to her fate in a strange house without even listening to anything she had to say in her defence? But apart from all this, the whole story does not ring true. Georgiane herself says that, when she arrived at the lodging that had been taken for her in Broad Street, Carnaby Market, she found that it was the house of her own mantua-maker, a Mrs. Mirvan, who did all in her power to help and comfort her. Such a convenient coincidence is a little difficult to credit, and it seems more probable that the circumstances of the affair were really such that it was Georgiane herself who decided to seek shelter with Mrs. Mirvan. At any rate there appears to have been no restraint on her, and there seems to have been no reason why she should not have walked straight out of the house and gone home. She says, indeed, that her family would have nothing to do with her and that all her letters to her mother were returned unopened. This may have been true after the scandal broke; but what was to prevent her going home before anything was known of her escapade? The town did not believe that she was as innocent as she claimed to be, and a flippant lampoon summed up what appears to have been the general opinion:

> *Ma belle amie*, I pry the esay,
> The first time thou wert stol'n away,
>   Without a bonnet,
> Why didst thou in the coach sit quiet?
> Why didst thou not kick up a riot?
>   O fie upon it!

It is, perhaps, understandable that Georgiane should have been "too much depressed by the public scandal to attempt a reinstatement in the theatrical line," though, if she was so entirely innocent of all fault as she says, it is singular that she did not hasten to seek the advice of her good friend, Quin. Was she, perhaps, too ashamed of herself to face him? Was it not possible that she had been a consenting party to the elopement in the sanguine expectation that it would be followed by marriage, and that, after having thoroughly compromised herself in the eyes of the world at least, she had backed out at the last moment on realising that no such ceremony was intended then or in the future?

Whatever may have been the true circumstances of the

affair, her experiences and their repercussions had no doubt been far from pleasant, and it is scarcely surprising that she should have fallen ill with what she describes as a slow fever. When she recovered, her doctor advised her to go to the country to convalesce. The kindly mantua-maker offered to lend her the money to do so, for she had none of her own. After much thought she decided to go to a Mrs. Clarke, a relative of her mother's who lived at Braintree in Essex. The Clarkes were Quakers, and there was little likelihood that the story of her disgrace would have reached them. Moreover, Mrs. Clarke's sister, who had recently died, had left Georgiane £300 on condition that she did not follow her mother's wicked example and go on the stage. Having already started on her theatrical career, she had not claimed the legacy, but, if her relations had not yet heard that she had taken this step, as seemed likely, it might still be possible for her to obtain the money, which would be a great help to her in her present trouble.

Chapter Three

GEORGIANE TRAVELLED DOWN TO ESSEX BY STAGE-COACH, and bearing in mind the Duchess of Queensberry's good advice, was careful to see that she was both simply and neatly dressed. This had the excellent effect, which she had not foreseen, of leading her relatives to suppose that she was what was known as a *wet* Quaker, a name tolerantly given to those less rigid members of the sect who allowed themselves to indulge within reason in ribbands, gauzes, and laces. Her explanation that she had come to the country to recover after a serious illness, borne out as it was by her extreme pallor, was readily accepted by her cousins, who made no further enquiries about the possible reasons for her unexpected visit. They also presumed that she had come to claim her legacy, and, on the day following her arrival, paid her the interest so far due on it, which enabled her to remit part of the debt she owed to Mrs. Mirvan. And a few days later, without asking whether she had done anything to forfeit it, they paid her the whole sum, which she had no compunction in accepting.

The peaceful existence in this quiet Quaker household was just what she wanted and needed at the moment, and for a time she was quite happy. She even enjoyed a meed of the admiration for which she always craved, for the Quaker apothecary who was called in to attend her fell in love with her and was not discouraged by her relations, who regarded him as a suitable match for her. At the time of the annual fair at Braintree this new admirer gave a party at his house in her honour. But as luck would have it a certain Mr. Zachary Moore happened to be staying in the neighbourhood with a friend of the apothecary's and was also invited. This eccentric character, whom Georgiane describes as being "as distinguished for his misfortunes as his dissipation", had run through a fortune that had at one time amounted to £25,000 a year, partly through swindlers and partly by his own extravagance. When the friend who had brought him to the party explained to him that Miss Bellamy was a *wet* Quaker, for whom their host the apothecary had an inclination, Mr. Moore, with an absence of tact surprising in one who called himself a man of the world, exclaimed in a voice loud enough to be heard by the whole company: "A wet Quaker, indeed! It is Miss Bellamy, the celebrated actress, who met with such applause the last winter at Covent Garden Theatre!"

Since Mrs. Clarke appeared to take no notice of what he had said, Georgiane devoutly hoped that she had not heard. Shortly afterwards her cousin ordered her carriage, which was to take the ladies home, but Mr. Clarke, who enjoyed his bottle of wine, elected to stay on for a while at the party and follow them later. They were giving a lift to another lady for part of the way, and during the journey home Mrs. Clarke still made no allusion to Mr. Moore's inopportune revelation. Georgiane began to feel more at ease. But when Mrs. Clarke stumbled on alighting from the chaise and Georgiane went to her assistance, she drew herself up with the air of a tragedy queen and exclaimed the one word "Avaunt"! At first Georgiane thought that the objurgation might be addressed to her cousin's dog, which had run to welcome her home; but when they got indoors Mrs. Clarke proceeded: "Avaunt! Thou art a child of iniquity! Thou hast sold thyself to the impure one! Thou art an impostor!"

Georgiane protested that she had told her no lies, which may have been literally correct, though she had certainly refrained from telling her the truth, and Mrs. Clarke seemed inclined to be somewhat mollified by her explanations, when Mr. Clarke unfortunately appeared, a little the worse for drink, and told them that he had heard the whole story of the Byron episode from Mr. Moore, and, having been assured that the world adjudged Georgiane innocent, had determined to intervene in the affair and avenge the ill treatment inflicted upon one of his dear wife's relations. His championship only served to arouse his wife's jealousy, and once again she attacked Georgiane in her picturesque Biblical language. "Avaunt!" she cried again. "Avaunt! Perdition will follow thee. Thou comest with all thy frauds to seduce my best beloved. Satan hath got hold of thee, as well as thy parent. Therefore, I pray thee, leave my mansion!"

Mr. Clarke thereupon expostulated with his wife, and when at last the argument between them had died down Georgiane said that, after what had passed, she could not think of spending another day under their roof. She was not offended at Mrs. Clarke's insinuation that she intended to seduce her beloved spouse from his conjugal fidelity, for she found that merely laughable, but she could not brook the insult offered to her dear mother, whose name she would not hear mentioned with disrespect. It was now growing late, and they all calmed down and went to bed. The next day the atmosphere in the house appeared to have resumed its accustomed serenity, but Georgiane still thought that it would be more prudent to leave, and, in spite of her cousins' persuasions, she decided to go to Ingatestone to visit a Miss White, a young Quakeress whom she had met down there and who had pressed her to come and stay with her. Mrs. Clarke obligingly sent her over in her chaise, and on parting presented her with a copy of Robert Barclay's *Apology*, the celebrated exposition of the Quaker tenets, which, she says, some years after proved of the most essential service to her.

Finding on her arrival at Ingatestone that the Whites were away in London, Georgiane ordered the chaise to take her to the best inn in the town and there dismissed it. While her dinner was being prepared, she went for a walk in the fields, and, ascending a hill to look at the view, observed a farm which attracted her by its neat and well-kept appearance. On her way home she encountered a snake and was so terrified that she fled from it and was climbing a stile when she was stopped by a small boy, who advised her not to proceed because there was a very vicious bull in the next field. But he was armed with a big stick and promised that he would protect her from the snake, so she willingly accepted his escort and arrived safely back at the inn, where she invited the landlady to share her dinner. During the meal the good woman entertained her with local gossip. She told her that Lord Petre had a noble house and estate adjoining the town, and added that his lordship's family was one of the worthiest in the world, although they were Roman Catholics. Georgiane could not help smiling at this reservation and admitted that she herself was of that religion, though an unworthy member of it. Then, to change a somewhat delicate subject, she asked who lived at the delightful farm she had seen from the hill. Her hostess told her that it belonged to a rich farmer, but that he and his family were Papishes. Georgiane was curious to know what difference there was between Roman Catholics and Papishes, to which the good woman replied: "Lord, Miss, surely you know the difference between a Hind and a Lord."

After her experience of a Quaker household, Georgiane thought she might fare better at the hands of her co-religionists, and she soon came to terms with Mrs. Williams, the farmer's wife. She removed to the farm that evening. They proved to be kindly and simple people, and they gave her a warm welcome as a member of their own faith. The good Catholic farmer obtained permission for her to attend Lord Petre's private chapel on Sundays and holy days. Although at this time the penal laws against Roman Catholics were still in force and most Catholics were obliged to meet in secret and envelope their proceedings in a certain degree of obscurity, a few ancient and highly-placed Catholic families, such as the Howards, the Cliffords, the Welds, and the Petres, were bold enough to flout the law and continue to worship more or less openly, if discreetly, in the private chapels of their great country houses, and even to extend the privilege to the humbler members of their faith who lived in the neighbourhood. But they were always liable to be denounced, and the credentials of strangers who professed to be Catholics had to be carefully scrutinised before they could be admitted.

Writing many years later, Georgiane professed to have revelled in these peaceful weeks of rustic simplicity in this calm retreat, where she enjoyed a tranquillity such as she had never experienced since she left the convent at Boulogne. Yet it was not long before the simple pleasures of the country began to pall and she was soon hankering to return to the theatre and the gaieties of an urban life. But how were her wishes to be accomplished? It appeared that she had cut herself off from it all, and none of her constant letters to her mother had met with a reply. Then, one day, when she was seated reading in a meadow, Mrs. Bellamy herself appeared before her with such suddenness that she at first took her for a ghost. The illusion was no doubt aided by the circumstance that the book she had been engrossed in happened to be Mrs. Rowe's *Letters from the Dead to the Living*. Georgiane "fell senseless on the flowery carpet of nature", or, in other words, promptly performed her customary faint. When she came to, her mother explained to her that her arch-enemy, the Irish relative, had maliciously intercepted and suppressed all her letters home and that, after her death, which had recently taken place, they had been found among her papers. The mystery of her daughter's apparent silence having now been cleared up, Mrs. Bellamy had hastened on the wings of maternal affection to atone for her unkind and inconsiderate behaviour. A touching and affectionate reconciliation followed, though Georgiane, always intent upon reiterating her complete innocence in the Byron episode, made a point of declaring that the voice of forgiveness could not have been more acceptable to her, had she really been culpable.

Mrs. Bellamy had brought with her some of her daughter's fashionable finery, and, on the following Sunday, when she attended Lord Petre's chapel, Georgiane could not resist the temptation to wear one of her London dresses, further adorned with some fine lace given to her by Mrs. Jackson. But the discovery that the neat and modest little crow they had been fostering in their midst was really a gay and sprightly peacock, lost her the affection and respect of the good, simple, farmfolk who now looked upon her and her modish mother with suspicious eyes.

A few days later Mrs. Bellamy went back to London, having arranged that Georgiane should follow her as soon as she had sounded Rich about re-engaging her at Covent Garden and, if he consented to do so, had procured a suitable lodging for her. But it so happened that, on her way to see Rich, Mrs. Bellamy ran into Tom Sheridan, who told her that he had come over to London to engage actors for the Smock Alley Theatre in Dublin, of which he had just assumed the management. Having heard of Georgiane's success at Covent Garden last season, he was very anxious to secure her for his company and pressed Mrs. Bellamy to persuade her to join him, but she sensibly replied that she could not do so until after she had seen Mr. Rich, to whom her daughter lay under the greatest obligations. On being consulted, Rich strongly advised her to accept Sheridan's offer. Georgiane would gain most valuable and much needed experience. Moreover, she would have the advantage of playing leading roles, which she could not yet hope to do on the London stage. At that time the principal parts in the plays which made up the established repertory were considered to be as much the property of particular performers as their weekly salary, and novices were only permitted to play them on special occasions as a trial of their talents. Mrs. Bellamy took his excellent advice and accepted Sheridan's offer on Georgiane's behalf.

Sheridan was so anxious to clinch the bargain that he was already waiting for Georgiane when she arrived at the lodging her mother had engaged for her in Chelsea, and the contract was speedily drawn up and signed. He insisted that she should leave for Ireland almost at once and allowed her very little time to make her preparations. She herself was not disposed to linger in London. Whether through bashful timidity, as she claims, or through consciousness that they really would have cause to blame and reproach her, she found herself unable to screw up enough courage to go and see either Rich or Quin before she left.

Sheridan himself shepherded his party to Parkgate, whence they were to sail for Ireland. Mrs. Bellamy accompanied Georgiane, and the other recruits for the company consisted of Mrs. Elmy and a promising actor called Lacy, who was to play the parts of romantic young lovers. Mrs. Elmy, now rather past her first youth, was already an established actress of fair repute. According to Georgiane, she was a humourist and possessed of great good sense, though her want of powers had always prevented her from making a really conspicuous figure on the stage. This description of her seems to be borne out by what Chetwood says of her: "She knows what she does as well as what she says," he remarks, but goes on to say that her voice was not powerful enough for the theatre and that consequently she shone more off the stage than on it, a quality of rather dubious advantage to a professional actress. Her maiden name had been Mors, and she had been married to a Mr. Elmy, of whom the sole fact that appears to be known is that he was born at Norwich. "But where he is now," says Chetwood, "I believe neither she nor I can tell." On this journey to Ireland Mrs. Elmy was accompanied by a humble admirer called Morgan who was in last stages of consumption, but Chetwood discreetly says that he did not know her well enough to be any judge of her morals. She seems, at all events, to have been a most lively and amusing companion, and Georgiane's filial feelings did not prevent her from being diverted by her constant tiffs with Mrs. Bellamy, at whose formality and pomposity she delighted in poking fun. She was for ever shocking her exaggerated propriety by her levity and low humour, both, as Georgiane thought, often assumed through

46

deliberate contrariness. The truth was that Mrs. Elmy was a real old trouper and was irritated by Mrs. Bellamy's excessively ladylike airs and pretentious assumption of the role of distinguished amateur.

During the journey they halted to change post-horses at a place in Staffordshire called Evisee Bank,* with which Mrs. Elmy was so enchanted that Georgiane laughingly dubbed her the Countess of Evisee. The unforeseen result of their keeping up this joke was that at all the inns the pretended Countess was given the best rooms, and more respect and attendance were shown to her than to the rest of the party. This so enraged Mrs. Bellamy that she told Georgiane that if she did not immediately "undignify her ladyship", she would insist upon their leaving the party and travelling separately for the rest of the journey.

When they arrived at Parkgate, they found that the wind was contrary and were told that there was no immediate prospect of their being able to sail. In the circumstances, Sheridan, who was fretting to get back to Dublin to look after his affairs, decided to go on alone by way of Holyhead. He left Mrs. Bellamy in charge of the party. But after they had remained at Parkgate for several more days and the chance of their sailing appeared to be as remote as ever, Mrs. Elmy urged Georgiane to persuade her mother to let them go on to Holyhead. Mrs. Bellamy was at first reluctant to ignore the manager's instructions, but at length was prevailed upon to consent, and horses and a guide were hired for the journey.

Georgiane had never ridden before, but she enjoyed the novel experience on the first day's journey, and on the next day their cavalcade was agreeably augmented by a party of Irish gentlemen whom they had already encountered at Chester. Among them was a middle-aged linen- merchant named Crump, who was returning to Dublin from Chester Fair, which he attended twice a year. Though somewhat hard-favoured, he was lively, obliging, and intelligent, and Georgiane was not at

* The real name of the place is Ivetsey Bank.

all displeased when he seemed disposed to pay assiduous attentions to her mother.

They had enjoyed fine weather until they reached Penmaen-mawr, when they were suddenly caught in a severe thunder-storm. At the very height of it, and when cataracts of rain were descending upon them, Mrs. Elmy held up their progress by falling off her horse in a road so narrow that they were obliged to ride in single file. Some of the gentlemen hastily dismounted and ran to her assistance, but she flatly refused to rise until she had declaimed what she considered to be some appropriate lines from the tragedy of *Jane Shore*.

> Fall then, ye mountains, on my guilty head;
> Hide me, ye rocks, with your secret caverns;
> Cast your black veil upon my shame, O night;
> And shield me with your sable wings for ever.

It was scarcely surprising that this impromptu performance, however spiritedly she may have delivered it, failed to appeal to the dripping cavaliers who had hastened to the lady's aid on a mountain-top in a downpour of rain. Fortunately Mrs. Elmy was not seriously injured by her fall, though she had cut her foot rather badly and had to halt at a cottage near by to bathe it with brandy. Georgiane good-naturedly offered to stay with her, but she herself was drenched to the skin in her thin riding-habit, and her mother insisted upon her accepting Mr. Crump's gallant offer to carry her pillion for the rest of the way. He was mounted on a swift hunter, and they so far out-distanced the rest of the company that they arrived at Bangor well ahead of them. Nor had any of them yet arrived when Georgiane, having changed into dry clothes provided by the landlady, descended to join Mr. Crump. Much to her embarrassment, he began to display what, to her already well accustomed eye, were unmistakeable signs of a disposition to make advances to her. She had no desire to dally with an elderly man whom she had been regarding as an appropriate suitor for her mother and adroitly anticipated his declaration by informing him that she was a female Narcissus and so very much in love with herself that she could not surrender her heart to anyone else. Mr. Crump's ardour was damped by this very patent discouragement, and he did not persist with his proposal. Soon after, and to her great relief, the rest of the party arrived. They were all soaked and sopping, and now at last Mrs. Bellamy had an ample revenge for all the pinpricks she had been suffering from Mrs. Elmy by being able to gloat over and even to contribute to her discomfort. She had been careful to provide herself with a change of clothing, and Georgiane had already secured every unemployed article belonging to the good landlady's wardrobe, so there was not a dry garment available for poor Mrs. Elmy, who was obliged to strip herself and go to bed in a sort of crib in a closet off the room which Mrs. Bellamy had appropriated for herself and Georgiane. And it was with great reluctance that Mrs. Bellamy consented to her being stowed even in that confined space. But if Mrs. Elmy suffered, the gentlemen fared still worse. There were no beds at all for them, and they were obliged to sit up all night. At five o'clock next morning they resumed their journey to Holyhead, where they arrived less than half an hour before the packet was due to sail. Georgiane was so fatigued that she went straightway to her cabin and fell into a deep sleep from which she did not awake until she heard the voice of the look-out on the ship crying that the Hill of Howth was in sight.

Chapter Four

As soon as she had recovered from the fatigues of her journey, Georgiane went to pay her respects to Miss O'Hara, Lord Tyrawley's elderly unmarried sister, who, she says, had not seen her since she was an infant. And, unfortunately, the poor lady was unable to see her now, for she had become quite blind. But she gave her a warm welcome, and since her distinguished brother had openly acknowledged this presentable young creature as his daughter, she was quite prepared to introduce her as her niece to her circle of fashionable and aristocratic friends. Though she did not approve of the profession the girl had chosen, this mattered the less because Georgiane went by the name of her mother's husband, to which alone, having been born in wedlock, she was legally entitled. At least her aunt could rest assured that the ancient and illustrious name of O'Hara would remain entirely untarnished by contamination with the theatre. The family affected to trace it back to Milesius, King of Spain, through his eldest son, Hiberius, who, with his brother Heremon, was supposed to have established a colony in Ireland sometime in the dark backward of the Celtic mists.

Georgiane's introduction into the high society of Dublin came even sooner than she had dared to hope, for, while she was still with her aunt, Mrs. Butler and her daughter were announced. The Honourable Mrs. Butler was one of the foremost leaders of Irish Society, as much by reason of her own personality as by reason of her husband's rank and position. The elder daughter and co-heiress of Duncan Cummin, M.D., she had been the widowed Mrs. Ormsby when, in 1730, she had married Colonel the Honourable Thomas Butler, younger brother of the first Viscount Lanesborough. She had been a toast of the town in her youth and still retained traces of her former beauty. Her daughter, Mary, only a little younger than Georgiane, was handsome, spirited, sensible, and good-humoured, and the two girls took to each other at once. Mrs. Butler readily agreed to extend her valuable patronage to Georgiane, and, before she took her leave, asked Miss O'Hara to bring her to dine and spend the evening next day at her house in Stephen's Green.

Delighted by this fortunate encounter, Georgiane hastened home and found that, while she was out, Miss St. Leger, whom she had met in the old days at Jones's shop in St. James's Street, had also called to ask her to come and see her next morning at Lady Doneraile's, where she was staying. Elizabeth St. Leger, who was some five or six years older than Georgiane, was also a person of rank and fashion, being the daughter of Sir John St. Leger and a near relation of Lord Doneraile. Thus the snobbish little Georgiane found, to her great joy, that she was, as she expresses it, "en train to be introduced into the first circle in Dublin."

She was so elated by the brilliant prospects that seemed to be opening before her that she suggested to her mother and Mr. Crump, who happened to be there, that, since her own professional and social engagements were likely to occupy most of her time, her mother should try to divest herself of her formality and persuade Mr. Crump to bestow all his leisure hours on her. Mr. Crump professed himself by no means unwilling, but Mrs. Bellamy, not surprisingly, was much displeased with her daughter for having taken such an unallowable freedom with her.

Next morning Georgiane breakfasted with Miss St. Leger, who received her with all imaginable politeness and invited her to stay on to dinner. Georgiane was probably not displeased to be able to tell her that she was already engaged to dine with Mrs. Butler. Miss St. Leger congratulated her; Mrs. Butler's acquaintance, she said, was the most desirable of any in Dublin.

Unfortunately, she herself was precluded from enjoying it, because Mrs. Butler and Lady Doneraile were not on speaking terms. The dinner with Mrs. Butler proved a great success; her hostess not only promised to act as her patroness, but also invited her to come to her house whenever her theatrical duties permitted. The culmination of her joys was reached when she discovered that the Viceroy was her father's old friend, the Earl of Chesterfield, who also promised her his patronage.

The curious name of the theatre at which Georgiane was to appear had a somewhat dubious origin. The proper name of the street in which it stood had been Orange Street, but, according to the prompter, Chetwood, it "took the appellation of Smock Alley from Mother Bungy, of infamous memory, and was in her days a sink of sin". But although the authorities had cleared the neighbourhood of its old population of thieves, murderers, and harlots, and it was now quite respectable, the street and the theatre still retained their disreputable nickname.

The theatrical season opened in September, but it was not until November 11th that Georgiane made her first appearance as Monimia, with Sheridan as Chamont, Spranger Barry as Castalio, and Lacy as Polydore. Her success was immediate. "This young and amiable actress . . . has a most admirable improving genius; therefore it will be no wonder if she soon reaches the top of perfection. She has a liberal open heart to feel and ease the distresses of the wretched. How amiable must blooming beauty appear, that forms the mind with every moral virtue!" says Chetwood, who seems to have fallen completely and genuinely under the spell of the "inchanting Bellamy", as he too calls her. She, in turn, was so flattered by his tributes to her charm and talent that she subscribed for twenty copies of his book on the theatre, which contained them, when it was published in 1749.

In Dryden's *All For Love* she played Cleopatra, with Barry as Antony and Sheridan as Ventidius. For this production Sheridan had provided for Georgiane a special costume which he had brought back from his recent visit to London. It was a superb dress of silver tissue, which had belonged to the Princess of Wales and had been worn by her only once on the occasion of the King's birthday. The princess was a woman of truly regal proportions, while Georgiane was a tiny creature with a remarkably slender waist, so Mrs. Bellamy sent her maid to the theatre to help the wardrobe mistress to take in the dress and also to sew on it a number of diamond ornaments which Mrs. Butler had lent to Georgiane for this great occasion. When the women had finished their work, they all went out of the room, foolishly leaving the door open. Mrs. Furnivall, an older actress in the company who was jealous of Georgiane and her success, espied the dress as she was passing by the door and whisked it off to her own dressing-room, determined to wear it in the character of Octavia, which she was to have played in the black velvet robe traditionally considered suitable for the part of the modest Roman matron. Since her proportions resembled those of the Princess of Wales rather than those of Georgiane, she set about unpicking the work that had just been done.

When Georgiane's maid returned to the dressing-room and found that the dress had vanished, she was as one distracted and rushed about the theatre trying to find out who had taken it. On discovering that Mrs. Furnivall had it, she went to her dressing-room and demanded it, and, when Mrs. Furnivall refused to hand it over, attacked her with such vehemence and fury that she might have done her serious injury, had not her cries brought people hurrying to her assistance. Georgiane's maid was hustled out of the room, while Mrs. Furnivall triumphantly retained possession of the costume.

On arriving at the theatre, Georgiane found her maid in tears, but she herself was more amused than annoyed. Nothing concerning a theatre, she says, could at that time affect her temper. Moreover, she admits that she enjoyed a secret pleasure at the thought of what the ultimate result was likely to be. She did, indeed, send to Mrs. Furnivall for the jewels, only to receive from her an insolent message that she should have them back after the play.

c

Thus deprived of her costume, Georgiane hit upon the ingenious expedient of making Mrs. Furnivall look still more ridiculous by appearing "as plain in the character of the luxurious Queen of Egypt as Antony's good wife ought to have been". She dressed herself in simple white satin with a few pearls in her hair. When she first entered the Green Room in this modest attire, and Sheridan asked her with some warmth why she was dressed like that, she replied that she had taken the advice Ventidius had sent to Cleopatra by Alexis and had parted with both her clothes and jewels to Antony's wife. Sheridan could not understand what she meant, but as the curtain was about to go up he had no time to pursue the subject.

Rumours had got around about the magnificence of the costume Miss Bellamy was going to wear in this play, so the audience was greatly astonished when she appeared in virginal white. Mrs. Butler, in the stage-box, was as surprised as the rest, but concluded that Georgiane purposed to reserve her regalia for the scene in which she was to meet Antony.

When Mrs. Furnivall made her entrance in all the magnificence of her borrowed plumes, Sheridan was so taken aback that he forgot his lines and just stared at her. At the same time Mrs. Butler loudly exclaimed: "Good Heaven! the woman has got on my diamonds." The audience naturally thought that Mrs. Butler was accusing the actress of robbing her, and there was great excitement, but as Sheridan, having recovered himself, went on calmly and smilingly with the play, they concluded that there must be some mystery and subsided until the end of the act. But then, after warmly applauding the other performers, they shouted: "No more Furnivall! No more Furnivall!" Mrs. Furnivall was so chagrined at being disappointed of her expected triumph that she promptly had a fit of hysterics, and her part had to be played for the remainder of the performance by Mrs. Elmy, who happened to be in the theatre, and who, says Georgiane with more than a touch of malice, should in any case have had the preference for the part.

On the following night the piece was repeated, and Georgiane, triumphant at having recovered her dress and her jewels, gave a magnificent performance. As she was making her exit, a young man standing by the wings, as privileged spectators were then permitted to do, took what she describes as "a very unallowable method of showing his approbation" by kissing the back of her neck as she passed. She instantly turned round and slapped his face before the whole audience. Lord Chesterfield, who was present, was delighted at her action and signified his approval by rising from his seat and clapping. The rest of the audience took their cue from the Viceroy and applauded also. At the end of the act His Excellency sent his aide-de-camp, Major Macartney, to the offending gentleman to require him to make a public apology, which he immediately did with penitence and a good grace. It appeared that he had been a little flushed with liquor, otherwise he would not have indulged in this sad lapse from decorum. His name was John St. Leger, and he was the elder brother of Georgiane's dear friend, Elizabeth. Georgiane does not say whether she knew who he was at the time. But the little incident had good effects in the long run, for it gave Sheridan an adequate excuse for issuing an order that, in future, no gentlemen were to be admitted behind the scenes. From the moment when he took over the management of the theatre, it had been his professed ambition to bring about an improvement in the behaviour of the audience, which of recent years had become increasingly rowdy and ill-mannered.*

Later in the season the company received a great accession of strength through the arrival on November 24th of David Garrick, who, having had a dispute with the management of Drury Lane and not being satisfied with the terms offered him by the rival house, had decided to accept Sheridan's invitation to join his company in Ireland. He was assured of an enthusiastic welcome in Dublin, for he had already appeared at

* Georgiane herself places the foregoing incidents in the following season of 1746–47, but she must have been mistaken, for by then Barry was no longer in the company, and Lord Chesterfield was no longer Viceroy.

the Smock Alley Theatre with Peg Woffington in 1742, and his fame and prestige had notably increased since then. The arrangement now was that he and Sheridan should both appear in all the plays, sharing the chief characters between them. Garrick opened as Hamlet on December 9th, with Mrs. Storer as Ophelia. It was not until later in the season that Georgiane first played this part. Garrick also took over the part of Chamont in *The Orphan* from Sheridan, who now played Polydore. Barry remained the Castalio. Barry, indeed, though a newcomer to the stage, was sometimes a formidable rival to the two other chief actors. In the *Fair Penitent*, in which Georgiane played Lavinia, Barry's performance in the usually unrewarding part of Altamont was so outstanding that his part seemed as consequential as those of the base seducer, Lothario, and the excellent Horatio, played by Garrick and Sheridan. The first performance of this play was on New Year's Day, 1746. The tall, handsome, silver-tongued Barry also shone as Othello. Garrick and Sheridan generously acknowledged that he surpassed them both in this role and decided to surrender it to him altogether and to take it in turns to play Iago. Georgiane was the Desdemona. She had already played the part with Sheridan as Othello. The yielding gentleness demanded of this heroine came easily to her, and she was afterwards accounted one of the best Desdemonas of her time.

A favourite play in the repertory this season was Vanbrugh and Cibber's the *Provoked Husband*, in which Garrick and Georgiane played Lord and Lady Townley. One evening when Georgiane was performing in this play she received a card from Mrs. Butler asking her to come to her house as soon as she was free. Being rather tired, she sent back a verbal message by the servant saying that she was sorry but she would be too fatigued after the performance to do so. But a little later she received another more peremptory note telling her that she must absolutely come the moment she had finished, without even waiting to change her dress. This aroused her curiosity, and, as it happened that one of the actors in the afterpiece, in which she was also to have appeared, was suddenly taken ill and another piece in which her services were not required was hastily substituted, she was able to get away from the theatre rather earlier than she had expected. And so she summoned her chair and hastened off to Stephen's Green, still wearing the very modish dress in which she had played Lady Townley. She arrived just as Colonel Butler and the gentlemen were joining the ladies after dinner. But to her great amazement her hostess greeted her with no more than a formal nod of recognition, and none of the other ladies spoke to her. Greatly upset by this cold and unaccustomed reception, she hastened to Miss O'Hara who was present, and asked her what was the matter. Her aunt replied that a few minutes would determine whether she herself would ever notice her again.

Among the gentlemen present was an extremely handsome and elegant young man whom she had not met before. Presently, since nobody seemed to talk to him either, he came up to Georgiane and entered into conversation with her. He told her that he had just returned from making the grand tour and had come back to take possession of his estate in Ireland. Relieved at having somebody to talk to, Georgiane conversed with him with as much animation and cheerfulness as she could muster in the trying circumstances. After a time Mary Butler came to fetch away her companion, who immediately sought out his hostess and asked her who the lovely stranger was with whom he had been talking. His question had been discreetly asked in a low tone, but Mrs. Butler replied loudly so that all in the room could hear her: "Surely you must know her. I am certain you know her; nay that you are well acquainted already." The young man, rather surprised, replied that he had never seen her before. "Fye! fye! Mr. Medlicote," said Mrs. Butler, "what can you say for yourself, when I inform you that this is the dear girl whose character you so cruelly aspersed at dinner?"

Mrs. Butler then explained the mystery to Georgiane. It appeared that this Mr. Medlicote had boasted that he had

received her favours in London, and that they thought it
necessary to subject her to this ordeal, so that his assertions
could be proved or disproved once for all. Had he seen her
first at the theatre, he might have maintained them to save his
own face, and some doubt might have remained. But her
character had been conclusively and triumphantly vindicated
by his utter failure to recognise her. The boastful Mr. Medlicote, covered with shame and confusion, hastily took his
departure, while Georgiane was made much of by the contrite
company. This is Georgiane's own version of the incident; it
may not have happened quite like that, and it is difficult not to
suspect that her account is considerably embellished. She
declares that this running of the gauntlet so upset her that next
day she fell ill, and it was some time before she felt well
enough to resume her duties at the theatre.

The feminine side of the company at Smock Alley was not so
strong as the male, and Georgiane had to appear almost every
night, sometimes, as she herself admits, in characters not very
fit for her. But she was not really the best judge of that. She
had, for instance, so set her heart on playing Constance in
Shakespeare's *King John* that she had actually stipulated for it in
her agreement with Sheridan. But Garrick, who was to play
the Bastard Falconbridge to Sheridan's King John, considered
Georgiane far too young to play Constance and sensibly
suggested that Prince Arthur was the better part for her. In her
Apology, written at the end of her career, she herself acknowledges that he was right, that she did not yet possess enough
experience to play Constance, and that, in any case, her slender
figure was more properly adapted for the lady's son, Prince
Arthur. But she did not think so at the time. Garrick remained adamant and insisted that Mrs. Furnivall should play
Constance. In spite of the agreement he had made with
Georgiane, Sheridan felt obliged to give in to his insistence.
And probably at heart he agreed with Garrick. But Georgiane
flatly refused to be fobbed off with the part of Prince Arthur,
and in the end it was played by Miss Orpheur, who, though

Georgiane's age, "from being hard-favoured, looked much older."

Georgiane was so chagrined at this frustration of her dearest wish that she flew to Mrs. Butler, who rather foolishly espoused her cause and requested all her friends not to attend the theatre on the night of the representation. A request of this kind coming from Mrs. Butler was almost a command, since nobody dared to run the risk of offending Dublin's most fashionable hostess and not being asked to her parties in consequence. On February 5th, 1746, the night of the first performance, therefore, the rank and fashion of Dublin kept away, the house was very thin, and the receipts did not amount to £40. Georgiane's ill-considered triumph was rendered complete when, on the play's revival, Garrick thought it more judicious to withdraw his objection and allow her to play Constance. The house was crowded, and people had to be turned away. Georgiane received an ovation, which she unhesitatingly attributed to her playing, though it is far more likely to have been due to amused appreciation of a young girl's victory over the increasingly powerful Garrick.

But before this happened Georgiane had continued to behave with a childish vindictiveness of which she ought to have been thoroughly ashamed. It had been agreed that Garrick was to have two benefits during the season, and for the first he chose *Jane Shore*, in which he was to play Hastings. Willing to make amends to Georgiane for the Constance incident, he asked her to honour him by playing Jane Shore. The spoilt young woman retorted that, if she was too young to play Constance, she was also too young to play Jane Shore. This time Garrick was astute enough to turn the tables on her by being the first to have recourse to Mrs. Butler, knowing that Georgiane was not in a position to refuse any request that came from her. But at the same time he was foolish enough to write Georgiane herself a very silly and sentimental note addressed: "To my soul's idol, the beautiful Ophelia," in which he informed her that, if she would oblige him, he would write her "a goody, goody epilogue, which, with the help of her eyes, should do more mischief than ever the flesh or the devil had done since the world began". Unfortunately, the idle servant to whom he entrusted this injudicious effusion handed it over for delivery to a porter in the street, and this man, completely puzzled by its superscription, gave it to his master, who happened to be a journalist and seized upon it with professional avidity. Next day it appeared in the public prints, much to the embarrassment of its author.

When the Butlers moved out to their country estate in the spring of 1746, Mrs. Bellamy took a furnished house near by at the sheds of Clontarf, where later in the summer Georgiane would be able to indulge in the newly fashionable diversion of sea bathing, which would be beneficial to her health. An intimate and sentimental friendship had by now been established between Georgiane and Mary Butler, and they doted on each other to such an extent that, though they usually dined together and spent the remainder of the day together, two or three notes would also pass between them before they met.

By this time Georgiane had become entirely reconciled with Garrick, who was a frequent visitor to the Butlers. Some days before the conclusion of the season, as Georgiane was walking on the terrace with Mary Butler, Garrick rode up and told them that he had come to bid them farewell, as he was leaving next day for England. This must have been at the beginning of May, for he left Ireland on May 3rd, and the season closed a fortnight later. On his departure, Mrs. Butler presented him with a mysterious package, saying to him: "I here present you, Mr. Garrick, with something more valuable than life. In it you will read my sentiments; but I strictly enjoin you not to open it till you have passed the hill of Howth." Fully expecting that he was receiving a valuable present, with, perhaps, an avowal of Mrs. Butler's concealed passion for him, Garrick took the packet "with a significant, graceful air". But when he had left after dinner, Mrs. Butler revealed to the rest of the company that she had been playing a joke on him and that the contents of the package were Wesley's *Hymns* and Dean Swift's *Discourse on the Trinity*. Georgiane says that, when they next met, Garrick told her that he had incontinently flung Mr. Wesley and the Dean into the sea and offered them up as a sacrifice to Neptune.

The prospects for the next season were not very bright. The loss of Garrick was bound to be severely felt, and, in addition, Barry, anxious to try his fortune in England, had broken his agreement and gone off without giving the manager any previous notice. Benjamin Victor, the theatrical historian, who was at this time deputy-manager and treasurer of the theatre, says that the company was so weak that Sheridan himself and Miss Bellamy were its only members of reputation and that, therefore, it was necessary to choose plays which could be supported by two characters only.

This did not perturb Sheridan unduly, for the great esteem in which he was held by Dublin audiences made him imagine that he was a more versatile actor than he really was. He began to play the roles of romantic lovers, for which, in spite of his good appearance, he was totally unsuited by voice, manner, and temperament. He particularly wanted to revive *Caius Marius*, Otway's queer adaptation of *Coriolanus*, in which the young lovers from *Romeo and Juliet* had been astonishingly introduced under the names of Marius Junior and Lavinia. Victor ventured to suggest that it might be preferable to revive Shakespeare's *Romeo and Juliet* itself, but Sheridan decided that he preferred *Much Ado About Nothing*, which, unhappily, lived up to its name only too well in his production. He and Georgiane played Benedick and Beatrice.

After this failure, he did consent to take Victor's advice and produce *Romeo and Juliet*, in which Georgiane had to play Juliet to his Romeo. This must have been a still odder version of Shakespeare's play than the usual eighteenth century 'improvement', for Sheridan, perhaps because he mistrusted the capacity of other members of his company, added to the part of Romeo other passages which appealed to him, including the famous Queen Mab speech which the poet had allotted to

Mercutio. Nevertheless, it was a very great success and was played for nine nights in succession to great houses, which, as Victor notes, was an extraordinary thing in Dublin. Georgiane's playing of Juliet added greatly to her reputation.

Sheridan also insisted upon playing Antony in Dryden's *All For Love.* "But, oh! what a falling off was here!" says Georgiane. "Instead of the silver-toned voice and bewitching figure of a Barry, which used to enchant the audience, formality and monotonous declamation presented itself. The difference was too conspicuous to escape the observation of the public. And every one regretted the loss of his great powers in the part of Ventidius, wherein, as I have before observed, he was truly capital; as indeed he was in all *sententious* characters." Georgiane herself played Cleopatra. During one of the performances of this play a ludicrous incident occurred, when Mrs. Kennedy, who had a ragged tail to her dress, entered dragging half a kettle-drum after her with a great clatter. Georgiane, who was in the midst of one of her intensest passages, could not contain herself and burst into a loud fit of laughter, in which the audience joined.

It was in this season that Georgiane first undertook the part of Portia in the *Merchant of Venice.* She had already started rehearsing the part when she happened to find herself seated next to the Lord Chief Baron Bowes at a concert in Fishamble Street. A gentleman, mistaking them for father and daughter, remarked on the great resemblance between them, and this gave her the mischievous idea of studying the Lord Chief Baron's bearing and mannerisms for her appearance as the young advocate in the Court scene. Her imitation was so exact that it created much amusement in the audience, and her distinguished victim, instead of bearing resentment, was flattered and delighted, congratulating her particularly on having even copied his habit of coughing in the middle of a long word. She did not think it necessary to reveal to him that she had achieved this effect quite inadvertently, having stumbled over the difficult word 'predicament'.

There were fortunately times when Sheridan himself seems to have doubted his capacity to undertake romantic parts, and it was this, so Georgiane believed, that induced him to revive Vanbrugh's *Æsop*, as a play "more suited to his scientific talents". There was no part in this play really suitable for Georgiane; that of the Young Lady was deemed to be too insignificant for her, while that of the Categorical Lady demanded more volubility than she could compass, and she was obliged to play that of Doris, the old nurse, an uncongenial role of immense length.

The house was very crowded for the first performance on January 19th, 1747. There had been considerable resentment about Sheridan's order excluding members of the audience from the stage, and during the first act a certain Mr. Kelly from Galway, rather the worse for drink, clambered over the spikes which now divided the pit from the stage and made his way to the Green Room, where he found one of the actresses, the eminently respectable Mrs. Dyer, to whom he proceeded to offer a series of indelicate insults. It chanced that Georgiane, who was not quite certain of her lines in the next act and wanted to go over them with Mrs. Dyer, came into the room just as he was trying to pin that unfortunate lady down in an armchair, and, when she expostulated with him, he turned on her, and addressed her in most indecent terms. She ran away, pursued by the abusive Kelly, and locked herself in her dressing-room. When she was wanted on the stage, she dared not come out, and Kelly was making such a noise trying to force the door that Sheridan himself came along to enquire what was happening. Kelly refused the manager's civil request to go away, and finally Sheridan felt obliged to order the attendants to conduct him forcibly back to the pit.

The play then proceeded smoothly until the first scene of the last act, when Kelly seized a basket from one of the orange-women and began pelting Sheridan with oranges. His aim at first was rather erratic, but at last an orange hit the Manager full on the false nose he was wearing, with such force that it made a dent in his forehead. Sheridan promptly stopped the play and went forward and addressed the audience. Then the curtain was dropped, and the rest of the play was abandoned.

The drunken Kelly now forced his way into the manager's office to demand satisfaction for the insult he said had been offered him—and received it in the form of a sound cudgelling from the oak stick which Sheridan had been carrying in the character of Æsop. The indignant drunkard finally took his departure, vowing vengeance and swearing that Sheridan should severely repent this usage to a gentleman. He betook himself to Lucas's Coffee House, the 'Brown Bear', which was the favoured resort of the 'Bucks', the rowdier and more Philistine young men in Dublin society, who, as Georgiane aptly puts it, "had a natural antipathy to all learning, except that kind of knowledge which enabled them to distinguish good claret from bad." There he enlisted the sympathy of his boon-companions by telling them, quite untruly, that Sheridan had had the audacity to declare that he was a better gentleman than anyone who had been that night at the theatre and also that he had been held down by the attendants while Sheridan beat him, which was also untrue. They decided to wreck the theatre and forthwith proceeded there in a body. But finding all the doors closed against them and securely barricaded, they had to abandon their intention for the time being and postpone action until the next night, when they proposed to go and create a riot at the theatre.

The play billed for that evening was Rowe's the *Fair Penitent*, in which Sheridan was to appear as Horatio. He fully expected that an attack would be made on his person, and being a man of courage, would have been quite prepared to face the threatened storm; but he received so many warnings from well-wishers that it would be dangerous to the point of madness for him to make an appearance that in the end he yielded to his friends' persuasions and remained at home. It was as well that he did so, for Kelly and his allies were present at the theatre in force and a very ugly mood, and, when it was announced that the manager would be unable to appear, pandemonium broke loose. They rose in their seats and shouted: "Out with the ladies and down with the house!" Some fifty of them scrambled upon the stage and proceeded to rampage all over the theatre, breaking open every door and searching high and low for Sheridan, whom they believed to be hiding somewhere on the premises. They ransacked the wardrobe, and, when they did not find him there, took a petty revenge by stabbing the stuffing of the padded costume he wore as Falstaff.

Meanwhile Georgiane had taken refuge in her dressing-room, and she had not been long there before two gentlemen came in and assured her that they were there to protect her from possible insult. But she did not trust their good intentions and told them rather tartly that her room was a very improbable place to find the person they were searching for, as she would certainly not undress, were there a gentleman in it. At this point Kelly himself burst into the room and cried out that she was the—who had occasioned all the disturbance. His friends, however, persuaded him to leave after she had permitted them to lift up the covering of her *toilette* to make certain that the manager had not concealed himself underneath it. One of the two gentlemen who first came in, a Mr. Hussey, insisted upon proving that he had acted in sincerity and good faith by walking by the side of her sedan-chair to see that she reached home unmolested.

Being apprehensive of further riots, the Lord Justices instructed the Master of the Revels to order the theatre to be closed for the time being, but the Dublin audiences soon protested that they could not do without their accustomed entertainment, and four weeks later Sheridan was persuaded to re-open the theatre with an assurance that he would receive protection. He chose *Richard III* for his reappearance and took good care that the theatre should be filled with his own friends and supporters. But Kelly and his rowdy friends managed somehow to gain admittance and attempted to start another riot. A member of the audience, a certain Mr. Charles Lucas, thereupon called for silence and proceeded to make a speech in which he stated that the audience had paid their money to see an entertainment, that therefore the actors were under their protection during the performance, and that every interruption and insult offered to them was also an insult to the public. He was enthusiastically supported by the bulk of the audience, and the interrupters had to withdraw discomfited so that the play could proceed. But Mr. Lucas was made to pay dearly for his intervention; two days later he was seized and severely beaten by ruffians in the middle of Sackville Street.

Sheridan thereupon closed the theatre again, and it was not until a few weeks later that he announced a performance of the *Fair Penitent* for the benefit of the Hospital for Incurables. The *élite* of Dublin society rallied to his aid, and the distinguished governors of the hospital also attended in the fond belief that there could be no disturbance in their august presence. But Kelly and his friends were not to be diverted from their intention. They began shouting as soon as Sheridan attempted to speak the prologue, and a free-for-all fight ensued between them and the students from Trinity College, who were there in force to support the manager, who had formerly been one of their number.

Sheridan had already started a prosecution against Kelly; but the young men of Trinity College decided first to take the law into their own hands. Having somehow inveigled Kelly, a Mr. Fitzgerald, and several other ringleaders of the riots into the precincts of the College, they proceeded to inflict summary and condign punishment by bestowing upon them liberal quantities of cold water from the College pump and subjecting them to other appropriate and humiliating ordeals.

Shortly afterwards, both Sheridan and Kelly were arraigned for assault before Mr. Justice Ward, in the presence of a full bench and Lord Chief Justice Maclay himself, who, suspecting that the jury might be 'packed', had given special instructions to the High Sheriff to provide a list of "sufficient and able" jurors who would not be bribed or intimidated by Kelly's friends. On hearing the evidence that Kelly had offered such provoking, abusive language to the manager in his own dressing-room, where, in any case, he had no business to be, that it had been necessary to beat him out of it, the jury acquitted Sheridan without leaving the box. Kelly, on the other hand, was found guilty, and, to the utter amazement and consternation of himself and his friends, was sentenced to three months imprisonment and a fine of £500. But a week in prison, presumably without the solace of his accustomed potations, cooled his head completely, and he made an abject apology and appeal to Sheridan, who magnanimously interceded for him and got the fine remitted and the prisoner set free.

Costly though this affair had been to Sheridan, it turned out advantageous in the long run, for the publicity, the sympathy felt for him, and the general admiration of his generosity towards those who had injured him raised both his popularity and prestige. And the incident was to have still more momentous consequences for the drama. Moved and delighted by some verses which appeared in *Faulkner's Journal* under the title *The Owls: a Fable* and an anonymous pamphlet, both of which extolled his conduct in this affair, Sheridan made enquiries about their author and discovered that she was a young lady called Frances Chamberlaine. He contrived to meet her, immediately fell in love with her, and shortly afterwards married her. She was to become the mother of Richard Brinsley Sheridan.

It appears to have been in the spring of this year, 1747, that Georgiane first met a family, who, in her own words, afterwards made "a very conspicuous figure in the great world". As she was returning one day from rehearsal she heard sounds of lamentation proceeding from a house at the bottom of Britain Street, and overcome by feelings of humanity or curiosity, or perhaps a mixture of the two, she pushed past some seedy-looking men who were guarding the door and went in. There she found "a woman of most elegant figure, surrounded by four beautiful girls and a sweet boy of about three years of age". In reply to her solicitous enquiries, the lady informed her that her name was Mrs. Gunning, and that she and her children were about to be turned out of the house by virtue of an execution. Her husband had been obliged to retire into the country to avoid being arrested for debt, and her brother, Lord Mayo, had remained deaf to all her entreaties for help in her distress. Georgiane, who had probably already had some experience of such matters and was, alas! to have a great deal more during the course of her career, had some eminently practical suggestions to offer. In the first place, as soon as it was dark she would send her manservant to wait under their drawing-room window, where he would collect and bring to her house everything that could be conveniently thrown out to him unobserved by the bailiffs. And while Mrs. Gunning herself went to her husband to help him try to settle their affairs, the children might come to her, since she and her mother had more room than they could conveni n ly occupy. The plan was embraced with grateful alacrity and duly carried out without hitch. Shortly afterwards, Mrs. Gunning's sister, Miss Burke, "a lady of exemplary piety," sent for the younger children, but the two elder girls remained with Georgiane. Only a few years later they were to become two of the most famous beauties of the eighteenth century and to contract brilliant marriages. At this time Georgiane confessed to a slight preference for the elder, Maria, later Countess of Coventry, whose disposition she thought more resembled her own—"all life and spirits", as she describes it. Betty, the younger, later successively Duchess of Hamilton and Duchess of Argyll, and the mother of no less than four dukes, was more reserved and solid.

If an exceedingly ill-spelt and ungrammatical letter from Maria Gunning is authentic, and there is no reason to suppose that it is not, Georgiane must have returned to England with her mother for a while in the summer of 1747, though she makes no mention in her *Apology* of having ever broken this stay in Ireland and, indeed, implies the contrary. But the allusion to Tom Sheridan's recent marriage conclusively dates the letter, and it is quite certain that Georgiane was playing at the Smock Alley Theatre again in the autumn of this year. The letter is addressed somewhat vaguely "To Miss Bellamy in England".*

"I recd my Dearest Miss Bellamy Letter at Last: after her long silence, indeed I was very Jealous with you, but you make me amen's in Letting me hear from you now, it gives me great Joy & all our faimely to hear that yr Dr mama and you Dearest self are in perfect Health to be sure all yr Relations where fighting to see which of them shod have you first and Longest with ym. I hope you are a most tird of england & that we shall soon have your sweet company in Ireland, where you will be heartily welcome, it gives me vast pleasure to hear you haves thoughts of coming over, my Lady . . . . To be sure I dont wonder at it, for you know her heart & soul was wrapit up in his, as to hows being the next heir I believe it will be how my Lord pleases, he is in ye Country & my Lady is with us she cant go to her own house I believe she will go strait to england to Miss Bour, I was very unfortunate to be in the country when our Vaux Hall was, if I was in Town I sho'd be thear & I belive I shoud be more delighted than at a publicker devertion, I am quite alterd since I saw you, there is nothing I love so much as solitude; I dont belive it was Mr. knox you read of at Bath, for he is hear and pray write me word when you saw or heard from Mr. Crump . . . . . is out Town this two months past ever . . . . in the country, Dublin is ye stupites place in the world I hope ye winter will be more . . . tho I see know great Lilihood of it, for I believe Shredian can get know body

---

* A note in the *Apology* (III, p. 197) states that "As it is much defaced by time, there are several breaks in it, but it is given in its present state, and at the same time *verbatim et literatim*." And in a footnote it is stated that the original is in the hands of the publisher. Surely, if this letter had been an invention or a forgery, it would be more complete, coherent, and comprehensible.

to play with him is doing all he can to get frinds for him sef to
be sure you have hread he is marrd for sirtain to Miss Chamber-
lan a sweet pare,

"Papa & Mama & Miss Betty & Miss Kittys sincer love and
compts to you and yr mama yr Littel Husband sends you ten
Thousand kisses he whisses he had you hear to give ym to you
he says they wod be swe . . . Lipes than on paper without
making . . . Compts he shakes me so I can't write . . . Miss
Bellamy will excuse this . . .

"I must bid a due & shall
only say I am my Dr your
ever affecnat.

M. GUNNING.

"Dublin august 31.
"Mrs. Jussy begs Leave to give her Compts to you, & is
rejoyes'd to hear you are well, she is in a very bad state of
health."

Georgiane relates that one day, at the instance of the two fair
sisters, she went with them to visit a female fortune-teller in
Dublin. The three of them disguised themselves in mean
clothes and went on foot. Georgiane wore a wedding ring. If
her recollection of the sybil's prophecies was not coloured by
later knowledge, it must be admitted that they proved
singularly accurate. Miss Molly was to be titled but far from
happy, while Miss Betty would be great to a degree and happy,
though her happiness would be marred by ill health. She told
Georgiane that she might take off the ring she was wearing, as
she never was, nor ever would be married, unless she played
the fool in her old age. Opulence, she said, would court her,
and flattery follow her, but through her own folly she would
be brought to indigence.

In September the company at Smock Alley was reinforced
by the arrival of Henry Woodward, who was accounted one of
the foremost comedians of the time. Georgiane was at first a
little nervous about meeting him again, for, during her first
season at Covent Garden three years before he had fallen in

love with her and asked her to marry him, and her light-hearted refusal had offended him. But he appeared to have recovered from his resentment, and they found that they liked playing together. They had not done so before, because he had been at Drury Lane while she was at Covent Garden. Woodward gave his much admired performance of Lord Foppington in the *Careless Husband*, and Georgiane played Lady Betty Modish. Sheridan insisted upon playing Sir Charles Easy, but Georgiane thought he should have been called Sir Charles *Uneasy*, so awkwardly did he play the part. In the hope of increasing both his popularity and his receipts he had arranged that all the characters in this play were to be dressed in fabrics of Irish manufacture.

Georgiane may have misdoubted Sheridan's capacity for comedy, but she seems to have had no qualms about her own abilities in that field. Woodward had brought over with him Garrick's new and uproarious farce, *Miss in her Teens*, which had been an enormous success in London. He himself repeated his superb rendering of the bogus bully, Captain Flash, and Georgiane did not disdain to play the coquettish Miss Biddy, thus, as she claims, convincing the town that she was "no less qualified to perform in low than in genteel comedy".

As the season drew to a close, Georgiane became more and more convinced that the time had come for her to leave Ireland. Her relations with Sheridan were now becoming increasingly strained, and she was no longer happy at the theatre. Moreover, the social life which she enjoyed so much would be sensibly affected by the departure of her great friends, the Butlers. Mrs. Butler had been seriously ill and contemplated taking a cure at Spa and then going on to the South of France for an indefinite period, taking Mary with her. Miss St. Leger, her other dearest friend, was already in England and was not coming back to Ireland. Miss O'Hara had now become so much an invalid that she never went out.

Her mother was not so anxious to leave Ireland, for she would regret parting from her friend, Mr. Crump, with whom she was now on terms of most intimate friendship. But she changed her mind when that gentleman, doubtless with his own interest in view as well as hers, advised her to invest the considerable sum of money she had managed to save while she was in Dublin in the purchase of Irish linens, which she would be able to dispose of most advantageously in London. And so she agreed that they should go back to England at the end of the theatrical season.

Georgiane's exasperation with Sheridan and her determination to leave Ireland were both increased when Mr. Victor, the treasurer of the theatre, brought her the account of her salary, from which a charge of £75 for orders for free tickets had been deducted. Her own explanation is that the receipts had been falling considerably and that Sheridan himself had asked her to give orders to all the young ladies of her acquaintance who would accept of them. She had done so with a lavish hand, but she did not see why she should be expected to pay for them herself, seeing that it was at the manager's own request that she had given them. Sheridan was most annoyed that she should take this attitude, and she retaliated by refusing to appear at the theatre any more. Next day Mr. Victor arrived with the balance of her account, but offered to pay the full amount if she would enter into a fresh engagement for the following season. But she had now made up her mind to leave Ireland at all costs. Victor describes her departure as an irreparable loss.

Another circumstance may have induced the Bellamies to hasten their departure. Lord Tyrawley was expected in Dublin on a visit to his sister. Seeing that Georgiane had not become reconciled with him, it is perhaps not surprising that she should have been anxious to avoid meeting him; but it is also extremely probable that she had been shamelessly exploiting her relationship to him in order to establish her position in Dublin society and especially with Miss O'Hara, and that she was afraid he would contemptuously prick the iridescent bubble she had blown.

Chapter Five

REMEMBERING UNEASILY that she had gone off to Ireland
without seeing Rich and without consulting or even informing
Quin, to both of whom she owed so much, Georgiane was
more than a little doubtful of the reception she might meet with
at Covent Garden and therefore resolved to try first to secure
an engagement at the other house. And so, as soon as they
were back in London, she got her mother to write and inform
Garrick of their arrival. He immediately invited them to dine
with him that very day at his apartments in King Street,
Covent Garden. He had now become a still more important
personage in the theatrical world, since in April of the previous
year he had acquired a half-interest with Lacy in the patent
of Drury Lane and was entirely responsible for the choice of
both plays and players there. According to Georgiane, he had
been so much impressed by the reports of her successes in
Dublin after he had left that he had wished to engage her for his
first season at Drury Lane and had deputed the actor, Dennis
Delane, who happened to be travelling to Ireland on family
affairs, to make her an offer of £10 a week, a handsome salary
in those days. She had declined it then and had since heartily
regretted her refusal. What she did not know at the time was
that Garrick had been so irritated by her conceit in turning
down so good an offer that he had sworn he would never
engage her upon any terms whatever. But he did not make any
allusion to this when they met, and received her and her
mother with his usual cheerfulness and civility. It was, he said,
because he had already engaged Mrs. Cibber, Mrs. Clive, and
Mrs. Pritchard, who would be playing all the principal

characters, that he could not at present offer Georgiane a place in his company. Concealing her disappointment as best she might, Georgiane chatted merrily with him about the experiences they had shared in Dublin, and they parted very good friends.

There being no vacancy for her at Drury Lane, Georgiane had no alternative but to try Covent Garden. She enquired after Quin and was informed that he was at Bath, where he usually retired for the summer recess. On this occasion, as it happened, he had retired there for considerably longer, having departed in high dudgeon after the season of 1746–47, when Rich had insisted upon engaging Garrick for Covent Garden and Garrick had had by far the greater success and had outclassed the veteran Quin in almost every play in which they had appeared together. He had not returned to the theatre in the autumn, and in November, 1747, had written to Rich: "I am at Bath. Yours, James Quin." Rich had replied with equal laconicism: "Stay there and be damned, Yours, John Rich." But this exchange of bitter badinage had not paid either of them. On the one hand, the Covent Garden company without Quin was feeble in the extreme, and the season had proved dull for the audience and unprofitable for the manager, while, on the other, Quin had not enjoyed his spell out at grass and was fretting to get back into harness again. It was rumoured that Covent Garden was to make a new start in the autumn with a really good company which would rival that at Drury Lane, and clearly there might be a great opportunity for Georgiane, if she could get in there again. And it seemed by no means impossible, could she only conciliate the all-powerful Quin, for Rich seemed to be well enough disposed towards her. As soon as he had heard of her return to London, he had sent his friend, the actor Bencraft, to ask her and her mother to pay him a visit at his country house, Cowley Grove, Hillingdon, where he was spending the summer.

Georgiane would have liked to accept this invitation at once, but Mrs. Bellamy insisted on going first to pay a visit to

74

relatives at Watford. Her step-sister, who had saved a certain amount of money in the munificent service of Mrs. Godfrey, had advanced her position in the world and had contracted an advantageous marriage with an attorney named Crawford. A few years later he had died, leaving a considerable fortune to his widow and three-year-old son. In due course the boy had grown up and himself become a prosperous lawyer. And he had increased his fortune by marrying a Mrs. Sylvester, a wealthy widow much older than himself, who, however, was not so elderly that she had not been able to present him with a son and heir. It was with these people that the Bellamies were to spend the next few weeks.

Georgiane took an immediate dislike to them both. Crawford was a short fat man with a specious air of heartiness and good humour concealing a character compounded of cunning and chicanery. His wife was ugly and stupid. When the Bellamies first arrived, Crawford, who delighted in assuming the airs of a country gentleman, spent much of his time in entertaining local sportsmen, with whom the fastidious, town-bred Georgiane found she had little in common; but, on realising that Mrs. Bellamy was willing to occupy herself with his wife and her baby, he betook himself off with increasing frequency to London, where Georgiane says, he regaled himself with his friends the sheriff's officers and ladies of easy virtue. Georgiane spent as much of her time as possible away from the uncongenial atmosphere of this household. Fortunately, her great friend, Elizabeth St. Leger, was staying with her uncle, Lord Doneraile, at the Grove, Watford, not far away, and she was able to visit her often and to borrow books from Lord Doneraile's extensive library. She would often take a book and spend hours reading in the vast domain of Lord Essex's seat, Cassiobury Park, which was quite near her cousin's house.

One day she was seated on a bank in the park reading Dryden's *Virgil* when an old gentleman came and seated himself beside her. They soon got into conversation, and, when the stranger enquired what she was reading, Georgiane did her best to impress him with a display of literary taste and erudition. The old gentleman was vastly amused and vowed that, if he ever had a daughter, he hoped she would be like her. Then pulling out his watch, he said: "I am sorry to leave you, Miss, but I must go to dinner, which I do not think I shall like, as the relative I am come to see is gone to London, and the good woman is in the straw." Concluding from this description that it must be the Crawfords he was going to see, Georgiane explained that she was on a visit to the same house, and they walked back together. It was not until they were approaching the house that the stranger disclosed his identity. He asked her to precede him and announce his arrival to Mrs. Crawford and informed her that his name was Sykes. Georgiane was terrified, for she realised that he was the brother-in-law of her late supposed father, Captain Bellamy. (She does not particularise the relationship, but presumably he had been married to Bellamy's sister.) She hastened to inform her mother, who was equally alarmed, and, fearing reproaches on her treatment of Captain Bellamy, wisely decided to keep well out of the way until the unwelcome visitor had left next morning. Since Crawford had not returned from London, the burden of entertaining the guest that evening fell entirely upon Georgiane. Although he never mentioned it, Georgiane felt that he must be aware of her identity, and she could not help thinking that he seemed to eye her at times with a glance of pity and suspicion. But he appeared on the whole to be pleased with her company, and paid her many compliments when he left early next morning.

Crawford came back that same day, and it appeared that he had encountered Mr. Sykes on the way, for the first thing he said to Georgiane was: "Well, Miss! I have blown you. The old codger was very inquisitive when I met him, yet, notwithstanding, he likes you. But——" Apprehensive that he was going on to say something that would offend her mother, who was present, Georgiane cut him short; but a little later he told her that unfortunately the old gentleman had had to leave

London immediately on pressing business. "Otherwise," he continued, "who knows but that by the help of your tongue and my cellar, we may have taken him in." Georgiane bridled angrily, and Crawford, seeing that he had gone too far in disclosing his true character, hastened to try to appease her. "Nay, don't blush," he said, "I only meant that we would have tried to get him to make a will in your favour."

Her dislike for her cousins was only one of the many reasons which made Georgiane long to go on to the Riches, and at length she was able to persuade her mother to cut short their stay. Rich kindly sent his carriage for them, and on their arrival at Cowley Grove they were received with great cordiality by him and his daughters, who were overjoyed to meet their former playmate again after so long an absence. But Mrs. Rich, who had been a Miss Priscilla Wilford, when the manager married her as his third wife in October, 1744, was far less cordial, and, in fact, received them with formality and reserve. She had no thought for anything but Methodism and money, which ought to have made her recognise Mrs. Bellamy as a kindred soul, but somehow did not.

A fellow guest at Cowley Grove was the beautiful Mrs. Ward, who had recently been acting with great success in Edinburgh, and whom Rich had already engaged for the coming season at Covent Garden. She was accompanied by "a frightful being, to whom she gave the title of husband". Georgiane, who justly scented in her a rival for the parts to which she herself aspired, describes her in terms not untinged with jealousy. "This lady had one of the most beautiful faces I ever beheld. But her figure was vulgar to a degree. By the stoop and magnitude of her shoulders, it might be imagined that she had formerly carried milk-pails. Her beauty would have been more conspicuous in that line, or with a chain and knife fastened to her apron-strings, than in the character of a queen or young princess. Yet, notwithstanding this dissimilitude of appearance, and being pregnant into the bargain, it was determined that she should debute in Cordelia, the

77

youngest daughter of King Lear." Georgiane, of course, rather fancied *herself* as Cordelia.

Georgiane had left it to her mother to make arrangements with Rich about her engagement at Covent Garden, and Mrs. Bellamy seems to have been rather casual about it. Since Rich made no comment, expressed no surprise, and raised no objection when she told him of the terms Garrick had offered her daughter through Delane the season before last, she took it for granted that he would be prepared to give her the same salary. Georgiane soon discovered, to her dismay, that she would be expected to play second fiddle to Rich's new discovery. He told her that he was anxious that Mrs. Ward should make her first appearance as soon as possible, "her pregnancy rendering such a step necessary," and that he considered Georgiane as a happy *corpse de reserve*. (Rich was never too certain of his words, and was popularly reputed to say *adjutant* when he meant *adjective*, and *turbot* for *turban*.) His leading lady in comedy was to be Peg Woffington, whom he had triumphantly enticed from Drury Lane, together with three of Garrick's best actors, Sparks, Delane, and Ridout. The rift between Delane and Garrick had been caused by Delane's unaccountable action in recommending Mrs. Ward to engage with the rival house, although he himself was a personal friend of Garrick's and a prominent member of the Drury Lane Company. Garrick never forgave him for this foolish piece of treachery, dismissed him from the company, and ever after cut him if he met him in the street. Besides Quin, there were two other members of the old company with whom Georgiane had played in the season of 1744–45, the whistling Ryan and the fading and increasingly corpulent beauty, Mrs. Horton.

When Georgiane and her mother were suitably accommodated in lodgings in Tavistock Street near the theatre, they were joined by Georgiane's half-sister, Lord Tyrawley's eldest illegitimate daughter, Miss O'Hara, who, so Georgiane says, "had by some means or other disobliged his lordship." It was not a very difficult thing to do, as Georgiane herself had

78

already discovered. The two girls got on very well together, and Mrs. Bellamy also welcomed the newcomer, who she hoped would help her in persuading Georgiane to accept the hand of her friend, Mr. Crump. That gentleman had made up his mind by now that his affections were really centred on the daughter rather than the mother, and Mrs. Bellamy had not been in the least offended. Her own heart and mind were wholly occupied by her religious and commercial activities. Mr. Crump's advice to her to invest in Irish linens had been proving most profitable, and she was content to regard him as a friend. Her satisfactory business association with him made her only too pleased to do all in her power to forward his suit. For her part, Georgiane had no wish to be united with the Irish linen-draper, and one day, when her mother was being un-usually importunate on the subject, she lost her temper and replied tartly: "I wish, Madam, you would marry him yourself. I can have no objection to him as a father-in-law, but have an insuperable one to him for a husband." Mrs. Bellamy was highly offended, but Georgiane's firmness did not cause her to abandon her cherished project.

As soon as Georgiane was informed of Quin's return to town, she hastened to wait upon him to make her abject apologies for her unpardonable neglect and ingratitude in having betaken herself to Ireland without asking him for his advice. To her great relief, she found that he was not alone, for she felt that the presence of several of his friends, with whom she was already acquainted, would make it difficult for him to bully her, as she both expected and deserved. But Quin embraced her and at once declared himself willing to forgive her. "My dear girl," he said, "I was hurt at your contempt and inattention, as I sincerely *had* your welfare at heart." Georgiane felt a little uneasy at the emphasis he appeared to place on the word *had*. But she was partially reassured when he professed his old interest in her career, and advised her to make her reappearance in the part of Belvidera. To this she was quite agreeable, for, with her usual conceit, she had no doubt of succeeding in any character she undertook.

The season opened with a series of comedies in which Peg Woffington, who was making her first appearance for seven years at Covent Garden, scored resounding successes, especially in her famous part of Sir Harry Wildair in the *Constant Couple*, in which she was unrivalled whether in her own time or before or since, and her favourite "breeches-part" of Sylvia in the *Recruiting Officer*. On October 3rd the other leading lady, the beautiful Mrs. Ward, made her first appearance in *King Lear*, in which she was expected to make a great impression as Cordelia. But, when she had been engaged, it had not been appreciated that she would be quite so far gone in pregnancy quite so soon, and, as Georgiane smugly remarked, "her situation, as well as her figure, being against her, she did not conclude the part of Cordelia with any degree of credit." Moreover, Quin's Lear could not stand comparison with that of Garrick, which was still fresh in the memory of the Covent Garden audience, so that the whole production was a dismal failure. It was played again two days later, but not revived that season, as had been intended. The truth was that Quin was not a good Shakespearean actor, except in the parts of Falstaff and Henry VIII, to which he was physically and temperamentally suited, and in which he excelled. He appeared in both these parts this season, playing Falstaff in the *Merry Wives of Windsor* as well as in *Henry IV*.

On October 22nd Georgiane was last announced, as she herself puts it, "to bring up the rear of our theatrical forces" as Belvidera in *Venice Preserved*. To her surprise and mortification, the house, which in her vanity she had expected to be crowded, was half empty. But her reception from the small audience that was there was enthusiastic enough, and at the end of the play her old supporter, Mr. Chitty, who had helped to save the situation for her on her first appearance, once again rallied to her aid. When the piece for the next evening was announced, he called out: "The same! The same!" and the rest of the audience took up his cry. Georgiane asserts that the piece was played to crowded houses for four successive nights, but this is not quite true, for two days later she was playing Monimia, and the day after that Marcia in *Cato*.

The part of Belvidera was then considered to be one of the supreme tests of the abilities of a tragic actress, and throughout her career it was always one of Georgiane's best parts and one in which she could hear comparison with her great rival, Mrs. Cibber, who was already famous. "Mrs. Cibber and Mrs. Bellamy had each singular merit in this part," writes Francis Gentleman, "however, the former, who had a countenance most exquisitely formed to express anguish and distraction, far surpassed her competitor in those scenes where deep and violent feelings occur, while the latter, from an amorous glow of features and utterance, excelled in the passages relative to conjugal affection; her description of the madness, such as it is, was preferable to Mrs. Cibber's because more disengaged."

Georgiane was distressed to find that, in spite of their apparent reconciliation, Quin did not now treat her with "that conspicuous tenderness and regard" he had formerly shown to her. He was no longer fatherly as he had used to be, he no longer gave her unsolicited but welcome advice, and, worst of all, he rarely if ever asked her to his supper parties. She was also rather perturbed because, although it was known in the theatre that *Tamerlane* was to be played, according to custom, on November 4th, with Quin as Bajazet, she had not been told yet what, if any, part she was to play in it. One evening she was summoned to Quin's dressing-room. Hearing voices within, she paused for a moment before entering and heard Quin say: "Why, my lord, we have Woffington at the receipt of custom, and who bids more! Ward, flatter than a half-baked pancake— and little Bellamy as cold as ice and as conceited as the devil!" Georgiane waited until the laughter at her expense had subsided before she went in, to find Lord Orford and two other gentlemen with Quin.*

* Georgiane says that they were the poets, Thomson and Shenstone. But Thomson was already dead at this time.

81

"My dear girl," said Quin, "I have a favour to beg of you, and desire you will not deny me."

Georgiane, who fully intended to play the principal part of Arpasia in *Tamerlane*, realised at once that Quin was going to try to coax her into playing that of Selima, and replied: "You can make but *one* request, Mr. Quin, relative to the theatre, which I can refuse you; and I beg you will not give me so sensible a pain as that of not being able to acquiesce in every request of yours."

Quin saw that she had divined his intention. "It is what you point at," he said, "and you had better comply with a good grace, for you *shall* and *must* do it."

But Georgiane was not to be browbeaten. With what she considered to be "the air of Queen Catherine", she firmly announced: "I revere you, sir, as a father, and esteem you as a friend; but if your request relates to *Tamerlane*, I must tell you that little Bellamy has too much conceit to play Selima to such a half-baked pancake as Ward."

Her assumed consequence so highly diverted the gentlemen that good humour was at once restored. Quin was delighted with her spirited retort, and she was fully restored to his favour from that moment and presided at his supper table that very night. She took advantage of the improved atmosphere to ask him why he had recently been treating her with such coolness. He told her frankly that her indiscretion in leaving a London theatre, after she had received so many marks of peculiar distinction from the public, deserved the severest reprobation. Whoever had been her adviser on that occasion had not been her friend. As she had had every reason to conclude herself the favourite child of the public, they would certainly have cherished her, and it was treating them, as well as herself and him, ill to desert them. He added that she could not avoid observing the difference of her present situation, and it would be a considerable time before she recovered the height from which she had fallen. He had felt the disappointment far more than she did, since he had set his heart upon her rivalling the women at the other house. The rest of the gentlemen present agreed with him, and this was a very salutary cold douche for the conceited young lady, who confesses that she went home "more oppressed by his friendship than she had been unhappy through his displeasure". However, it made her resolve not only to work hard to retrieve her position, but also always to consult her valued friend in future. She does not reveal whether she made atonement by agreeing to play Selima after all, but certain it is that the part of Arpasia was given to the half-baked pancake, Mrs. Ward.

Perhaps Mrs. Ward's condition prevented her from showing her person and talents to the best advantage; perhaps Georgiane did take Quin's advice to heart and worked hard, or perhaps she really was the better actress of the two. Whatever may have been the cause, she did succeed in supplanting her rival before the end of the season. When Mrs. Ward returned to the theatre after the birth of her baby, she found Georgiane in possession of most of the best parts in the tragedies and was unable to dislodge her.

Besides playing her former parts of Monimia in *The Orphan*, Marcia in *Cato*, and Eudocia in the *Siege of Damascus*, Georgiane now began to play many of those principal parts in the traditional repertory with which her name was to be associated for the next decade or more: Belvidera in Otway's *Venice Preserved*, Imoinda in Southerne's *Oroonoko*, Indiana in Steele's *Conscious Lovers*, Leonora in Young's *Revenge*, Athanais in Lee's *Theodosius, or the Force of Love*, Almeyda in Dryden's *Don Sebastian*, Celia in Ben Jonson's *Volpone*, Lady Percy in *Henry IV*, and Anne Boleyn in *Henry VIII*. Alicia in Rowe's *Jane Shore*, in which this season Peg Woffington played the name-part, was to become one of Georgiane's best known roles and always remained a favourite with her. She also excelled as Statira in Lee's *Rival Queens*, which was revived after a lapse of eight years and henceforth taken into the repertory. The other leading part, that of Roxana, was played by Mrs. Ward, but in subsequent seasons was taken over by Peg Woffington, who was often to be Georgiane's rival Queen in the future. Another revival, Aphra Behn's farce, *The Emperor of the Moon*, in which Georgiane played Elaria, though produced at considerable expense on December 26th, failed to please the public and was thereafter relegated into the oblivion whence it came. But the only new play introduced this season, Thomson's posthumous *Coriolanus*, was an outstanding success and was acted ten times. Thomson had died on August 27th of this year, but Quin happened to have the manuscript of the play in his possession and resolved to have it produced as a last tribute to the memory of his dead friend. And since Thomson had died a poor man and left his two elderly sisters unprovided for, Quin and Rich generously decided that a number of performances should be given for the benefit of these distressed ladies. A moving prologue was written by another of the dead poet's friends, Lord Lyttelton, and affectingly spoken by Quin, who was unable to restrain his genuine emotion.

Georgiane played Volumnia. Unlike Shakespeare, Thomson had preferred to follow the authority of Livy and Dionysius Halicarnassensis rather than that of Plutarch, and had made Volumnia the young wife of Coriolanus, giving his mother the name of Veturia. This part was played by Peg Woffington, who, with true altruism, offered no objection to making herself up as a very old woman.

Although Georgiane had managed to oust Mrs. Ward from her position as chief tragic actress in the company, in comedy she could not hope to compete with Peg Woffington, and in most of the comedies she did not appear at all. But she played Harriet in Etherege's *Man of the Mode*, Lady Froth in Congreve's *Double Dealer*, and Lady Fanciful in Vanbrugh's *Provoked Wife*, with Quin as Sir John Brute and Peg Woffington as Lady Brute. Quin's rendering of Brute was utterly different from Garrick's and far less gentlemanly, and the town was divided on the merits of their respective performances. Tate Wilkinson thought that the author, had he been living, would have allowed them both to be right. Yet had Quin attempted

Garrick's mode, or Garrick Quin's, each would certainly have failed. But Garrick was the rising, Quin the fading star, and Drury Lane was now perhaps the more fashionable of the two theatres, though Covent Garden was in general well attended. It did possess two great advantages over the rival house. Rich's pantomimes, which were so often played as the after-pieces, were always excellent, and the standards of dancing and music were higher than at Drury Lane. And Covent Garden enjoyed the valuable patronage of the Prince of Wales, who was a fervent admirer of Quin's. Whenever he ordered a command performance, it was always at Covent Garden.

As she stepped on the stage as Athanais in *Theodosius*, Georgiane experienced a great shock when she saw her would-be abductor, Lord Byron, seated in the stage-box. She was so taken by surprise that she turned pale and for a moment stood motionless and unable to speak her lines. Alarmed at her pallor, Rich hurriedly left his box in the front of the house and came round to find out what had upset her. He was at no loss to account for her agitation when he encountered Lord Byron, who by this time had left his seat and was standing beside one of the side-scenes in full view of the audience. "Well, Rich," said Byron boldly, "I am come to take away your Athanais." Rich took him aside and tried to remonstrate with him, but, making no headway, finally took a firm line with him. He told him that he would not stand tamely by and see his performers insulted and asked him to quit the scenes. Reluctant to have an open quarrel with the manager and perceiving that the audience was beginning to resent his conduct, Byron prudently retired first to his former seat and later to an even less conspicuous position at the back of a box in the front of the house.

Quin, who had not been at the theatre that night, was of course informed of this unpleasant incident, and when he arrived at the theatre next evening was told by somebody— Georgiane says it was Thomson, but it cannot have been he, for he was no longer alive—that, as he was passing the back of the stage, he had overheard a snatch of conversation between two persons and that one of them, whom he believed to be Lord Byron, had said to the other: "I will speak to her tonight, or I will shoot my . . ." He had not heard the rest of the sentence, but had concluded from what he had heard that Byron meant to carry off Georgiane that evening. Quin agreed that this seemed likely, and, sending for Georgiane, told her that she must not return in her chair that evening. He himself would escort her home and take his supper at her lodgings. He arranged that her chair would be carried from the stage door in Bow Street with all its curtains drawn so that it might be supposed that she was in it, while they were to go through the front of the house and on foot by way of the piazzas to Tavistock Street.

This plan was carried out, and they reached Georgiane's lodgings without mishap. When the chair arrived shortly afterwards, the chairmen told them that they had been stopped on the way by a man muffled up in a great coat. He had peremptorily ordered them to set down the chair, and when, after making a show of protest, they had obeyed him, he had lifted the top of the chair and thrown a letter into it, swearing that, if the answer were not favourable, he would destroy himself. Then he had lowered the lid and ordered the chairmen to carry the lady home. One of the chairmen added that he was sure the poor gentleman meant no harm to Miss, as he was one of the best men in the world. "And pray," asked the astonished Quin, "who is that gentleman?" "Why, sir," replied the chairman, "it is his honour Mr. Bullock." Quin asked Georgiane's permission to read the letter, though she was not very willing to let him do so, for she had realised that it must be just another of the numerous notes she had recently been receiving from a lovelorn Cambridge undergraduate. But Quin insisted, and the contents of the letter were found, as Georgiane expected, "to breathe nothing but love and madness." Quin, who knew young Mr. Bullock's father, put the letter in his pocket and promised to bring the young man himself to reason.

They had just sat down to supper when a waiter arrived from the Bedford Head coffee-house with another letter addressed to Georgiane. This one proved to be from Lord Byron and far less innocuous than Mr. Bullock's amorous meanderings, since in it he made her proposals of a nature which, considering that he had recently married, could not but be dishonourable. Quin undertook to deal with this missive too, and, sending for pen and paper, wrote the following note: "Lieutenant O'Hara's compliments to Lord Byron, and if he ever dares to insult his sister again, it shall not be either his title or cowardice that shall preserve him from chastisement." This note was dispatched to the Bedford Head and so effectively scared Lord Byron that he quitted the coffee house forthwith and next day sought the safe sanctuary of his country seat in Nottinghamshire. Nor did he ever trouble Georgiane with his importunities again.

But although she had thus got rid of two of her unwanted admirers, Georgiane had still to cope with the more honourable, if no less unwelcome, persistence of Mr. Crump, who in his correspondence with her mother was continually urging his suit. Georgiane could not help knowing of this from what Mrs. Bellamy told her, though she protests that she had never read any of his letters which her mother carelessly left lying about, until one day she happened to do so almost inadvertently. Her maid had found a letter in the parlour and had handed it to her, thinking it was one she had dropped. She had hastily put it into her pocket with three others she had just received, and, on taking them out, the following words in Crump's letter happened to catch her eye: "Dear Madam, I believe your loved daughter cannot withstand the power of——" She could not understand what this meant or what the dash signified and threw the letter aside without reading any more of it. And for the time being the matter passed from her mind.

Chapter Six

ONE EVENING, when Georgiane was feeling particularly pleased with herself because the applause of the audience showed her that she was making a great success in the part she was playing,* her old admirer, George Montgomery, suddenly entered the Green Room of the theatre. Much to the amusement of her fellow players she did not attempt to disguise her joy at seeing him again. He told her that he had come into a good estate by the death of his mother, whose maiden name of Metham he had consequently assumed. And he left her under no doubt that the passion he had formerly declared for her was still as strong as ever. But observing that the pressing attentions of so fashionable a young gentleman were exciting the jealousy of Peg Woffington, who, she says, "expected to have the tribute of admiration first paid to her," Georgiane hastily put an end of their conversation. Metham, however, was not discouraged. After the performance he again approached her and begged permission to wait on her next morning. She replied that she could not grant this, because her mother would not consent to her admitting any male visitor in the quality of a lover, but she softened his disappointment by acceding to his request that he might write to her.

Next evening Georgiane was playing Alicia. This must have been on December 3rd or 5th, 1748, for both earlier and later in the season that part was played by Mrs. Ward. As she came off the stage, Quin came up to her "with a pleasure sparkling in his fine eyes which she had never seen them express

* The play cannot have been the *Double Dealer*, as she says it was, for it was not put on until April 5th, 1749, the night of her own benefit.

before off the stage", and told her to stop and kneel to the
first person she met in the scene room, by which she had to
pass on her way to her dressing-room. At first she did not
understand what his meaning could be, but reflecting that
there were few persons in the world to whom she could be
expected to pay such a tribute, she divined that this visitor
could be nobody but her father, and, summoning up all her
courage, she entered and, as she had expected, found Lord
Tyrawley awaiting her. Overcome with emotion, she threw
herself at his feet, crying: "My dear Lord, forgive me!" Lord
Tyrawley, seemingly no less affected than herself, raised her up
and embraced her. He then told her to hasten home, as he and
Quin proposed to sup with her that evening. His old friend
Quin's account of her had, he said, given him the highest
satisfaction and had corroborated what he had heard of her in
Ireland from a person, who, *when alive*, had loved her as well as
he did. Georgiane guessed from these words that old Miss
O'Hara was dead, and burst into a fresh paroxysm of tears.
But her grief was somewhat assuaged when Lord Tyrawley
presented her with two rings which he said Miss O'Hara had
left her. One of these was a large pink diamond of considerable
value and the other a fancy ring. Georgiane opined that this
was not the whole of her legacy, but says that, as his Lordship
made no mention of anything else, she could not with propriety ask him. The belief that she was left large legacies of
which she was unscrupulously deprived by interested parties
was a positive obsession with Georgiane and recurred at
frequent intervals throughout her life.

Neither Mrs. Bellamy nor Miss O'Hara was present at the
little supper party which followed, Lord Tyrawley having
enjoined Georgiane never to request him to see either of the
ladies of her family, as he was determined never to speak to
them or know them. And in the belief that the father and
daughter would have a great deal to say to each other after so
long a separation, Quin made a very late appearance at the
supper table. Lord Tyrawley regaled them with reminiscences

of his embassy to Russia, and the party did not break up until
the small hours of the morning. Tyrawley announced his
intention of supping with Georgiane three or four times a week
and begged Quin to join them as often as possible. But
although the two men were very good friends and highly
appreciated each other's conversation, their tastes were very
different. Quin loved his good fat capon, his ale and orange,
and *ungartering*, as he called it; but Tyrawley was not fond of
the bottle, and the pleasures of the table meant little to him.
So the three of them rarely met together for a meal. Georgiane
would receive her father alone, but would sup with Quin at his
own lodging whenever she could.

It was probably at this time that Lord Tyrawley first introduced this natural daughter of his to his wife, with whom he
remained on fairly friendly terms and who was quite indifferent to his peccadilloes. Lady Tyrawley received the girl
with great kindness, and often invited her to come and see her
in her apartments at Somerset House, which were always filled
with innumerable cats, dogs, and monkeys. Indeed, one of her
guests suggested that she might be collecting this assemblage
of animals against a second flood. She would divert herself by
dressing up the monkeys, and there were never less than three
or four of them clad in regimentals or as fine ladies and gentlemen. The visitor was invariably greeted by a pack of yelping
dogs, and, on the authority of Tate Wilkinson, "an affront to
any one of those favourites was truly so to her ladyship and
not to be forgiven." Tate Wilkinson, who some time later
often visited her and used to meet Georgiane there, gives a
vivid description of this amiable but eccentric lady. "Though a
woman of high sense and breeding, she could not boast of any
personal attraction, as she was short-sighted, squinted, and was
in her person bordering on the extravagance of caricature, but
was friendly, generous, sensible, and humane." Before long,
she took Georgiane to her kindly heart, and was ever after a
true friend to her, treating her as if she were indeed a daughter
of her own.

Restored to the good graces of both Lord Tyrawley and Quin, and loved almost to adoration by the man, whom, though she was not yet certain that she returned his love, she acknowledged that she preferred to all others, Georgiane had never been so happy. She had convinced herself that Metham loved her truly. He showed himself so respectful both in his letters and in his behaviour that she did not think there was any imprudence in her accepting the attentions of a man who had formerly told her that it was not in his power to pay his addresses to her on honourable terms. In fact, his openness and candour on that occasion and his retirement to the country in order to avoid the peril of her attractions had so impressed her that she confesses she was now lulled into a false security. The opposition he had expected from his parents, upon whom he was then entirely dependent, had formerly prevented him from offering her marriage, but, now that he was free and wealthy in his own right, she assumed that his intentions towards her must be both sincere and honourable. He was not, as a matter of fact, quite as wealthy or as free as she imagined, for, though he had come into his mother's property, his father, from whom he had the greater expectations, was still alive, even if he *had* already written his own epitaph. On the slab over his wife's grave in the chancel of the church at North Cave he had placed the following lines, which he must have composed himself:

> *In the Vault lies Barbara*
> *Hugh Montgomery, Esq's Wife,*
> *Who ne'er was Angry in her life:*
> *As Daughter, Sister, Wife or Mother*
> *You'l rarely hear of such another.*
> *She died the 26th of May in the 59th year of her age,* 1747.

And beneath this the bereaved husband had added:

> *My Father a North Briton*
> *My Mother Rutlandshire*

From Dublin their Son
  Hugh Montgomery, Esq.
When my race is run
  Shall rest me in this Choir,
In hope, as he begun,
  God will raise me higher.

Aet 68. A.D. 1748.

About this time Georgiane was invited to a masquerade, at which Metham was also to be present, and, as she had never attended one of these functions before, she asked him how those who were there could discover one another if they were masked. The infatuated Metham unguardedly replied that her eyes would light him and his intuition would prevent any mistake. In a spirit of mischief Georgiane decided to put this boast of her lover's to the test. Accordingly, instead of wearing the elegant disguise he would naturally expect of her, it was in a voluminous black domino with a large hood that she went to the ball with her friends, the Miss Merediths, who were habited as Savoyard girls. In this guise she approached Metham and asked him what fair one kept him waiting. She made her voice sound elderly, and Metham completely failed to recognise her and tried to shake off the unwelcome presence of one whom he took to be an old and doubtless unattractive female. She told him that he had better accept the offer of her company, which she assured him she had the vanity to presume would be fully as agreeable to him as the person he was expecting. Furious at being thus importuned, Metham abruptly left her, and she maliciously watched his disquietude as he anxiously scanned the passing masks in an endeavour to discover his loved one.

Not being hoodwinked by love like Metham, Count von Haslang, the elderly Bavarian Ambassador, who was a great friend of Lord Tyrawley's, had had no difficulty in penetrating Georgiane's disguise and had revealed her identity to the

Spanish Ambassador, General Wall, whom she had already met on several occasions when he had come behind the scenes at the theatre. The General, who was well aware that Metham was her professed admirer, had been amusedly observing her little comedy with him, and now mischievously suggested that he should join her in the baiting of her unfortunate lover. And so they approached him again, and this time he could not take to flight to escape from her railleries, for the ambassador was unmasked and he could not well abruptly leave a person of such consequence. Moreover, he could not be certain that the mysterious mask with his Excellency was not some lady of high rank whom it would be injudicious to offend.

At four o'clock in the morning, Lord Tyrawley, who had been supping with a private party, returned to the great room, and having found Georgiane and the two other girls, suggested that he should see them to their chairs, since he was leaving himself and could not think of letting them remain in such a place unchaperoned. Georgiane, who was thoroughly enjoying herself, would have liked to stay longer, but Lord Tyrawley was insistent, and her companions, who had been dancing all the evening, were tired, so she had to agree to leave. As she passed Metham she just had time to say to him: "What is become of the brilliancy of those eyes, which with your blessed intuition, were to render every other information unnecessary?" Metham, wholly taken aback at this last minute disclosure and cursing his own stupidity, pursued her to the door, trying to speak to her and beg her pardon. But this time it was she who shook him off.

In spite of her perverseness on this occasion, Georgiane was beginning to fall in love with George Metham, and now she had more frequent opportunities of seeing him, for, the season of Lent coming on, both of them devoutly attended at Benediction every Wednesday and Friday evening at Count von Haslang's chapel in Warwick Street, Golden Square. At this time Roman Catholics had no other places of worship available to them in London but the chapels allowed by diplomatic privilege to foreign ambassadors from Catholic countries.

Metham professed to be deeply in love with her, and she says that she trusted so implicitly in his honour and his respect for her that, if he happened to be indisposed, she made no scruple to visit him in his lodging. She is particularly and defiantly insistent upon conveying the impression that nothing untoward happened on such occasions and that she had no reason to repent of her condescension. George Metham, she avers, never attempted even to kiss her. But at the same time she admits that, as she now regarded him as her future husband, she saw no reason why she should not accept the presents he was continually offering her—and they seem to have been such as a young lady would not normally accept from a member of the opposite sex. Her mother was not at all perturbed by this sudden increase in the luxury of her wardrobe, for she believed that Georgiane was receiving a good deal of money from Lord Tyrawley, who, whenever he visited her, would always divide the contents of his purse with her so that he might contribute to the expense of his own entertainment. But Mrs. Woffington and Mrs. Ward were not so unsuspicious and did not put so favourable a construction on Georgiane's sudden apparent affluence. "Being unwilling to account for the elegance of my dress by imputing it, as my mother had done, to an allowable source, they thought it could only proceed from my having formed an unallowable connection with Mr. Metham." And, in spite of Georgiane's bland protestations of innocence, they were probably right.

Because of Lord Tyrawley's generous help with the household expenses and the considerable profits she herself had been making by the sale of the linen she was importing from Ireland, Mrs. Bellamy had for some months past been in no want of ready money, and had therefore not sent to the theatre for any part of Georgiane's salary; but now, having occasion to send a remittance to Ireland in payment for a fresh consignment of linen, she wrote to the treasurer of the theatre asking him to let her have what was due to her daughter. Imagining that

Georgiane's salary had been fixed at ten pounds a week, she was greatly surprised to receive only half the amount she was expecting, and she was so indignant at what she, rather unjustifiably, considered to be Rich's duplicity that she returned the money to the treasurer and forbade Georgiane to appear any more at the theatre. Since Georgiane's pride, too, was piqued by what she regarded as a gross undervaluation of her true worth, she was quite ready to comply with her mother's behest, even though she suspected that the dispute was not altogether unwelcome to Mrs. Bellamy as being likely to advance her favourite project of marrying her to Mr. Crump.

When rumours of Georgiane's intention to resign reached the company at Covent Garden, Peg Woffington, much as she disliked and despised Georgiane, was not as delighted as might have been expected. In fact, she did not relish the prospect at all. The time for the yearly benefits was approaching, and the withdrawal of one of the principal actresses at this juncture would be most embarrasing and inconvenient to the rest of the Company. She was naturally unwilling to plead with Georgiane herself, so she deputed a great friend and admirer of hers, Mr. MacSwiny, to endeavour to dissuade her from her intention. But his persuasive eloquence had no effect on Georgiane, who declared that her decision in the matter would depend entirely upon the advice given to her by Mr. Quin. It would have been unlike Quin to let the theatre down, and it is not surprising that he urged her strongly to continue to perform for the rest of the season, especially as it was drawing to a close. She must remember that she was to be in all the pieces that had been commanded every Thursday by the Prince and Princess of Wales, and her abrupt withdrawal might give offence to these exalted personages as well as to the public. In his opinion no pecuniary motive should induce her to refuse to play for the short remainder of the season. Georgiane wisely bowed to his advice, and all the more readily because her consenting to continue would redound to her credit.

Lord Tyrawley, however, somewhat unexpectedly took the

opposite point of view, and, when he came to sup with her that evening as usual, seemed displeased that she had not carried out her first intention to resign from the Company. And his reason for wanting her to be free soon became apparent. "Pop," he said, "you do not love me so well as you did even some weeks ago." Being only too conscious that it was true that all her thoughts were now concentrated on her lover to the exclusion of everyone else, Georgiane blushed and remained silent. "Why do you not speak?" Lord Tyrawley went on. "If your heart is engaged to a proper object, I will give him your hand." There was a pause, then he added meaningly: "I flattered myself indeed, that your affection for me was so unbounded, that you would have left the choice to me."

The truth suddenly dawned on Georgiane, and in an enlightening flash she realised that Lord Tyrawley, too, was concerned in the scheme to marry her to Crump. The mysterious dash in the linen-draper's letter to her mother was now explained. It could only stand for Lord Tyrawley's name. He was the one person whose power Crump thought she would not be able to withstand. But she hastened to tell her father at once that, though she loved and revered him much, she would freely and sincerely acknowledge that she felt a strong presentiment in favour of another, though she could not yet reveal to him the name of that person. Lord Tyrawley told her with an oath that she might rest assured he would never consent to a union with her admirer. She afterwards discovered that, having heard the story of the note thrown into her chair, her father assumed that she must mean young Mr. Bullock, but at the time she imagined that he knew about Metham and was referring to him. His apparent opposition only served to increase her predilection for her lover, which now became a "violent impetuous affection".

On April 5th her benefit took place. Quin considered that the Covent Garden company this season was strongest in comedy and had advised her to choose Congreve's *Double Dealer*. Maskwell was a part in which he himself excelled; Peg

Woffington was known to be admirable as Lady Touchwood; and the part of Lady Froth would, he thought, afford ample room for the exertion of Georgiane's fancy and humour. She affected to be diffident about undertaking "a part the inimitable Clive had long been in possession of", but met with better success in it than she had dared to hope. And this was all the more creditable because Kitty Clive had lately been playing the part at Drury Lane, so that comparisons were bound to be made.

Although her former patronesses, the Duchess of Queens-berry and Lady Cardigan, once again graced the occasion with their presence in the boxes, the financial result was not quite as gratifying as it had been at her first benefit four years before. Georgiane herself thought this was partly because those who had encouraged her while she was still considered as a young performer did not think their assistance so necessary now that she was established, especially as the story of her origin was now an open secret and they imagined that Lord Tyrawley must be providing amply for her. In addition she suspected that many gentlemen who would have been willing to express their admiration for her in financial form had she been known to be heart-free were kept at a distance by a belief that Mr. Metham was her favoured lover.

Some days after her benefit Lord Tyrawley came into her room all smiles and apparently delighted with himself and breezily announced to her: "Pop, I have got you a husband." Georgiane's heart sank, for she thought she knew what was coming, but she calmly replied: "I hope then, my Lord, you have found out my choice." Tyrawley's countenance clouded, and he brusquely threw a letter down on the table, exclaiming: "There, read that. I have given my word, which I will not break for you nor the whole world; therefore no trifling, for I will be obeyed." With this he stumped out of the house, leaving her to read the letter. It proved, as she had expected, to be from Mr. Crump, and made it abundantly clear to her that her marriage had already been settled between her father and him even before Lord Tyrawley had left Dublin. Mr. Crump announced that he was to be in London next evening—which was that very day—and intended to do himself the honour of meeting his lordship at his daughter's apartments in Tavistock Street.

Seething with indignation, Georgiane sat down and wrote a note to George Metham. When she had first divined her father's intentions about her marriage, she had written to him telling him that she was very unhappy about something which had happened, but had not then further explained herself. But now she frankly told him all and admits that she left him no room to doubt that he was the entire master of her affections.

Her anger had one good effect in that she felt no difficulty in assuming the air of disdain proper to the character of Lady Fanciful, which she played on that fateful evening of April 20th, 1749. And the presence of Mr. Crump seated in the front row of the pit raised her anger almost to boiling-point. Metham, too, was at the theatre and stood behind the scenes, his usually florid face so pale and dejected that he looked more like the disappointed lover than the favoured one, and Peg Woffington concluded that there must have been some lovers' quarrel between them, especially as he did not follow Georgiane to the Green Room as usual whenever she left the stage. Nor was it until she was crossing the back of the stage behind the scenes in order to be ready on the opposite side for her entrance in the fifth act that he at last approached her, begging her to let him speak one word to her in the hall. Georgiane consented, knowing that the prompter did not ring the bell for the musicians to stop playing until he saw all those who were to begin the act ready to go on; but she was no sooner out in the passage than Metham lifted her in his arms and carried her out to a coach which his valet had waiting for him. The coach rapidly drove off and took them to a house in Leicester Street, where he had engaged a lodging for them. Georgiane had not expected that he would act quite so impetuously and was taken by surprise, but she candidly acknowledges that she was by this time so much in love that she was neither sorry nor offended at the step her lover had taken.

Meanwhile, at the theatre, the *entr'acte* music had continued so long that the audience had begun to be restive and showed its impatience so noisily that Quin came out of his dressing-room to enquire the reason for the din and disturbance. Eye-witnesses were able to tell him exactly what had happened, but it could not be more felicitously expressed than in Georgiane's own delightfully ingenuous phrase: "a real rape (if a running away with, where there is no resistance, might be so termed) had interrupted the progress of the play." And Quin, who must have been well aware both of Metham's infatuation and of Georgiane's feelings towards him, seems to have assumed from the first that she had been a willing party to the elopement. In the circumstances he judged that the best thing was to tell the truth to the impatient audience. Accordingly, he came on the stage in his character of Sir John Brute, and aptly making use of some of Lady Fanciful's own lines in the play, with which his audience may be supposed to have been thoroughly familiar, informed them that he was come to beg their excuse for the fantastical girl of quality, whose company they would un-fortunately be disappointed of at the conclusion of the piece, as she had left Heartfree upon finding an admirer that was made on purpose for her. This whimsical and good-humoured explanation given by a favourite actor seems to have not only appeased but also amused an audience always disposed to be indulgent towards romance.

Chapter Seven

AT FIRST, at any rate, George Metham seems to have done nothing to disabuse Georgiane of her belief that he intended to make her his wife. He introduced her openly to his sister, Mrs. Dives, and his whole circle of friends. One of these, Major Burton, was courting Georgiane's aristocratic friend, Elizabeth St. Leger, and hoped to marry her, and, on his assuring her that Georgiane's marriage with Metham would speedily take place, she did not break off her friendship with Georgiane and continued to visit her. But others were more censorious; the circumstances of the elopement were common knowledge, and everybody was well aware that no marriage had as yet taken place. Mrs. Bellamy's rigid Methodist principles forbade her to condone her daughter's conduct, but they did not prevent her from retaining Georgiane's salary for her own use, on the pretext that she would have no occasion for money, now that she had found herself a wealthy protector. Miss O'Hara, however, was allowed to take her her ornaments and clothes, which were very necessary to her, seeing that she had been abducted in her stage costume and had had to be supplied for the time being with more suitable apparel by Mrs. Studwick, the landlady of her new lodging. Believing that to obtain Lord Tyrawley's forgiveness would be as difficult as trying to remove the Colossus from Rhodes, Georgiane made no attempt to do so. Moreover, his Lordship, who still had an eye for beauty, had "enlisted under the banner" of Peg Woffington, a circumstance which, so Georgiane thought, seemed likely to render a reconciliation even less attainable. Nor could she rely upon Quin's support on this occasion. He had always been averse to

Lord Tyrawley's project of marrying her to Crump, but Tyrawley had silenced his remonstrances by rudely hinting that he had designs on her himself, and he did not feel inclined to exasperate his old friend still further by espousing her cause now. But he wrote to tell her that, though he could not wait upon her now in deference to Lord Tyrawley's attitude, he would pay her a visit later in the summer, when he supposed that they would go to Yorkshire.

Shortly afterwards, she did, indeed, accompany Metham to York, where he had taken a house for her. But though he seemed as devoted to her as ever, he soon showed that he had no intention of altering his habitual mode of life on her account. He was a keen sportsman and spent much of his time in sporting pursuits with his great friend, Lord Downe, while his numerous other friends in the country and his father, Mr. Montgomery, who lived some forty miles from York, claimed so much of his company that Georgiane had very little of it. She would, indeed, have seen nobody but her servants had she not made friends with the nuns of the convent which abutted on the garden wall of her house.

Seeing that Roman Catholicism was at this time outlawed in England, it may seem surprising that it should have been possible for such an institution to continue unmolested in a populous city such as York. But the convent had now been there for well over fifty years. The nuns belonged to a teaching order originally founded early in the seventeenth century by a Yorkshire woman, Mary Ward. In 1669, after many vicissitudes, including the suppression by the Vatican of the original foundation in 1630, some of its members had come to London and had established a convent in St. Martin's Lane under the protection of Queen Catherine, the Catholic consort of Charles II. Later they had removed to Hammersmith, whence they sent out a colony to Heworth in Yorkshire, where their foundress had spent her last years and was buried. In 1686 the nuns moved from Heworth to York to a house in Blossom Street at the corner of Baggergate Lane bought for them by a devout Catholic lady, Mrs. Paston, in order that they might establish there a seminary for Roman Catholic young ladies of good family. "The site, gardens, and agreeable walks made it very convenient for that purpose." It prospered and has remained at Micklegate Bar to this day.

Although the prejudice against papists was still rampant in England, Roman Catholicism at this time was fairly strong in Yorkshire, and York itself was a centre resorted to by the best Catholic families. The existence and activities of this establishment, though it may not have been known that it was conducted by professed nuns, seem to have been known to the outside world. A writer about this time remarked that it had of late been "much enlarged by elegant buildings backwards, which proves that the number of scholars has greatly increased". At the petition of Barbara Babthorpe, fourth chief superior of the Order, their rule was approved in 1703 by Pope Clement XI, and it was then that the "Institute of Mary" was given to the congregation as its official title. It was a non-enclosed Order, and the nuns took simple vows of chastity, poverty, and obedience. In the penal times, when Georgiane knew them, they wore no special habit, but were attired in the ordinary secular dress of the period.

Georgiane first made their acquaintance through their chaplain, Father Blunt, a gentle, learned man, to whose kind instructions she says she was indebted for a return of those sentiments she had early imbibed in her loved cloister at Boulogne. She herself admits that the nuns themselves at first fought shy of her, as her character was doubtful, but when she informed Father Blunt that Mr. Metham fully intended to marry her, they consented both to receive her and to visit her, and treated her with the utmost kindliness.

The ground on which her house stood had once belonged to the convent, and there was still a communicating door on the terrace, though it had been walled up. With the consent of the community Georgiane ordered it to be unblocked, and by means of it they were able to exchange visits whenever they felt so disposed. In their kindly treatment of her the good nuns certainly showed a broad-mindedness and a most charitable compassion for the frailty of this weaker sister of their faith, for, as the months passed by, she could not well have concealed from them that she was far advanced in pregnancy.

In the autumn Metham's absences grew more and more frequent. He went away to shoot grouse; he went away to hunt; he went away on visits to his friends, Viscount Downe, the Earls of Burlington and Scarbrough, and the Marquess of Rockingham. It is true that he did once remain at home for a whole week—York race week—but then he filled the house with guests. Owing to his high rank, one of these, a noble peer, was always seated in the place of honour of his hostess's right hand, and Georgiane could not help noticing that he was staring at her fixedly. At first this flattered her greatly, then it began to embarrass and disconcert her, and finally she complained to Metham of his friend's rudeness. Metham burst into peals of laughter and assured her that she was flattering herself unduly and that his Lordship must be acquitted of any improper scrutiny of her charms, as the eye that appeared to be unremittingly fixed on her was an innocent glass eye, which was immovable by day and rested very quietly on a table by night.

On December 6th Georgiane was suddenly taken very ill, and the nurse who had been with her for some time declared that she was in labour. Metham, who was away at Ferrybridge, was sent for at once, and, on his arrival, wanted to send for a man-midwife to deliver the child. Out of modesty Georgiane would not agree to this, but she became so ill that eventually her life was in danger, and she was obliged to have recourse to the help she had refused. She says that her son was born on the eleventh day of her illness, which according to her own reckoning would have been December 17th, though he himself in a letter written to her many years later says that his birthday was December 22nd. But a few days one way or the other matter little; what is more to the point is that, unless

George Montgomery Metham was a seven-months child—as, of course, he may have been—Georgiane's virtue was as weak as her arithmetic, and she must have become Metham's mistress, as Peg Woffington believed, and as she herself strenuously denied, for some time before he had eloped with her from Covent Garden.

If Metham had been guilty of neglecting her recently, he made full amends now and was like a man distracted until she was pronounced out of danger. When Georgiane first fell ill, he had written to her mother to ask her to come to York, and to their great surprise she came. But she straightway informed Metham that she could not become reconciled with Georgiane until he had promised to marry her, and she never gave him a moment's peace until he had satisfied her scruples by a solemn promise. She insisted upon taking charge of the child during Georgiane's convalescence and showed amazing bravery and self-sacrifice in having him to sleep with her in her bed when he developed small-pox, though she had never had the disease herself and had always dreaded it.

About this time Georgiane received a letter from Quin, apologising for not having visited her in the summer according to his promise and urging her to return at once to London, as he had induced Rich to offer her an engagement at Covent Garden on such terms as would compensate her for his failure to pay her adequately last season. He had agreed to give her seven pounds a week with a free benefit, and, in spite of the fact that she had not been there, the salary was to be reckoned from the date of the opening of the season. Georgiane, who now had a craving for domesticity and was beginning to pride herself upon the way she ran her household, wanted to refuse the offer, but Metham's long spell at home during her illness had made him restive. He was bored with the dullness of York, and was languishing to return to London. His insistent pleas in the end overcame her reluctance, and she consented to accept the offer.

Georgiane herself says that they did not set off for town until the beginning of February and were delayed by floods on their journey, but here once more she is slightly at fault with her dates, for her return to the stage was made in the part of Belvidera on January 23rd, 1750, and she appeared again as Marcia four days later.

Finding several notes from Quin already awaiting her at the furnished house Metham had taken in Lisle Street, Leicester Fields, Georgiane sent at once to inform him of her arrival, and soon after he came in person to greet her. He told her that the very announcement of her return had caused so much interest that he almost regretted having made the engagement for her, as she would have been able to ask even more favourable terms for herself. She was not sorry to hear from him that Lord Tyrawley was away in Ireland. It would have been awkward for her to meet him, for he had assured Quin that, though he might forgive Georgiane herself, he would never become reconciled to Metham, even if he did marry her.

Georgiane received an enthusiastic welcome from the audience on her first appearance after her return, and her success was greater than even her own most sanguine hopes or Quin's prognostications had given her reason to expect. That Rich had re-engaged her because he really needed her support soon became apparent. Except for Peg Woffington, who continued to draw the town by her brilliant playing in comedy, the company had been woefully deficient in female talent. Mrs. Ward, believing that Georgiane was to return in time for the opening of the season and despairing of wresting from her those parts she most wanted to play, had allowed herself to be persuaded by Garrick to break her articles with Rich and join the Drury Lane Company, which Mrs. Cibber was leaving owing to a difference with Garrick.

At Covent Garden the parts that Georgiane or Mrs. Ward would have played had so far been rather inadequately undertaken by Mrs. Vincent. Mrs. Horton was still in the company, but the zenith of her beauty was long past, her acting had now become too old-fashioned to appeal to the public, and she was relegated to playing minor parts of elderly ladies. At the end of the season she was to leave the stage. Rich no longer thought her worth the salary he had been paying her, but out of kindness offered to retain her still at a salary of £4 a week. This she indignantly refused, preferring to subsist in retirement on a small annuity, the memory of her former triumphs, and the illusion that she still retained all her beauty. To the last she dressed like a girl of twenty.

The company was much stronger on the male side. Besides Quin it still included such first-rate actors as Bridgewater, Delane, Ryan, Ridout, and Sparks, and it had also been reinforced by Lee, who had deserted Garrick in violation of his articles, and two promising newcomers in Barrington and the young Irish actor, Dyer, who played mostly in comedy and was a good singer and an excellent mimic.

Besides her old parts of Belvidera, Marcia, Imoinda, Almeyda, and Indiana, Georgiane this season added several new ones to her repertory, including those of Almeria in Congreve's *Mourning Bride*, and the not very penitent Calista in Rowe's *Fair Penitent*, which she played for the first time at her own benefit. Being obliged to appear far oftener than she would have wished before she had fully recovered, her strength failed her and she was pronounced to be in danger of a galloping consumption. Quin insisted upon her consulting Dr. Thompson, an eccentric and unorthodox physician in whom he had great faith, and he speedily restored her to health, to the great relief of Metham, who was blaming himself for having insisted upon bringing her back to London and the theatre against her inclinations.

During this season Rich put on one of his characteristic pantomimes, *The Fair*, in which he introduced a dancer on the tight wire. Both Quin and Peg Woffington regarded this act as degrading to the prestige of the Theatre Royal, Covent Garden, and flatly refused ever to appear in the same bill with it. Opposition of this sort always riled the usually easygoing Rich and he declared that nothing would induce him to eliminate the act to which they so unreasonably objected. Georgiane's sympathies were with him; she could not see how the performers in the main piece could be affected by the nature of the after-piece, and said she would always be willing to play. She suggested that, while Quin and Mrs. Woffington continued in their obstinacy, he should revive what she curiously calls "*Romeo and Juliet* as altered by Mr. Sheridan from Otway's *Caius Marius.*" This would have been like piling Ossa on Pelion.* The play produced on this occasion was probably that version of *Romeo and Juliet* which Sheridan had concocted when she was acting with him in Ireland. Her advice proved sound; the play appealed to the public and was kept on for five nights in succession. Georgiane scored a great success as Juliet, with Lee as Romeo and Dyer as Mercutio. To Rich's great delight Georgiane even consented to make an appearance in the offending pantomime itself.

For his own benefit Quin had chosen Dryden's *All For Love*, in which he played Ventidius. As in her first appearance in this play in Dublin—an occasion she was never likely to forget— Georgiane was attired in white satin, but this time more appropriately, for she was playing Octavia. Peg Woffington was the Cleopatra, and, says Georgiane with unwonted generosity, "appeared *most characteristically* as the enchantress of all hearts. Her beauty (for I must give everyone their due) beggared all description." It was probably at this performance, in which he took the part of Antony, that Georgiane played for the last time with Dennis Delane. He was taken ill after playing Piercy in *Virtue Betrayed* on March 22nd, and a few days later he was dead. He was a great loss to the stage, for he was a good actor, though over-inclined to animate and sustain his talents by a too liberal recourse to the bottle.

The Duchess of Queensberry was present at Quin's benefit and expressed a wish to be taken afterwards to the Green Room, as she had heard that after the play it was a rendezvous for the greatest wits in town. Georgiane offered to escort her,

* See pp. 61–62.

and accordingly, when her own part in the play was concluded, she threw a cloak over her theatrical costume and went to the Duchess's stage-box, where she was bidden to take a seat behind Her Grace. She was thrilled by the stir caused in the audience at this flattering mark of condescension bestowed on a mere actress by one of the greatest ladies in the land. But her sense of triumphant exaltation was to be brief. On the conclusion of the performance she ushered the Duchess into the Green Room, but instead of finding it filled, as she had expected and as it usually was, with persons of quality exchanging witty persiflage or nonchalantly playing at *Woman or Head* for huge sums against the chimney-piece, a very different scene met their gaze. Around a table covered with mutton-pies the players were seated, while Peg Woffington, still in her costume as the Queen of Egypt, was waving a pot of porter and crying out "Confusion to all order. Let Liberty thrive!"

Whether or not this picturesque scene had been deliberately and maliciously staged by Peg for Georgiane's especial discomfiture, in the knowledge that she was bringing an illustrious guest, it is not to the credit of either Georgiane herself or the Duchess that they were outraged by it. For a moment the Duchess stood aghast, then exclaiming: "Is hell broke loose?", she turned about, hurried out of the theatre, and was carried home in her chair. As for Georgiane, her snobbish soul was cut to the quick at the notion that her exalted acquaintance should have received so disgusting an idea of the inside of a theatre.

Georgiane's frequent appearances left Metham with too much time on his hands, and he chose to kill it by gaming and lost so heavily that he decided to go and recruit his finances in Yorkshire. Although Mrs. Bellamy was still there, looking after the baby, Georgiane was either unable or unwilling to accompany him and took a small house in Knightsbridge for the time being. Metham had left her no money, but their friend, the Hon. Mr. Brudenell, lent her enough to live on pending her lover's return. His absence was not long. In the country his luck had changed for the better and soon he had won enough to come back to London and take a large house in King Street, St. James's, where he and Georgiane proceeded to dissipate his winnings by living in a high style and entertaining on a scale that they could not afford. Their house was much frequented, for since Metham's sister, Mrs. Dives, and her family appeared to accept Georgiane, the people she had known before her connection with Metham had no objection to renewing their visits.

Georgiane makes the quite unwarrantable statement that it was at this time that the famous parliamentary contest at Westminster between Lord Trentham and Sir George Vandeput took place, and that she took a very great interest in its daily progress and indeed gave public breakfasts on the occasion. This election had actually taken place in the late autumn of 1749 when Georgiane was having her baby in Yorkshire; but it is quite possible that she did come in for some of its repercussions, since the result was challenged and petitioned against, and hot disputes and even riotous clashes between the rival parties continued to enliven the City of Westminster for over a year afterwards.

An unpleasant fracas had occurred when Lord Trentham's political opponents had tried to make capital out of his alleged foppishness, his frenchified manners, and his patronage of the company of French players who had been brought over by the actor, Monnet, to perform a series of French plays. They had engineered a riot at the Haymarket Theatre, and, although the intruding rabble had been put to ignominious flight by more cultured members of the audience, the popular prejudice against France and everything French still endured. This was the cause of a ludicrous incident when the brother of Georgiane's friend, Elizabeth St. Leger, that same gentleman who had once behaved towards her with such impropriety at the Dublin theatre, but had since become a friend of hers, came to call upon her on his return from his travels abroad. She happened to be standing at her window when she saw him

approaching the house, attired most extravagantly in the latest
French fashion, "A White surtout, with a crimson cape, a
French waistcoat, his hair *en papillote*, a feather in his hat, a
couteau de chasse by his side with a small cane hanging to
his button, and attended by two greyhounds." As he
espied Georgiane at her window, he called out to her
"*Bonne nouvelle! Bonne nouvelle!*" This extraordinary exhibition
attracted the attention of some scavengers in the street, and one
cried to another: "Tom, smoke Mr. Red heels!" But, unfortunately for them, Mr. St. Leger's dandified apparel belied
his true character. He may have been a coxcomb, but he was
no coward, and with easy nonchalance he stepped up to his
insulter, caught him up, and chucked him bodily among the
rubbish in his own cart. Then, with the utmost *sang froid*, he
walked into the house.

Even though she was not married to Metham, the conditions of her life with him had given Georgiane an exaggerated
sense of her own social prominence and had increased her
innate propensity towards extravagance. She herself admits
that she had contracted a taste for expense, and it was "without
considering that she was not entitled to gratify it equally with
the persons of fashion with whom she was intimate" that she
now took a house in the Vineyard on Richmond Hill. One of
her main reasons for doing so was that Lord Tyrawley was now
living there, and that, though she knew that he disapproved of
her association with Metham, she hoped to be able to overcome his inflexibility and rekindle his old affection for her.
Metham himself was not with her, but everyone imagined that,
if she was not already his wife, he meant to make her so, as he
had shown by leaving his two nephews and his niece under her
care. And she badly needed such financial support as her father
could be induced to give her, for though she had a good salary
and her benefit that year had been lucrative, and though
Metham's generosity, when he had any money himself,
was unlimited, her expenses were very heavy, and she frequently found herself without a guinea in her purse. Somehow

or other she managed to bring about the desired reconciliation with her father.

The ill-success of the French players at the Haymarket had so reduced their resources that they were now stranded and penniless. Georgiane, who had become very friendly with them, got up a subscription for them and raised a considerable amount. And she took a particular interest in one of their number, Madame Brillant, whom she accommodated with an apartment in her house in town. It was partly with the object of helping Madame Brillant that she fell in with a suggestion made to her by the Marquis de Verneuil, an amiable French nobleman who had been introduced to her by Metham. The Marquis proposed that they should engage the Assembly Room at Richmond and perform a series of French plays there. The idea appealed greatly to Georgiane, who prided herself on her command of the French language, which she had learnt in her childhood at the convent at Boulogne. It happened fortunately that both the guests she had staying with her, the widow of Dennis Delane, the actor, and Miss Hilyard, an illegitimate daughter of Lord Frederick Cavendish, could also speak French, and she could rely upon the enthusiastic co-operation of her friends, the two Miss Merediths, both of whom spoke French like natives. And she sent for Madame Brillant. The plays they performed were Racine's *Andromaque*, *Zaïre*, and *Athalie*. Georgiane had often played in the English versions of the first two. Unfortunately, she gives no further details about the performances or the performers.

This 'frolic', as she herself styles it, seems to have been regarded by both Georgiane herself and the Marquis less as a means of raising money than as an opportunity to give lavish entertainments to the nobility and gentry of the neighbourhood, and it proved exceedingly expensive. The Marquis had undertaken to pay for the rooms, light, music, wine, and servants, but Georgiane had made herself responsible for the wardrobe and the refreshments, and in the end she found herself £300 in debt. And, just at this juncture, when she did not know where to turn for ready money, she received a disquieting letter from Metham. He had had a run of bad luck in his gambling at Scarborough, and his father, who deprecated his extravagance, would give him no help. The date of his return to London would therefore be uncertain, and she must give up the house in town and take a temporary lodging until he could raise enough money to return to her. He added meaningly that, while staying with Lord Burlington, he had met Garrick, who had expressed a very great opinion of her talents, and wished to have her in his company at Drury Lane.

Georgiane was very worried. She could not move at once, because little Hugh Dives, Metham's nephew, was ill, but, as soon as he recovered, she returned to London and took a small furnished house in Frith Street, Soho. Few of her friends were in London, and she speedily became bored and conceived the fancy to go to Tunbridge Wells to visit what she was pleased to call "the estate of my progenitor, Mr. Seal", which, but for her grandmother's imprudent marriage to Busby, might one day have been her own. She decided to journey down to her 'ancestral home' in style, and thinking that it would derogate from her consequence if she were to travel with less than a set of horses, she hired four bright bays to add to her own pair and set off for Tunbridge in her coach-and-six with her maid, O'Bryan, and two mounted footmen.

She had already sent to have lodgings taken for her at Mount Sion, where most of the people of rank and fashion then stayed, and where, according to a contemporary account, "there are a great many good houses built in regular confusion, and so beautifully intermixed with trees and groves, that they cannot fail of having a most pleasing effect on a stranger. At a little distance, it bears the appearance of a town in the midst of woods, and conveys to the imagination the soothing idea of a rural romantic retirement, while it actually affords all the conveniences of a City life."

Her first visitor after her arrival was her old acquaintance, John St. Leger, but, to her great surprise, he seemed ill at ease

and oddly cold and reserved in his demeanour towards her.
When she ventured to enquire the reason, he explained that he
was paying his addresses to Miss Mary Butler, whom he hoped
soon to marry,* and that he had come with a message from
Mrs. Butler, her former friend and kind hostess in Dublin.
Mrs. Butler, it appeared, had heard conflicting rumours about
her association with Mr. Metham and wished to know if she
was really married to him, for, if she were not, she regretted
that it would not be in the power of either herself or her
daughter to take notice of her. St. Leger hinted that this
meant that she might receive a very mortifying reception at the
Rooms, since a number of the Irish nobility and gentry whom
she had known in Dublin happened at that time to be at the
Wells and would naturally follow Mrs. Butler's lead.

This was a humiliating shock to Georgiane, but she had not
a moment's doubt about the wisest course for her to pursue.
A public rebuff from a lady of quality was the one thing in the
world that she could never endure. And so she thanked Mr.
St. Leger for having avoided awkwardness for her by his timely
visit, and sent a respectful message by him to Mrs. Butler and
her daughter, saying that she should ever retain the most
grateful sense of their goodness to her when she was in Ireland,
but she felt she could not repay them with deception and must
acknowledge that, though she had every reason to believe that
Mr. Metham was going to make her his wife and he had,
indeed, given her leave to assume that character, there had as
yet been no marriage ceremony. Since, therefore, she could not
yet hope for the honour of Mrs. Butler's notice, she proposed
to return immediately to London. St. Leger suggested that she
should defer making her decision until next day, when he
would have had an opportunity of making Mrs. Butler
acquainted with her "unexampled sincerity", for he believed
that her complete frankness would have a much better effect
than if she had endeavoured to deceive the ladies. But Georgiane
wisely decided not to run the risk of being snubbed and

* He did marry her later—on July 23rd, 1754.

arranged to go back to London next morning. She might have been obliged to do so in any case, for that night, playing at cards, she lost nearly the whole of the £200 she had brought with her. But perhaps she might have played a more skilful and less reckless game, had her mind been at rest.

And so, next morning, she set out on her return journey with only one solitary half-guinea in her purse, and, at Bromley, where they halted to dine, she was obliged to borrow from her maid to pay the reckoning at the inn. She had not a shilling left when she arrived at Frith Street and was faced with the problem of paying for the four coach-horses and the two saddle-horses she had hired for her footmen. But, fortunately, she knew that Mr. Brudenell, who had financed her during Metham's first absence, was in London, and she sent to him to borrow the money. In the meantime the coach and horses had to wait outside her door.

Some time previously Georgiane had taken pity upon a ragged and starving boy who lived opposite to her and had taken him into her service. Neither she nor her servants had been able to get anything out of him beyond the facts that his name was Peter and that he came from Bruges. But he had shown great gratitude for her kindness to him and had developed a dog-like devotion to her. This Flemish boy was now posted at the door, awaiting the return of the messenger she had sent for the money.

The sight of so magnificent an equipage standing outside the door of a small house in such a neighbourhood as this naturally attracted much attention, and the elder of two gentlemen who were passing by wondered aloud whose it was. Peter pertly replied: "My mistress's." "Ah!" said the gentleman, "I should be glad to know who is to pay for it!" Peter was much upset by this implied insult to his beloved mistress and ran in to tell her of this impertinence. But Georgiane was rather amused and merrily asked him why he had not told the rude man that the privilege could belong to him, if he had no objection. Peter took the jest quite seriously, and when, a short time after, the two gentlemen came by again and the elder repeated his comment, the boy blurted out word for word what Georgiane had said. The gentleman promptly replied that he could not have the least objection, and without ceremony he and his companion entered the house and walked upstairs, to Georgiane's great astonishment.

Georgiane recognised the elder of them at once as the Secretary at War, Henry Fox, whom she knew only by sight, though she had once been presented to his wife, Lady Caroline. Fox introduced himself by saying, with courtly grace, that he hoped the whimsicalness, in the first place, and the irresistible temptation, in the second, would plead as an apology for his intrusion. He introduced his companion, Mr. John Calcraft, who, with less assurance than the experienced statesman and man of the world, stood by blushing and awkward. Georgiane explained hastily that she had not intended her joking remark to be taken seriously; she was temporarily short of money and had had to send for some to be able to discharge her coach. Luckily for her, her messenger now returned bringing twenty guineas from Mr. Brudenell, and she was able to disabuse Mr. Fox of the notion he might have entertained—and probably did entertain—about her virtue. Her standing was still further confirmed by the arrival of Count von Haslang and General Wall, who, having noticed in passing that her house was lighted up, had decided to pay her a call. After a little conversation, Fox took leave with his companion, but, before he left, asked if he might have the pleasure of calling on her again. He explained that business kept him in town and he was much alone, since Lady Caroline's delicate state of health obliged her to remain in the country. Georgiane replied that she would be happy to have the honour of seeing him whenever he had leisure.

As soon as Fox and Calcraft had gone, her diplomatic friends were eager to know how it was that she was receiving a visit from somebody of Mr. Fox's eminence. Georgiane made no secret of it and told them of the ludicrous incident that had occasioned it. General Wall was very much amused; but Count von Haslang, who knew his Georgiane still better, smiled and asked whether Mr. Fox, upon hearing of her situation, had given her "de monies". Georgiane indignantly protested that he could certainly not suppose that Mr. Fox could be guilty of such ill manners, but Count von Haslang shrugged his shoulders and grunted, which, Georgiane says was "the only mode by which the Comte usually expressed either his approbation or dislike".

Georgiane asked them to stay on to play cards and sent for two ladies to join them. While the gentlemen were waiting they went over to the chimney-piece to look at some Chelsea figures the Count had recently presented to Georgiane, and found lying there a piece of paper which looked like a bank-bill. Georgiane disclaimed all knowledge of its existence or how it had come there, but on examination they found that it was, indeed, a bank-bill for £50. Georgiane concluded that Mr. Fox had taken this method of relieving her present necessities without offending her delicacy. But she declared that she intended to send it back at once, as she did not wish to be beholden to a person who was almost a stranger to her. Count von Haslang told her not to be a fool. By returning it she would offer the highest affront to the giver of it. Would she be displeased with such a mark of approbation at her benefit? Why, then, should she now? Many persons, at different times, made her presents, and she need not be more scrupulous about receiving them from Mr. Fox than from the General, or himself, or several others, who offered them merely as a tribute to her talents, without having any design upon her person. This was the sort of reasoning that appealed to Georgiane; she was not sorry to confess herself convinced by it, and decided to keep the banknote and consider herself indebted to Mr. Fox for a bounty so delicately bestowed.

This was a lucky evening for her. Before it was over she had doubled her resources, having added to the mysterious bank-note fifty more pounds won from her guests at the card-table.

Her diplomatic friends were so impressed by her skilful play that they proposed that for the few weeks before the theatres opened again, and, perhaps, occasionally afterwards, they should combine to set up a Faro Bank with the Marquis de Verneuil, who was daily expected from Yorkshire, where he had been visiting his friend, George Metham. Georgiane was delighted with the idea, though it meant that she would have to raise £1,000 as her share of the capital needed to set it going. But, if she had no money, she had her diamonds, and she believed that she would have no difficulty in raising the requisite sum.

Chapter Eight

FULLY EXPECTING TO BE RE-ENGAGED for the forthcoming season at Covent Garden, Georgiane now decided to go and spend a few days at Richmond before she had to instal herself in town for the autumn. She had scarcely descended from her chaise when Mr. Lacy, joint-manager with Garrick at Drury Lane, was announced. Since they were on friendly terms and he lived not far away at Isleworth, she supposed that he was merely paying a casual call on her. But, to her great surprise, he told her that he had come expressly to inform her that Mrs. Cibber had been engaged for Covent Garden and that Quin, in disgust, had quitted the stage. He had, therefore, come to offer her a three years engagement at Drury Lane. Georgiane confesses that she ought to have been suspicious, because Quin wrote to her regularly and would surely not have left her in the dark about events which were of so much consequence to her own theatrical situation. But she was so enraged at this apparent proof of renewed duplicity on the part of Rich that she impetuously signed the agreement Lacy had brought her. No sooner had she done so than Lacy admitted to her, with what she describes as a "malignant grin of self-approbation," that the report of Mrs. Cibber's engagement was current, but that he could not vouch for the truth of it. "However," he continued, "at all events you must be a gainer by playing with my partner, whose consequence stamps merit where there is none, and increases it where it is." Georgiane was furious at being thus tricked, even though she was by no means displeased at the prospect of her new engagement.

Shortly after Lacy had left, Rich and his friend, Bencraft,

arrived to see her, and Rich informed her that he had already engaged Barry for the coming season and had brought articles for her to sign. Georgiane had to confess that, having been told by Lacy that Mrs. Cibber had been engaged for Covent Garden, she had signed articles with him that very morning to act at Drury Lane. Rich protested that Lacy had lied to her. While he admitted that it was true that Mrs. Cibber had offered to come to Covent Garden for £700, which was less than she had received last time she had played at Drury Lane, and that Barry had been insistently urging him to accept this tempting offer, he said that out of regard for Georgiane he had steadfastly rejected it and had brought with him articles for her to sign for a three years engagement at five, six and seven hundred annually. He complained bitterly that, now she had let him down so badly, he would be obliged to give Mrs. Cibber any terms she chose to ask.

Georgiane was quite as distressed as Rich himself, and sincerely wished that she could recall what she had done, not only because she had apparently misjudged Rich, but also because the terms she had agreed with Lacy were much lower— £300 annually for the three years. And she would have enjoyed playing romantic parts with that most romantic of lovers, Spranger Barry.

Though this account of Georgiane's engagement for Drury Lane may not have been quite true, for she always made her stories as favourable as possible to herself, there was certainly some substance in it. Mrs. Cibber, who had quarrelled with Garrick, undoubtedly did want to go to Covent Garden, and Lacy was probably quite right in thinking that Rich was likely to close with the advantageous offer she was making him. For this reason he had intended to make quite certain that Rich would not also have the services of Georgiane Bellamy, who was already the next best actress of such parts as Mrs. Cibber played, and, under Garrick's tuition, might even become a formidable rival to her. The whole incident provides interesting evidence of Georgiane's exact standing in the theatre at the time.

On her return to town she found that her friends, the Ambassadors, were as keen as ever on their plan to run a Faro Bank, and she threw herself into the project with her usual extravagant ardour. Determined that everything should be done in style, she engaged Goundu, the most eminent cook of the time, and took on his wife as her French woman. By borrowing money she managed to raise the £1,000, which was her share of the capital. The scheme started off in a splendid manner and promised to be a great success. The '*petits soupers*' provided by Goundu were a great attraction and brought the fashionable world to her house. Moreover, she herself had such a splendid run of luck at the tables that she was able to redeem her jewels, pay off all her debts, and put some hundreds of pounds in her pocket, in spite of her great expenses. She was, in fact, fully convinced that she would have made her fortune if Verneuil had not gone off to Paris and she herself had not been obliged to return to the theatre. But after Garrick's return to London she had to devote herself entirely to the duties of her profession. The manager of Drury Lane was a severe taskmaster, and expected from others the same attention to the business of acting as he exacted from himself.

The rivalry between the two houses was bound to be more intense than ever this season. Rich had got together a very strong company at Covent Garden. Apart from his triumph in securing the services of Mrs. Cibber he had also attracted from Ireland the great Spranger Barry, Macklin and his wife, and Georgiane's old friend, Mrs. Elmy. And, of course, Quin and Peg Woffington remained with him. Although Garrick had done his best to revenge himself on Rich for his capture of Mrs. Cibber by trying to entice Quin to Drury Lane, Quin had preferred leading at Covent Garden to playing second fiddle at Drury Lane. But he had not scrupled to make use of Garrick's offer to him as a lever to extract from Rich a salary of £1,000 a year, the highest salary yet paid in the theatre.

At Drury Lane, Mrs. Pritchard and Kitty Clive were twin towers of strength, and Garrick possessed two excellent

comedians in Woodward and Shuter. Mrs. Ward was still in
the company, but Garrick did not like acting with her owing to
her fidgetiness, and Georgiane was to play his younger
heroines. She fully realised that she had a formidable task
before her, for it was not easy for her, at the best of times, to
compete with Mrs. Cibber's dazzling talents and greater
experience, and now the fact that Mrs. Cibber had been absent
from the stage for a year made her a still greater attraction.

Garrick had decided that Georgiane should make her first
appearance at Drury Lane as Juliet in a superb production of
Romeo and Juliet, with himself as Romeo. Following the usual
custom at that time, Rich promptly announced that he would
produce the same play on the same day. Both productions
were staged on September 28th, 1750. At first the whole town
flocked to both houses, eager to compare the rival performances. Rich had determined, if possible, to outshine
Garrick in every way, and it was universally conceded that
Covent Garden had the advantage as regards spectacle. The
particular piece of pageantry devised by Rich on this occasion
was the Funeral Procession of Juliet, set to music specially
composed by Mrs. Cibber's celebrated brother, Dr. Arne.
Georgiane avers that Rich spent almost as much on this scene
as the whole play brought him in. Not to be outdone, on the
third night Garrick also introduced an additional scene
representing the funeral procession to the tomb of the Capulets.
But his procession was less imposing than Rich's, and the
music was not by the composer of 'Rule Britannia'.

The town was very much divided over the merits of the two
Romeos, but, on the whole, Barry's rendering seems to have
been considered rather better than Garrick's. In Georgiane's
opinion, there was only one scene, that with the friar, in which
Garrick exceed his rival. No doubt Garrick was the better
actor of the two, but Romeo is the most romantic of parts, and
Barry possessed the manly bearing and the beauty of person
and voice that the part demands. Garrick had all the grace, but
lacked the stature. On the other hand, Woodward's subtle and

whimsical playing of Mercutio at Drury Lane was considered to be immeasurably better than the elderly Macklin's staid and matter of fact version at Covent Garden.

Georgiane had played Juliet before both in Ireland and at Covent Garden, but on this occasion she had had the advantage of special tuition from Garrick. Mrs. Cibber was incomparably the better actress of the two, but she was now thirty-six, and Georgiane had the appeal of real youth to help her. Francis Gentleman, in his *Dramatic Censor*, published anonymously in 1770, says that both actresses had great merit in this character. "One excelled in amorous rapture, the other called every power of distress and despair to her aid; Mrs. Bellamy was an object of love, Mrs. Cibber of admiration; Mrs. Bellamy's execution was more natural. Mrs. Cibber's more forceable; in the former there were traces of nonage; in the latter too much of the woman." This must be accounted high praise for Georgiane; it must be remembered that Gentleman was an exceedingly forthright critic, more lavish with brickbats than bouquets. If he considered Mrs. Cibber to be the better actress of the two, he regarded her as the greatest tragic actress of her time, and he placed Mrs. Bellamy not very far behind her. It was almost always with Mrs. Bellamy's performance that he first compared Mrs. Cibber's before going on to estimate those of other actresses. In his final summing-up of their comparative merits in all the famous tragic parts which both of them played, he says: "Mrs. Bellamy trod close on the heels of Mrs. Cibber, she had, we think, the more amiable countenance of the two, though it was not marked with so much sensibility, her person though small was very satisfactory, and her expressions of rapture beyond any thing we have ever heard; she came nearer comedy than her great competitor, but never deserved much praise in that stile."

Romeo and Juliet continued to be played at both theatres until not only the performers themselves but also the town became sick of it, and the managements had to be generous with free seats if they were to fill their houses. After twelve consecutive nights Rich took off his production, but Garrick, merely for the satisfaction of having the last word, kept his on for one more performance. On the last night Kitty Clive spoke a special epilogue in which she poked fun at the difference in stature between the two Romeos, the towering Barry and the diminutive Garrick.

> I, Catherine Clive, come here t'attack them all,
> And aim alike at little and at tall.

The piece was later revived at Drury Lane and played nineteen times in all this season. It was played twenty-three times at the rival house.

Georgiane's next parts were all familiar to her: Belvidera at the end of October, and in November Cordelia and Alicia. In December there was a very successful and highly profitable production of Congreve's *Mourning Bride*, in which she played Almeria, with Mrs. Pritchard as Zara. Garrick was Osmyn, and Georgiane remarked that, though his playing of the part was "beyond description", and deservedly met with unbounded applause, he was not too pleased that her success as Almeria was as great as his own. "I believe," she says, "he would gladly have sacrificed both his reputation and his profit, sooner than I should have acquired the approbation of the public as I did in the character of Almeria." As usual, there was a rival production at Covent Garden. Once again Gentleman considered that Georgiane should not be placed far behind Mrs. Cibber: "Her painting of distraction was more faint, but love and tenderness she always expressed with admirable feeling." Tate Wilkinson, who also saw both productions was by no means favourable to Georgiane: "Garrick was not in my secret opinion as enchanting as Barry— Mrs. Bellamy was very inferior indeed to Mrs. Cibber—but Mrs. Pritchard's Zara struck me with admiration."

Towards Christmas Metham returned to town, bringing with him Mrs. Bellamy and the baby. Georgiane's house at

Frith Street was far too small to accommodate them all, so a lodging near by was procured for Mrs. Bellamy, and Metham installed himself in rooms in Pall Mall. Georgiane is careful to record that this arrangement was purely practical and was not due to any slackening in her lover's affection for her. On the contrary his passion for her was increased by his satisfaction in seeing her so much admired as an actress and successfully standing a comparison with Mrs. Cibber, whom she describes as the "first female tragedian in the world". But, as Gentleman has pointed out, Georgiane could enchant the heart and senses as Mrs. Cibber with her greater talent never could. As Calista in the *Fair Penitent*, which they both played at the beginning of 1751, it was in the passages of love and tenderness that she excelled Mrs. Cibber.

On February 23rd Garrick produced *Alfred*, a play based by Mallet on his own and Thomson's *Masque of Alfred*, which had been first played before the Prince and Princess of Wales at Clieveden in 1740. In the masque the best part had been that of the Hermit, which had been specially designed for Quin by the authors, but in the new version the principal part was that of King Alfred himself, played by Garrick. Georgiane says that he excelled even himself in it and especially impressed the audience by his delivery of the line: "I fear God and have no other fear." Her own role of Eltruda, the part created by Mrs. Horton in the original production, was, she thought, as mediocre as it was short, and she attributed any success she had in it to her appearance and her dress. In spite of its lavish mounting and in spite, too, of the patriotic strains of 'Rule Britannia', the play did not appeal greatly and was acted only nine times in the whole season. Georgiane did not appear in the final performance on April 19th. Her last appearance this season was as Belvidera in her own benefit on March 18th.

The Prince of Wales died on March 20th, and both theatres were closed for a time. Georgiane did not return when they were re-opened, and the parts usually allotted to her were played by Mrs. Pritchard. Her absence may have been due to her grief over the death of her beloved friend, Miss Conway, who had indiscreetly drunk lemonade after overheating herself at a ball and had expired a few hours later in the most excruciating pains. The loss of this friend so upset Georgiane that she fell ill herself and was overcome with such lassitude that she did not feel equal to undertaking the journey to the south of France, where she had been invited to pass the summer with another friend, Elizabeth St. Leger, who was now married to Major Burton. Instead, she remained quietly at home, neither giving nor attending parties, but enjoying the 'placid society' of a few friends. She herself says that "Nothing material happened this summer".

The company at Drury Lane this autumn was augmented by two actors who were making their first appearances on the English stage. Henry Mossop, an Irishman with a fine voice but an uncouth manner, had had a great success in Dublin and was now to appear in some of the parts usually played by Garrick, including Richard III and Macbeth. In contrast to him, David Ross was a handsome and elegant young man, who both looked and spoke like a gentleman, but too often allowed his love of conviviality to take precedence over his work and consequently played with a languid indolence born of fatigue. Georgiane remarked that it was fully in his power to do a part justice when he did not choose to walk over the course. But when he could be bothered to do so, he played the parts of young lovers to perfection, and Garrick allowed him to essay Romeo at his benefit on March 31st, 1752. Georgiane was his Juliet; she had already played the part with Garrick as Romeo six times in the season.

In the production of the *Fair Penitent*, which was extremely popular, Georgiane played Calista, with Garrick as Lothario, Mossop as Horatio, and Ross as Altamont. She also made occasional appearances in many of her familiar parts—Monimia, Imoinda, Cordelia, Andromache, Almeria, Mrs. Sullen and Rutland—and several that were new to her. With Mossop she had two great successes, first in Young's *Revenge*, in which she played Leonora and he Zanga, and later in *Phædra and Hippolitus*, which had not been acted for twenty years and was now revived with Mossop as Theseus, Mrs. Pritchard as Phædra, and Georgiane as the young Ismena.

Another outstanding success was Thomson's *Tancred and Sigismunda*, in which Georgiane appeared for the first time as Sigismunda on February 13th, 1752. Garrick played Tancred. This was a fairly new play, the original production having taken place in 1745, when Mrs. Cibber had played Sigismunda. Unfortunately, Gentleman has left no description of the rival merits of the two actresses in this play. Georgiane said that Mrs. Cibber was "most capitally great in the performance of that character", but felt that she had not acquitted herself too badly in the part. At any rate she succeeded in it much beyond her hopes. She seems, indeed, to have been satisfied with her own performance, since she chose it for her benefit on March 14th, with the *Anatomist* as after-piece. This benefit was very lucrative, and she records with pride that the ladies of the Earl of Essex's family were added to the list of her habitual patronesses.

On the other hand, there were two conspicuous failures this season. Rowe's *Lady Jane Gray*, in which Georgiane played the name-part, was revived after a lapse of seven years and ignominiously withdrawn from the repertory after the second performance. And on February 17th, 1752, Garrick found that he had greatly overrated the merits of *Eugenia* or *The Supposed Daughter*, a play in blank verse by a friend of his, Dr. Francis. In spite of Garrick's own efforts as Mercœur and Georgiane's as Eugenia, it was played "to empty benches and a dead silence" on the first night, and the public voted it appallingly complicated and excessively dull. Garrick, who had had great hopes of it, kept it on for six performances with no better result and then reluctantly withdrew it. It was never revived.

Towards the end of the season Georgiane appeared several times as Desdemona, and on April 20th she had the pleasure of playing Rutland for her old friend from Covent Garden, Mrs.

Horton, who appeared as Queen Elizabeth at a benefit given to her by Drury Lane.

By this time Georgiane was beginning to become seriously worried because Metham still showed no signs of making her his wife. Her mother was continually urging her to speak to him about it, but she did not find it easy to broach the delicate question. However, one day a favourable opportunity did at last present itself, and she asked him "without any circumlocution" whether he would marry her. Without answering, he abruptly left the room, which surprised her because he was usually most polite. She was so offended that, as soon as he had left the house, she rang the bell and gave her maid instructions not to admit him next time he came. But an hour later she received a card from him informing her that he and his brother-in-law, Mr. Dives, proposed to dine with her that evening and asking her to ensure that they should be alone, as they were coming on business. Assuming that their business was to discuss the marriage, she consented to receive them.

When they arrived they brought with them another gentleman, hitherto unknown to her, whom she presently discovered to be an attorney. After much beating about the bush Metham produced a document in which he agreed, in case he should die without legitimate issue, to settle the estates he had already inherited from his mother and those he expected to receive on the death of his father, upon his sister, Mrs. Dives, and her husband and their heirs. Mr. Dives was to join with him in securing Georgiane an annuity of £300 a year, with the sum of £2,000 to George, her son by Metham.

Although the purport and purpose of this deed should surely have been clear to the meanest intelligence, Georgiane declares that she imagined Mr. Dives's acquiescence in securing this annuity to be an act of disinterested generosity on his part. But as soon as her mother saw the document she speedily disabused her of this notion, pointing out to her that, under cover of making a disinterested provision for her and her child, he was really securing the estates for himself and his family.

127

She did then realise that the whole thing was an artful plan to induce her to give up her expectations of ever marrying Metham.

She hastened to consult Quin, who told her that, if she really loved Metham, as she assured him she did, it would be better for her not to make herself or him unhappy by pestering him to marry her. In any case she could not go by his name while she continued on the stage, which, for financial reasons, she would be obliged to do so long as Metham's father was alive. He said he could not see what difference the actual ceremony would make, since it was generally believed that they were already married and that the marriage was being kept secret "for prudential reasons". It would be wiser to leave the whole question to Metham's honour and affection, which would doubtless come into play in course of time. Somehow it is difficult to believe that it could have been with sincerity that Quin gave her such bad advice; if he really did so, it must have been because he saw through Metham's machinations and did not like to tell her straight out that it was obvious that her lover had no intention of marrying her. Georgiane says that, in consequence of Quin's advice, she concealed her wishes, though she could not altogether suppress them. She was conscious that her character received a stain from the nature of her connexion with Metham, which her sincere affection for him and her belief from the first that it would culminate in a more honourable union could not altogether expunge, though she managed to persuade herself that "in the eye of heaven such a connexion, when conducted with this propriety, may not need the repetition of the nuptial ceremony". Unfortunately, this was but one of several occasions in her career in which Georgiane's certainty that she was conversant with heaven's views on the desirability or otherwise of a marriage ceremony was to prove disadvantageous to her from a purely mundane point of view. On this occasion she had come off with a meagre settlement and no wedding ring.

In the autumn of 1752 Georgiane was in constant demand at

the theatre and played Belvidera, Juliet, Leonora, Monimia, Imoinda, and Cordelia. The company had lost Mrs. Ward, who, however, according to Tate Wilkinson, was "neither wanted nor regretted; as Miss Bellamy's youth, fashion, dress, etc., aided with Mr. Garrick's powerful assistance, enabled her to make a tolerable stand in tragedy against Mrs. Cibber, which Mrs. Ward was by no means equal to". In fact, although the powerful combination of Barry and Mrs. Cibber was at Covent Garden, that theatre did not do so well this autumn as Drury Lane, which was "constantly attended". Mrs. Ward's place was filled by two new actresses, Miss Davies, from Dublin, and Miss Haughton, a pretty and promising young actress a little handicapped by a lisp and traces of a Newcastle accent, who made her first appearance at Drury Lane as Amanda in *Love's Last Shift* on December 18th, 1752. For some weeks at the beginning of 1753 Georgiane did not appear, and the two new actresses shared her parts, Miss Davies playing Imoinda and Miss Haughton Monimia and Juliet.

Chapter Nine

SINCE SHE HAD BEEN SO CONSTANTLY at the theatre, Georgiane had not been seeing so much of Metham of late. He was spending most of his time at White's or some other coffee house, gambling and usually losing his money. But she now arranged to give a party for him on January 30th, which was his birthday. It was a convenient date, for by tradition the theatres were closed that night, the anniversary of the execution of King Charles I.

Metham brought with him John Calcraft, with whom he had become very friendly. He was a young man of about twenty-seven, the son of a Grantham solicitor, who was Town Clerk and political agent to the local territorial magnate, the Duke of Rutland. Through the influence of Rutland's son, the Marquess of Granby, young John had obtained a clerkship in the Pay Office, and, at the age of nineteen or twenty, he had already held a responsible position, being stationed at Newcastle to receive the Excise from the Collectors of the northern Counties, with which to pay the forces engaged in suppressing the Jacobite Rising in Scotland. Even at that time he could already describe as his "particular friend" the powerful Henry Fox, the Secretary at War, with whom he could claim some slight relationship through his mother's family. Fox took an interest in this distant kinsman, and, recognising in him great financial ability and an unscrupulousness equal to his own, provided him with sundry opportunities to exert both in their mutual interest. By now John Calcraft was rapidly building up a future and a fortune for himself.

The high social position that he also coveted was rather

more difficult to obtain, for his manners were still uncouth and provincial, and his deportment was by no means elegant. Georgiane maintains that his appearance was unpleasing and that his figure was not unlike that of a drayman, but she was a very biased witness, and her account of him is not borne out by the pleasing joviality of his portrait at Rempstone, nor by an otherwise hostile article in the *Town and Country Magazine*, which, after stigmatising him as one of the "state-vultures that prey on the nation's vitals", describes him as "a tall handsome man, with a ruddy complexion, an easy address, and a facility of speech that greatly recommended him". But it is true that this account dates from 1769, by which time he had had leisure to acquire polish. He was not at this time very well known to Georgiane, although, since he had met her on that strange occasion with Henry Fox, he had become an assiduous attendant at the theatre.

Another guest was Metham's great friend, young Lord Downe, with whom Georgiane had first become acquainted in Yorkshire, where one of his seats was situated. She says that, though she had every reason to believe that he was in love with her, he had never told her so, and, in fact, never admitted to it so long as she was under the protection of his friend, George Metham. But Metham, too, had apparently divined his secret and was consumed with jealousy.

In her desire to make the birthday party a great occasion, Georgiane sent for the celebrated chef, Goundu, to dress the dinner and Robinson, the fashionable confectioner, to provide a magnificent dessert. The 'desserts' of the eighteenth century could be most elaborate affairs, and often exceedingly costly. Sometimes they would consist of medieval castles or oriental temples built of sweetmeats and peopled with tiny sugar-figures. At the christening of Prince Henry Frederick during the Jacobite rising of 1745 the citadel of Carlisle had been reproduced in sugar, and the Prince of Wales's guests had been invited to bombard it with sugar plums. At a great dinner given by the ugly but devout and prudish wife of one of the

German Ministers, somebody observed that all the sugar figures in the dessert were girls, upon which the Minister replied: "Ça est vrai; ordinairement les pettis Cupidons sont des garcons; mais ma femme s'est amusée toute la matinée à en ôter tout ça par modestie." The Duke of Newcastle once had a dessert representing Vauxhall Gardens illuminated with hundreds of little lamps of different colours.

Regrettably, Georgiane has left no description of the dessert Robinson provided for her on this occasion, but it must have been particularly sumptuous, as it caused so much comment among her guests that she began to have qualms about it, realising that the ordering of it seemed to reflect no great honour on her prudence and economy. But she attempted to laugh the matter off by observing that she was not in fear of visiting the new buildings in St. George's Fields—the debtors' prison—on account of it, but if ever she should, she hoped some one or other of them would release her. Whereupon Metham, who must undoubtedly have been very drunk, or very jealous, or both, rose from his seat and declared that she might rot there before he would release her. For a moment a dead silence followed this astonishing outburst, then Calcraft turned to Metham and remarked: "I hope, sir, you will not be angry with those that will." But a damp pall of awkwardness had settled on the company, and the remainder of the evening was dreary in the extreme.

Lord Downe, who entertained a suspicion that Metham's insult was indirectly aimed at him, took his leave as soon as he decently could, and Metham was prevailed upon to do so too. But, unfortunately, since all public places of entertainment were closed that night, the rest of the company had nowhere else to go and stayed on until the small hours of the morning. It would have been better for Georgiane in her hysterical and overwrought state if they too had left, for she was so upset by Metham's behaviour that, when some of her friends tried to make excuses for him and persuade her to forgive him, she dramatically dropped to her knees and made a sacred vow that, if he now offered her his hand, she would refuse it. Not content with this, she also swore solemnly that from that time to her dying hour she would have no connexion whatever with him.

When she at last retired after her guests had gone, Georgiane was still far too discomposed to sleep and wandered restlessly about her room. Whenever she approached the window and looked out she perceived a man pacing the street below in much the same agitated manner as herself, but she was so engrossed in her own troubles that the reason for his presence there did not at the time arouse in her more than a passing curiosity.

In the morning a very contrite Metham came to call on her. He apologised for his rudeness, imputing it to a momentary frenzy which he could not control, but which, he assured her, proceeded from the excess of his love for her. But Georgiane's pride was still smarting; she would not listen to anything he had to say in his defence or to any of the promises he made, and in the end he went away in a state of utter dejection. After a few days, finding that she still persisted in her refusal to resume her connexion with him, he appeared to be resigned to it and asked a friend of theirs, Colonel Sandford, to intercede for him and persuade Georgiane at least to admit him as a friend. This she consented to do, but she had, she said, formed a firm resolution to have no more love-affairs, and to dedicate herself henceforth entirely to her profession. She wrote and told Quin of this resolution, and in his answer he thoroughly approved of it.

A few days later Georgiane's maid brought her a packet which had been left at her door. On opening it she found it contained ten bank-bills of £100 each. But there was nothing to indicate who was the sender. Georgiane was inclined to suspect that the money had come from Lord Downe, but believing in any case that so munificent a present could only come from somebody who was greatly interested in her and who would therefore inevitably reveal himself in time, she decided to lock up the packet and not to use the money until her unknown benefactor should disclose his identity.

In the spring of 1753 Garrick decided to produce *The Brothers*, a tragedy by the Rev. Dr. Young, the celebrated author of *Night Thoughts*. This play had actually been written nearly thirty years before and put into rehearsal in 1726, but had been withdrawn when its author entered holy orders. The fame of Young's *Revenge* raised great expectations that this piece might be even better.

Georgiane, who was well acquainted with the author, had the temerity to send to him and ask him if she might read the manuscript of the play, on the plea that she wanted to study the part intended for her, which she had been told was very long. The truth, however, as she well knew, was that it was very short, for Garrick fully intended that the principal part of Erixene should be played by Mrs. Pritchard. But Dr. Young, assuming that Georgiane was to play Erixene and approving of the idea, readily assented to her request. Garrick was, not unnaturally, furious, and was provoked into writing her the following letter: "Since you have humbugged the town, I suppose you think you are intitled to do whatever you please. The liberty you have taken in asking to peruse Doctor Young's piece, is unwarrantable. And I will convince you that I *alone* am the person to be addressed in whatever concerns the theatre. I shall find means to repay the contempt you have been pleased to show me."

Far from being abashed by this rebuke, as she should have been, Georgiane sent the manager a tart reply, informing him that she had not meant to infringe upon his authority, or to lessen his great dignity, but that, notwithstanding she was to be governed with the greatest ease by complacency, no power on earth should rule her with a rod of iron.

When she entered the Green Room rather late for the first reading of the piece, Garrick came up to her angrily. "Ah, ah, ah, madam, you are come at last. It was unfortunate for us that the doctor insisted upon your being his heroine." Georgiane blandly agreed. The haughtiness the part demanded was not in her line, and she was sure that his favourite, Mrs. Pritchard, would do it much better. She was, therefore, quite ready to give up the part. But to Garrick's further exasperation Dr. Young himself intervened and insisted that the part should be played by Georgiane. The play was then read, and Georgiane, all cock-a-hoop with her triumph over the manager, offended the author himself by objecting to what he considered to be one of the best lines in the part of Erixene: "I will speak to you in thunder." But then realising that she had perhaps gone too far, she released all her youthful charm and cajoled the doctor into such a state of complacency that, to Garrick's astonishment he took up a pen and struck out the line she had criticised. And after the reading was over he invited himself home to dine with her.

Georgiane also invited Quin, who happened to be in London on one of his rare visits from Bath, where he had settled on his final retirement from the stage two years before. Dr. Young greatly diverted the old actor with an account of the dispute in the Green Room. "Oh, Doctor," said Quin, "if you knew what that girl could do as well as say, you would not be surprised at anything relative to her." Georgiane did not quite know how the doctor might interpret this rather equivocal compliment, but he was by now so much under the spell of her charm that he said he had been informed of the goodness of her heart, which induced him to impute what she had uttered to sincerity; whereas, he should otherwise have esteemed it conceited impertinence. And he would have been right.

The play, produced on March 3rd, 1753, was not a success, and this was partly because Miss Bellamy was not suited to her part. Both Garrick and Mossop were excellent. There were only eight performances, and the profits, which Dr. Young had arranged to give to the Society for the Propagation of the Gospel, were so meagre that he himself generously made them up to £1,000 out of his own pocket. Considering the sacred purpose to which the emoluments of his piece were to be devoted, Dr. Young was extremely annoyed when, on the last night, Garrick, possibly to take a subtle revenge upon him for his championship of Georgiane, added a somewhat ribald epilogue spoken in her naughtiest manner by Kitty Clive. There was a decided coolness for some time between the reverend author and his old friend, the manager of Drury Lane.

Although Georgiane had declared her willingness to receive Metham as a friend, she did not intend to be left alone with him, and accordingly, when he was to dine with her one evening, she asked Colonel Sandford to come too, explaining that she thought a *tête-à-tête* in this present situation would be "awkward and not very agreeable to both". Metham, possibly for the same reason, brought his new friend Calcraft, with him. The party was completed by Mrs. Lane, Rich's second daughter, who happened to call and was invited to stay on to dinner. The conversation turned on the pantomime, *Harlequin Sorcerer*, which had been revived this year with an additional fountain scene which was reputed to surpass any pantomime trick that had ever been devised. It was drawing crowded houses every night. Georgiane lamented that she had so far been unable to get any seats for it. The remark was probably intended as a hint to Mrs. Lane, who at any rate took it up and offered to procure her seats for any evening she chose to name. Georgiane selected the following Saturday, as she did not happen to be acting that night. Since they were not to accompany her in any case, Georgiane did not think it odd when Calcraft later proposed that Metham and Sandford should accompany him on a party of pleasure to Oxford. Both accepted, and it was agreed that they should set out next morning.

On the Saturday, as had been arranged, Georgiane went to the pantomime with Mrs. Lane and the Dives children. To her great surprise, shortly after the performance had begun, they were joined by John Calcraft, who explained that he had been called back to London on business and had left Metham and Sandford to continue their journey to Oxford. Georgiane naturally accepted this plausible explanation of his presence, and thought no more about it. She says that it never occurred to her that he could have the presumption to conceive any design on her or the vanity to attempt to rival Metham and take his place in her affections.

At the end of the performance Calcraft handed the ladies to their carriage and asked permission to see them home. Georgiane consented, and on their arrival at her house invited him to stay to supper. They did not rise from table until two o'clock in the morning, and, as her carriage had been dismissed and Mrs. Lane had none of her own, Calcraft offered to send her home in his chair, which was waiting for him. Mrs. Lane lived some distance away, in Carey Street, Lincoln's Inn Fields, so that Calcraft was obliged to stay for a considerable time before his chairmen could return. This, says Georgiane procured him a *tête-à-tête* with her, "which otherwise he could never have obtained."

It was perhaps only natural that they should have talked of the impropriety of Metham's behaviour towards her, and anyhow Calcraft had determined that their conversation should proceed on these lines. He said that Metham's insult to her could only be excused by considering it as the madness of jealousy. It was his friend's hasty temper that had led him to make use of a brutal expression, which Calcraft was sure he regretted and which had made him miserable. Calcraft's stout defence of his absent friend gave Georgiane a most favourable impression of him, and, growing expansive, she told him in confidence about the money that had been sent her, and showed him the packet. Calcraft declared that, had he himself been in the position to do so, he would have made the same gesture "without any interested views", and he strongly advised her to abandon all scruples and make use of the money. He then asked her whether she thought that Metham intended to marry her, and she frankly told him that, if he did offer her his hand now, nothing would induce her to accept it. She had fully determined never again to enter into any engagement of any sort with any man. By this time his chair had come back, and after requesting that he might have the honour of waiting upon her again when she had leisure, he took his leave. Georgiane retired to bed, without, she claims, reflecting at all upon her indiscretion in sitting up alone until the small hours of the morning with a young man whom she scarcely knew.

On the following night at the theatre, as Georgiane was standing in the wings about to make her first entrance, she was rudely jostled by a drunken Irishman. Calcraft, who happened to be near by, resented the insult and knocked the stranger down. And as soon as he was able to get up, Calcraft asked him to come outside as he wanted to speak to him. A few minutes later he returned, looking thoroughly pleased with himself, so that everyone concluded that the affair had been amicably or at least satisfactorily settled. But the little incident brought Georgiane to realise that Calcraft must be in love with her, and she began to regret that she had invited him to a supper party she was giving after the play. However, he treated her with distant respect all the evening and left before anyone else, so she concluded that she was probably mistaken.

Next morning, as she was walking in the Park, a servant of Metham's came up to her and told her that his master had returned to town and desired to speak with her immediately at his lodgings. Since they were situated in Pall Mall close at hand she proceeded there at once. At the door she met Calcraft with the Irishman who had insulted her the night before. It appeared that Calcraft had insisted that he should either fight a duel with him or apologise to Miss Bellamy, and that, having been so drunk that he could not recollect anything at all about the events of the night before, he had wisely preferred to make the apology. They had called at her house for that purpose, and finding that she had gone to the Park had followed her there and thence to Pall Mall. The Irishman made an awkward apology in the presence of both Metham and Calcraft, and then gratefully took himself off. But, to Georgiane's great surprise, Metham turned to Calcraft, and, instead of thanking him for having protected Georgiane from insult during his absence, demanded from him what right he had to enlist himself as her champion. But the reason for his displeasure soon became apparent. On his return to London he had immediately called at Georgiane's house and had been told by her maid not only that Calcraft had stayed alone with her at her house until a most unseasonable hour in the morning, two nights before, but also that he had walked in the street below her window all night after her party on January 30th. Until that moment, so she says, she had had no inkling of the identity of that mysterious stranger. Metham having thus discovered his alleged friend's duplicity, an altercation ensued between the two men, and Georgiane accomplished one of her convenient faints. She says she was told afterwards that a challenge had been issued in consequence and that Major Burton and Colonel Heywood were to be the seconds, but it seems a little odd that she did not know whether the duel ever took place.

For the next few days, Georgiane was so occupied with rehearsals for the various benefits that she did not see either of her admirers. On March 22nd she appeared as Almeria in the *Mourning Bride*, which she had persuaded Kitty Clive to choose for her benefit. The great comic actress herself essayed the part of Zara, and, in Georgiane's opinion, she played the part with infinitely more judgment that Mrs. Pritchard. But the public did not like this great favourite of theirs to desert her accustomed field, and her performance was not received with favour. For her own benefit, two days later, Georgiane played Belvidera in *Venice Preserved*. The afterpiece was the *Oracle*, a farce written by her rival and friend, Susanna Maria Cibber. All the parts in this agreeable trifle were played on this occasion by children, and Georgiane herself spoke the epilogue. In the playbill for this evening it was announced that "No part of the pit will be laid into the boxes, nor any building on the stage".

Garrick had set his face against the inconvenient practice of building extra seating on the stage itself to accommodate the larger audience on benefit nights. It was a wise step in itself, though it may be significant that Garrick should have chosen the exasperating Georgiane as the first victim of a reform which was bound to have the effect of restricting the number of the audience on such occasions. Georgiane, however, states that the house was crowded and the applause uncommon. Mr. Murray, afterwards the famous Lord Chancellor Mansfield, was so enthusiastic about her performance that he said: "I came to admire Garrick, but go away enchanted with Bellamy." This flattering remark was repeated to her by Henry Fox in the presence of Garrick, and she says that it confirmed the dislike he had already conceived for her.

Next morning she was so fatigued that she lay in bed longer than usual. She had given orders that Metham was not to be admitted if he came, but he arrived in a frantic mood and, forcing his way into her bedroom, besought her to live with him again. And, when she steadfastly refused, he drew his sword and swore he would kill himself and take her with him. Her little boy, who was playing in the room, was so frightened that he screamed, and this brought Metham temporarily to his senses. But he soon renewed his threats and imprecations, and, finding these made no impression upon her, resorted to prayers and entreaties, and finally to promises to marry her out of hand. But Georgiane was not to be either frightened or cajoled into submission, and finally induced him to leave her for a time to allow her to recover, promising that he might return in two hours time. Metham consented, but before he left the house gave the servants strict orders not to admit anyone to see her.

Georgiane had been really frightened by Metham's violent behaviour, and she was determined not to face him again in his present mood. Telling her maid that she felt so ill that she would have to remain in bed, she sent her out on a sleeveless errand, but, as soon as she had gone, she flung on the first clothes that came to hand and rushed out of the house in a state of distraction which she says must have amazed the good people coming from church. She knew that it would be useless to go to her mother or any of her intimate friends, for Metham would be sure to look for her there, so she made her way to the house in Southampton Street, where she had lodged when she first came back from Ireland. Mrs. Smith, the landlady, took her in and did her best to comfort her, and, having given her some breakfast, went herself to tell her mother where she was. Metham was already at Mrs. Bellamy's lodgings, raving like a madman. He had been to Calcraft's house, but Calcraft had been able to convince him that Georgiane was not there. Calcraft imagined that she must have taken refuge with Lord Downe, and was as jealous and distracted as Metham himself.

Having got rid of Metham with an assurance that she would let him know where her daughter was as soon as she herself discovered it, Mrs. Bellamy hastened to Georgiane. Since both she and Georgiane had been striving their utmost for months to persuade Metham into marriage, Mrs. Bellamy was, not surprisingly, inclined to think that the offer should be accepted now it was made, but she did not altogether disapprove of Georgiane's flight, for she admitted that Metham might be dangerous in his present frantic state. Georgiane does not relate how she avoided meeting either him or Calcraft during the next ten days or so, during which she made at least one appearance at the theatre, as Desdemona in *Othello*, which Mossop had chosen for his benefit for the second year in succession.

The following week was Passion week, and, as the theatres were to be closed by order of the Lord Chamberlain, in deference to a request from the Bishops, Georgiane decided that it would be a good opportunity to avail herself of a long-standing invitation to visit some friends at Donyland Hall, near Colchester. This was the country residence of an eccentric old gentleman named Daniel Gansel and his wife, whose admiration of her acting had impelled them to seek her acquaintance. One evening, when she was playing Juliet, the doorkeeper had come into the Green Room and informed her that an elderly lady and gentleman were asking to see her. She had given orders that they were to be admitted. Mr. Gansel had explained that in his youth he had been a fervent playgoer and had frequented Drury Lane in the great days of Booth, Wilks, Colley Cibber, and Mrs. Oldfield. He was now spending a short time in London and had brought his wife to his old haunt. They had both been enchanted by her playing of Juliet, and they had, moreover, heard such glowing accounts of her personality and character in private life from their landlady that they were eager to know her.

Georgiane was flattered by their interest and enthusiasm and said that she would wait upon them next day, but nothing would satisfy them but that she should sup with them that very evening at their lodging in Southampton Street, the same house where she herself had stayed when she first returned from Ireland. The acquaintance thus casually made had soon ripened into friendship. Gansel was a cultured and much-travelled man. He had formerly been a Member of Parliament, but now suffered so badly from gout that he had retired to enjoy a quiet country life. His wife was a simple and gentle creature, who devoted herself entirely to running the household and keeping her husband happy and comfortable. In her present distracted and worried condition Georgiane thought that she would be both safe and happy in the home of these kindly people. Accordingly she set off in a hired post-chaise in the company of Mrs. Smith, the landlady of the house in Southampton Street, who also had been pressed by her lodgers to pay them a visit when she could spare the time. They were received with the greatest cordiality by the old people.

Donyland Hall, which Georgiane erroneously calls Donnalan Park, was a charming old moated house, built early in the seventeenth century and reconstructed about 1700. Mr. Gansel had further improved and embellished the house and enclosed the park about 1735. At this time it was described as "a neat mansion near the confluence of the small river Roman with the Colne."*

Georgiane was struck by the oddity of the dinner served on the first evening. The main course consisted entirely of chickens, three boiled, three roasted, three broiled, and a cold chicken-pie. The dessert, however, though equally plentiful, was more varied. Mrs. Gansel, who, Georgiane noticed, had appeared somewhat gloomy during the meal, showed her to her room afterwards and explained the strangeness of the repast. It appeared that Mr. Gansel had in his youth made an oath that he would never have more than one main dish at his table, and that she had been obliged to conform to his humour. Georgiane was much amused but was curious to know how, unless they roasted a whole ox, it was possible to carry out Mr. Gansel's requirement when they entertained a large number of guests, as it appeared that they frequently did. Tonight only eight had sat down to dinner. Mrs. Gansel replied that her curiosity would be gratified on the morrow, since the local magistrates were dining with them. And, sure enough, the main course at dinner next day consisted entirely of venison—a large haunch at the top of the table, another at the bottom, and a pasty on each side. Georgiane had imagined that she did not like venison, but good manners forced her to partake of it, and she found it delicious. At the end of the meal, when the wine began to circulate, she rose to retire, but Mr. Gansel restrained her with a gentle tap, saying: "Sit still, my dear girl; we never say anything women would blush to hear. And I can see no reason for ladies retiring after the first or second glass, without it arises from an apprehension of something of that nature, or that the men propose to make themselves brutes."

Next day, as they were walking in the Park to view a white bull which Colonel Gansel, the son of the house, who had joined the party the night before, had brought down as a

* The house is now known as East Donyland Hall.

present for his father's private menagerie, a message was brought to Georgiane that Mr. Gansel would like to see her immediately. To her great astonishment she found John Calcraft with her host. Mr. Gansel took her by the hand and said: "Here, my dear, is your protector from a madman. This is a gentleman of honour, and he proposes, with your consent, to make you happy for life."

Calcraft's proposition, if it can be believed, was certainly most extraordinary. He had told Mr. Gansel that he loved Georgiane to distraction and wished to protect her from Metham, but that, much as he longed to marry her, it was not in his power to do so immediately because of his dependence on Mr. Fox. His patron had enjoined him, upon pain of his displeasure, and the loss of his support, not to enter into a serious engagement with a woman in public life, and he had promised not to do so. He owed his present affluence entirely to Mr. Fox, and his future prospects depended upon him. But he had drawn up a paper in which he contracted under forfeiture of £50,000 to make her his wife within six or seven years, when he was certain to be in a position to avow his situation. This, he said, was the only way in which he could secure Georgiane and at the same time keep his word to his patron. But it was, as a matter of fact, entirely untrue that Fox had made any such stipulation. What John Calcraft did with his private life was his own affair, and whether this assistant of his, who merely hovered on the fringes of high society, married an actress or kept one as a mistress cannot but have been a matter of complete indifference to that easy, tolerant man of the world, Henry Fox. But Georgiane did not discover this until long afterwards. Nor was she aware of the still more important and disturbing fact that Calcraft already had a wife.

If Mr. Gansel really did not understand the implications of his bargain, he must have been extraordinarily naïve; they were certainly clear enough to Georgiane herself. She told Calcraft that she was firmly resolved never to form any connexion whatever. Having said this, she haughtily attempted to leave the room, and when Calcraft tried to bar the way, she lost her temper and struck him. Then she burst into tears. Mr. Gansel endeavoured to soothe her. He expatiated upon Metham's ungentlemanlike treatment of her. By promising to marry her, allowing her to pass as his wife, and then not keeping his promise, he had caused her veracity to be doubted; her reputation was blasted, and she was every moment liable to fall a sacrifice to a madman's jealousy. Calcraft had evidently convinced him that Metham was dangerous. The old gentleman became so eloquent that Calcraft came to the conclusion that the very best thing he could do was to leave his cause in his hands, and he took his departure, saying that he would not come again until Mr. Gansel sent him word that Georgiane had consented to be his. He ended by repeating that she must have a protector if she returned to London.

This peculiar interview had upset Georgiane so much that she was not well enough to return to London at the end of the week, and Mr. Gansel wrote to his son asking him to wait on Garrick and tell him that she could not come back to the theatre for some days. In the meantime he continued to use every art to induce her to accept Calcraft's offer of protection. At this juncture she received a letter from her mother. Mrs. Bellamy wrote that she had let Metham know where she had taken refuge and that he had seemed quite satisfied. In her opinion, he was suffering more from wounded pride at supposing that he had a rival than from the fervour of his affection for her. She had heard, indeed, that he had renewed his association with a former mistress of his. And she concluded by saying that, judging from the indifference with which she had heard he spoke of her, he did not mean to marry her, even if she did relax from her severity.

Georgiane, who was still in love with Metham, however angry she might have been with him, had by this time begun to relent towards him, but this 'fatal letter', with its news of his silence and indifference towards her, even though he knew where she was, renewed her resentment against him and put the finishing stroke to her undoing. Out of pique she began to listen to Mr. Gansel's arguments and eventually allowed herself to be persuaded by them. Calcraft was sent for. He came at once, and the contract was signed. In her letter to Calcraft, which was suppressed in 1767, but which she published in an appendix to the fifth volume of her *Apology*, Georgiane printed this document, which she says, was left in Mr. Gansel's charge and sent to her after his death by his son. The original, she adds, was in Calcraft's own handwriting and was available for inspection by any of his friends (if he had any) who were desirous to prove the authenticity of it, as his hand was as well known as his face.

"Know all men by these presents, that I, John Calcraft, of Brewer-street, Golden-square, in the county of Middlesex, Esquire, am held and firmly bound unto Georgiane Bellamy, of Frith-street, Soho, Spinster, in the sum of fifty thousand pounds, of lawful money of Great-Britain, to be paid to the said Georgiane Bellamy, her certain attorney, executor, administrator, or assigns, firmly by these presents, sealed with my seal, dated this 22nd day of January, 1752.

"The condition of this obligation is such, that whereas the above-bounden John Calcraft, and the above-named Georgiane Bellamy, have mutually agreed to marry with each other; and therefore the above-bound John Calcraft, shall and do marry the said Georgiane Bellamy, according to the rites and ceremonies of the Church of England; and shall not intermarry with any other person whatsoever, save the said Georgiane Bellamy; then this obligation to be void, or else remain in full force.

"Signed. JOHN CALCRAFT."

Georgiane draws attention to the fact that the document was dated some few days *before* her quarrel with Metham, which took place on January 30th. This could only mean that

Calcraft already had the intention of trying to supplant the man whose friend he pretended to be.*

According to Georgiane, old Mr. Gansel was as happy and proud at having succeeded in this negotiation "as if he had married his daughter to an hereditary prince". It seems curious that she has no reproach to make to him for his part in this highly immoral transaction, but on the contrary implies that he was deceived by Calcraft. Is it possible that the old gentleman was really so innocent as not to realise that it meant that Georgiane was to live with Calcraft until the marriage ceremony should take place; or was he so convinced of the rectitude of Calcraft's intentions and so trustful of his honour that he was indifferent about their immediate relations so long as they married in the end?

Calcraft declined Mr. Gansel's pressing invitation to stay on for a few days at Donyland Hall and insisted upon their leaving at once on the plea that urgent business demanded his presence in London. When Georgiane was seated with Mrs. Smith in the chaise, he informed her that the real reason for the immediate departure was that he had brought her mother down with him and that she was awaiting them at Ingatestone. He had assured her that they were really being married. And when she met her mother, Georgiane was too ashamed to confess to her that they were not.

As soon as she arrived back in London, Georgiane wrote to Metham to let him know that she had now placed an everlasting barrier to any future union between them. But it was not for a few days that she discovered the full extent of Calcraft's cunning and deceit. Far from being callous and indifferent about their separation, Metham had been so overcome with grief and despair that he had been ill in bed with a high fever and had only been restrained from taking his own life by the

* All the evidence goes to show that these events took place early in 1753. The error in the year-date may well be due to understandable carelessness, for the change from the Julian to the Gregorian calendar had only just taken place, and 1752 was the first year which began on January 1st instead of March 25th as hitherto.

devoted attentions of his friend, Major Burton, and his faithful valet, Sherrad, who now came to call on Georgiane and begged her to become reconciled with his master. She had to tell him that it was too late. Had she known in time of his true feelings, it might have been different. But she had been deceived by Calcraft's calumnies and the account of his indifference in her mother's letter, which, it now transpired, had been furnished by her own maid, who had been bribed to do so by Calcraft.

But however devoted he may have been to Georgiane and however chagrined he may have been at her breaking with him, Metham was not the man to retire to the solitude of his Yorkshire home and nurse a secret sorrow. Instead, he took the obvious method of consoling himself for a lost love by seeking another of the same kind, and soon Georgiane heard that he was in Paris, where he had "dropped his handkerchief at the feet of the Goslin,"* one of the prettiest and most talented of French actresses.

The excitement of all these events, the loss of the man whom at heart she still loved, and the way in which she had been tricked and cajoled into an association with a man she did not care for, all combined to lower Georgiane's spirits. Hearing that she was ill and unhappy, her old friend, Quin, made a special visit to town to see her. After she had told him all, he urged her to try to make the best of things. He admitted that she and Calcraft were not "congenial souls", but, in common with almost everyone else, he entertained a high opinion of "honest Jack Calcraft's" probity and rectitude, and he thought that, as his affection for her was so great, it might soon be in her power to bring him to her bent. Georgiane cared little about this, for she was not, and knew she never could be, in love with him. Had she been able to return his love, she would have abandoned everything for him, but, as it was, she insisted upon resuming her theatrical career, and during the month of May she continued to appear at Drury Lane, playing Almeria, Cordelia, Leonora, and Juliet.

* Mlle Gaussin.

Chapter Ten

WHEN THE THEATRE CLOSED at the end of the season (1752–53) Calcraft took a small house called Ragman's Castle, at Twickenham, where they spent the summer. Georgiane did not pretend to be in love with him, but his passion for her seemed to be increased by her indifference. If they ever went to town, they stayed in their separate houses. Georgiane preferred this, and, in any case, there would not have been room for her at Calcraft's house in Brewer Street, which he shared with his friend, Mr. Digby.

Since Georgiane had given Garrick a good deal of trouble and vexation, especially during the last season, it might have been thought that he would have welcomed the expiration of her contract, but she maintains that he was anxious to re-engage her and sent an intimate friend of his, Mr. Clutterbuck, to her with advantageous proposals. But the reason she advances for this action on his part is certainly plausible. He had already engaged Mrs. Cibber, and he was unwilling that Rich should be able to secure the services of the one actress who could stand up to her, at any rate in the eyes of the public. To do her justice, Georgiane herself always acknowledged the supremacy of her rival. It was, in fact, because she was "conscious of the great superiority of that inimitable actress, which I thought would throw me at an infinite distance" that she had stipulated in her articles that she should never be required to play with Mrs. Cibber. But off the stage she had always remained on the friendliest terms with her, and Mr. Clutterbuck now told her that Mrs. Cibber was willing to resign to her the parts of Juliet, Calista, and Desdemona.

Garrick also offered her an increase of salary. But Rich was eager to secure her for Covent Garden, and she closed with his offers and rejected those of Garrick, in spite of the advice of her friends, which she afterwards acknowledged to have been right. Had she continued to play with the great Garrick, her acting would have improved, and, in the event, it appeared that Mrs. Cibber's frequent indispositions would have made it possible for her to appear in principal roles far more often than she had expected. Already in the previous year Mrs. Cibber had been attacked by the stomach complaint which was so soon to kill her.

On their return to town in the autumn, Calcraft, being apprehensive that Metham might return from abroad and recapture Georgiane's affections, which he had never really lost, prevailed upon her to go and live with him at his house in Brewer Street, where she could now be accommodated, since his friend, Digby, had left to go abroad. She consented "as she thought it incumbent on her to oblige him in every thing that lay in her power". They went into a committee of finance, and she was surprised to discover that his present income was less than her own. He asked her what allowance she thought would be necessary for the housekeeping, and, without giving the matter any thought at all, she suggested a hundred guineas a quarter, to which he readily agreed.

Since the anonymous benefactor who had sent her the £1,000 in notes at the time when she broke with Metham had never revealed himself, she thought she could now make use of them, and she discharged all her debts and spent the remainder on jewellery and plate.

The account she gives in her *Apology* of the ensuing two or three years is hopelessly inaccurate, for she confounds events during the following seasons almost inextricably. She says that she appeared very successfully as Juliet with Barry as Romeo, but, although this is perfectly true, it did not happen until two years later. In this season of 1753–54 Juliet was played by Miss Nossiter, a very beautiful but not very talented young actress,

who had been well educated at the expense of Lord Cholmondeley, to whom her mother was housekeeper. She was
completely infatuated with Barry, and he with her.

Barry was quite determined that she should be the chief
actress at Covent Garden, and, knowing that he could not
break established theatrical custom by giving her parts which
were Miss Bellamy's perquisite, hit upon the expedient of
reviving several old plays in which she could not claim the
principal part as her right and some new ones in which Miss
Nossiter could play the lead without fear of challenge. One of
these, the ludicrous and inept tragedy of *Philoclea*, by an
obscure Irishman called McNamara Morgan, was received
with such derision by the audience, that it had to be hastily
withdrawn.

Georgiane had several good reason for not taking umbrage
at this arrangement. In the first place, she had stipulated in her
articles with Rich that she was to have a larger salary than any
other female performer at the theatre, and, as Barry had
insisted that Miss Nossiter should have £500, her own salary
was raised to 500 guineas. Secondly, she could not help liking
the charming and inoffensive Miss Nossiter, who was a
delightfully modest girl and had no desire to eclipse her or any
other actress, but simply to play with her beloved Barry.
Moreover, Rich had tactfully asked her permission for Miss
Nossiter to make her début in Juliet, and, as this formality had
been complied with, she had readily consented. But her best
reason for not objecting to the part of Juliet being played by
another actress was that she was pregnant and was expecting a
child in March. As it was, several of the characters she did play
were scarcely appropriate to her condition. Tate Wilkinson
had some rather ribald comments to make on the subject. Her
first appearance this season was made, he says, on Tuesday,
November 20th, "in a very improper character; as was her
second on Thursday, November 22nd (her situation considered). She was thus announced in the bills: Athanais,
Miss Bellamy, her first appearance this stage three years. After

the chaste Athanais, the pure Monimia followed, which led to strange ideas that Castalio most certainly had been acquainted with that lady long before the third act." Other parts she played this season were Eudocia, Calista, Celia and Andromache.

The complete failure of his tragedy, *Eugenia*, which Garrick had produced at Drury Lane two years before and in which Georgiane had appeared, had not discouraged the literary parson, Dr. Philip Francis, from further dramatic efforts, and he had persuaded Rich to put on his new tragedy, *Constantine*. The first performance was on February 23rd, 1754. Barry played Constantine and Georgiane the Empress Fulvia. But the public apparently did not share the author's confidence that this play would be better than the last, and they stayed away. The company played to almost empty benches. Dr. Francis, who had been counting on a resounding success and a brilliant career as a dramatic author, was overcome by this unequivocal dashing of his hopes, and Georgiane was so sorry for him that she took him home to supper and introduced him to Henry Fox, whom she begged to find him some ecclesiastical preferment, for which she believed his genius to be more suited. Fox promised that he would do so, and in the meantime forthwith made him his domestic chaplain and tutor to his children. "Well, Doctor," he said cheerfully, "who knows but your damnation as a playwright may be the means of your promotion as a divine." It must not be supposed that Fox was buying a pig in a poke when he thus casually engaged a tutor for his son, Charles James; he must have known that Francis, while still a curate in Dublin, had produced a translation of Horace which had the reputation of being second to none.

Constantine was played four times, and on the very day after the last performance, Georgiane gave birth to a daughter. She was christened Caroline Elizabeth, and Henry Fox, his wife, Lady Caroline, and Lady Tyrawley stood sponsors in person. Both the ladies, according to Georgiane, believed at this time that she was actually married to Calcraft. He was delighted

with his daughter, all the more because he hoped that this
pledge would insure to him Georgiane's affection in future.
He certainly gave her the impression that he intended to marry
her. Alarmed now at renewed reports that Metham was about
to return to England, he requested her to return the annuity
her former lover had settled on her, alleging that it was
improper that a woman who was to be his wife should have a
settlement from anyone but himself. In recompense for this
surrender, he proposed that an estate of £120 a year at
Grantham, which he had recently inherited from his grandmother, should be settled on her for life with remainder to her
daughter, and he also told her that by his will he had left her
the interest of £11,000 in the funds.

Georgiane's benefit this year had been arranged for March
23rd, but was postponed because of her 'illness'. She made her
re-appearance as Indiana on March 26th, and chose *Jane Shore*
for her benefit on March 28th. Tate Wilkinson thought that
the penitent mistress of Edward IV was a truly appropriate
part for her at this moment. Perhaps she thought so too, for it
was the first time she had played it; she usually played Alicia,
which on this occasion was taken by Mrs. Gregory, a young
actress who had made her first appearance on the stage a month
or two before as Hermione in the *Distressed Mother*, with
Georgiane playing Andromache.

Although she did not love Calcraft and never pretended to
do so, Georgiane was determined to do all in her power to
further his career. Not only was it presumably in her own
interest to do so, but also the way in which she could best
assist him happened to be extremely congenial to her, for it
consisted in entertaining politicians, peers, and, above all,
high-ranking military officers. Those who had command of
regiments were fed, flattered, and cajoled into giving Calcraft
their agencies. Henry Fox, the Marquess of Granby, and
General Hervey were regular guests at her breakfast, dinner,
and supper parties. With her usual heedlessness she assumed
that her expert cook must also be an excellent manager, and she

therefore left the financial side entirely to him. She did realise vaguely that, since they were giving dinner and supper parties every day, they must be spending considerably more than Calcraft was allowing her, but she was doing so much business for him thereby that she took it for granted that he would readily discharge any debts which were contracted in his interest.

At the end of the season Georgiane was feeling thoroughly ill. Acting, entertaining, and having a baby as well had reduced her to a state of exhaustion. Her doctor thought it necessary for her to have a complete change and advised her to go to Bristol Spa for a few weeks to recuperate. She set off, accompanied by her friend, the former Mrs. Delane, who had recently married one of Calcraft's clerks, named Walker. To her great surprise, as her chaise drew up at the Castle Inn at Marlborough, her old acquaintance, the actor Ryan, ran out to greet her and told her that Quin was staying there and would of course want to see her. He would go and awaken him. Since it was eight o'clock in the evening, Georgiane naturally concluded that her old friend must be ill, but John Beard ,who was also there, explained laughingly that he was merely sleeping off the effects of good cheer. He was now settled at Bath, and, unwilling to undergo the fatigue a visit to London would entail, he had arranged for certain of his old friends to meet him every summer at this famous hostelry,where they were all to remain until they had got through a certain quantity of wine. Georgiane could not remember exactly how much this was, but it was certainly a prodigious amount, and in her opinion, enough to have lasted them a whole year.

As she went out into the lovely garden behind the inn, Quin appeared at his window in his night-cap and called to her that he would be with her at once. A few minutes later he joined her, and they were able to have a long and intimate talk. He insisted upon her remaining to dine with him and in her honour caused the landlord to scour the town for delicacies and provide a banquet fit for a Lord Mayor. Twenty-six of them sat down to the feast. Georgiane herself retired to bed at three in the morning, leaving the rest of Quin's guests still at table, where, or under it, they still remained when she resumed her journey early next morning.

Because of the delicate state of her health she had taken her journey in leisurely fashion, and on her arrival at Bristol she found a letter from her maid already awaiting her with alarming news from home. Calcraft was laid up with a violent attack of gout in the head, her baby had developed small-pox, and her mother, who had insisted upon nursing it in the same reckless manner as she had nursed little George Metham, had also shown symptoms of the disease. She at once ordered two additional horses to be harnessed to her chaise and hastened back to London. At Marlborough, where she arrived at two o'clock in the afternoon, she found that Quin was not yet up, and she sat by his bed and talked to him while her horses were being changed. Fortunately, on reaching London she found that the reports had been greatly exaggerated; her little daughter's attack was a mild one, her mother's symptoms had disappeared, and Calcraft's indisposition had only been due to deep potations.

On her return to the stage this autumn Georgiane for the first time dropped the virginal 'Miss' and henceforth figured in the playbills more appropriately as 'Mrs. Bellamy'. As Tate Wilkinson remarked, the change was not made too soon. She made her first appearance this season as Lætitia in the *Old Bachelor* on October 14th. Four days later she played Desdemona with a new actor, Arthur Murphy, as Othello. He was to take the place of Barry, who, disgusted because Rich refused to comply with the exorbitant demands he made for his favourite, Miss Nossiter, had carried her off to Ireland, confidently predicting that Rich would be ruined by his desertion. Murphy could not hope to compare with the great Barry in the part, but he was easy and natural, and was favourably received. Georgiane thought he had some talent, but said that he was a better critic than an actor, and equally as good as a playwright as a critic.

But if Covent Garden had lost Barry to Ireland, Ireland had restored Peg Woffington, who now returned to Covent Garden and was rapturously received by a great house on her first appearance as Maria in the *Nonjuror* on October 22nd. Another unexpected arrival was that of Tom Sheridan. In consequence of a great riot at the Smock Alley Theatre in February of this year, he had thought it advisable for him not to appear in Dublin for a while, and he determined to come over to England and try to obtain an engagement at the same theatre as Mrs. Woffington, with whom he had enjoyed playing. Rich was only too pleased to get him. Georgiane had not forgiven him for his shabby treatment of her over the free tickets, and did not want to act with him, but Rich refused to release her from her articles, and she was obliged to appear with him on many occasions, since he played the principal male parts in nearly all her accustomed tragedies. She played Juliet to his Romeo, Leonora to his Zanga, Marcia to his Cato, and Belvidera to his Pierre, with Murphy as Jaffier. But before the end of the season Sheridan ceased playing Romeo, which was played by Smith on April 3rd and Dyer on April 11th.

The old hostility between Georgiane and Peg Woffington still persisted, and tiffs between them were always occurring. On one occasion, a rehearsal of the *Distressed Mother* had been called. Georgiane, who was usually very punctual, happened to arrive rather late and, to her great surprise, found Mrs. Woffington rehearsing the part of Andromache. This had always been one of her own parts, and she promptly protested. Mrs. Woffington replied that Mrs. Bellamy's youth and elegance better suited the part of Hermione, and that, so that she might enjoy the happiness she knew she would have in showing her new Paris finery, she herself had been induced to take the part of the Queen. Georgiane did not deign to answer, but sent for Rich, who immediately reinstated her in her character. Mrs. Woffington had to appear as Hermione, and Georgiane adds with triumphant malice, "to her very great mortification, in a dress that was not over-clean."

In Dryden and Lee's *Œdipus* (produced on January 10th, 1755), Peg Woffington obtained the leading part of Jocasta, which Georgiane coveted, and Georgiane had to take the minor role of the young Eurydice. Georgiane, however, managed to mar the performance by fainting on the appearance of the ghost. She herself says that, though so long used to the stage and its feigned terrors, she was so overcome by the horror of the piece that she was carried off in a state of insensibility; but Genest unkindly remarks that, if she had been well sluiced with a bucket of cold water, she would never have fainted at a stage Ghost again. Her name is in the playbill of the performance on the following night, though she may not have appeared; but when it was played again four days later, the part of Eurydice was played by Mrs. Vincent.

Georgiane's efforts to obtain regimental agencies for Calcraft were very successful. She secured those of General Campbell, afterwards Duke of Argyll, and Sir John Mordaunt, and the promise of that of Colonel Honeywood, who was expecting shortly to be given a regiment. The ill-fated General Braddock, an old friend of her father's whom she had known when she was a child, offered her his agency when he was appointed to command in America. On the eve of his departure he came to supper with her, accompanied by his two aides, Major Burton and Captain Orme. Major Burton was a sorrowing widower, having just lost his wife, Georgiane's old friend, Elizabeth St. Leger. The short, stout, coarse old General was very depressed about his mission. "Dear Pop," he said, "we are sent like sacrifices to the altar." He was convinced that he would never come back and deposited his will with her when he left. She says that, convinced that she was married to Calcraft, he left him his sole executor, giving to her personally all the plate he had received as the usual perquisite from government on his nomination.

Unless, indeed, he left this plate behind him in Georgiane's care, as is possible, this is not quite accurate. General Braddock, who made his will on November 25th, 1754, just before he sailed for America, left everything of which he died possessed to "his two good friends, Mary Yorke, the wife of John Yorke, a Lieutenant in the Royal Regiment of Artillery, now on duty at Gibraltar, and John Calcraft, of Brewer Street, in the parish of St. James, Westminster" to be equally divided between them. Calcraft proved the will on September 3rd, 1755, and administration was granted to him on his undertaking to deliver her share to Mrs. Yorke.*

This season saw yet another version of *Coriolanus*, compiled, apparently by Sheridan himself, from portions of both Shakespeare's and Thomson's plays on the subject. Sheridan played Coriolanus, Peg Woffington Veturia, and Georgiane Volumnia. It was fairly successful and was acted eight or nine times. The only entirely new play produced this season was *Appius*, a dull and inept tragedy by Robert Moncrieff, in which Georgiane played Virginia; but for her benefit she chose a play which was new, at any rate, to her, and had never been acted at Covent Garden before. This was the tragedy of *Alzira*, translated from Voltaire's *Alzire* by Aaron Hill. At her request, Murphy, who was to play the part of Zamor, made some alterations in the play, for she considered that it had too little incident and too much declamation to please an English audience.

Fox had been glancing through a copy of the play in Georgiane's dressing-room one morning, and suspecting from the style that Murphy was the true author of certain satirical verses of which he was curious to know the author, came to her house that evening and asked her to leave her other guests and withdraw to another room with him to discuss the matter. This private conclave threw Calcraft into a fever of apprehension; he had heard that Fox had already spent some considerable time in Georgiane's dressing-room that morning and jumped to the erroneous but alarming conclusion that she had been complaining about him to his patron and might even

* Somerset House, Paul, *f.*, 233.

have revealed to him the true nature of their connexion, which was the last thing he wanted him to know. But Georgiane was not aware of this at the time; she imagined that Fox was fully conversant with the situation and merely subscribed out of politeness and consideration for her to the common assumption that she and Calcraft were really married.

Georgiane did, indeed, endeavour to conduct herself as if that were her position. She ran Calcraft's house, acted as hostess to his friends, and took a sisterly interest in his brother, Tom. This young man, whom Calcraft had brought up at his expense at the school in Leicester where he himself had received such education as he possessed, was generous in disposition, genteel in figure, and would have been handsome, had his face not been so badly marked by small-pox. He had, in fact, nothing in common with his elder brother except an inordinate love for the bottle. Calcraft obtained him a commission in the army, but when he set off to join his regiment in Scotland, gave him nothing but his fare and two guineas. On Georgiane's remonstrating at this meanness, Calcraft curtly remarked that she was making the boy as extravagant as herself by her indulgence. On his return from Scotland, he was given a commission in the Guards, and Georgiane, who liked him and to whom he was in turn devoted, took some pains to polish him.

About this time Calcraft, whose wealth was rapidly increasing, bought a country house called Holwood Park, near Keston in Kent. The house, which was later to become the younger Pitt's favourite home, was at this time a 'plain, rectangular building' of no architectural merit, and, as it had not been occupied for four years, needed many alterations and improvements. Since this meant spending money and Calcraft had given her to understand that he would settle the house on her and her daughter, Georgiane was nothing loth to supervise the work, and she spent four months, from February to May, putting the place to rights. The grounds were beautiful, and she improved the eleven acres of garden and built a range of greenhouses and an ice-house. General Campbell, who was a keen horticulturalist, supplied her with a collection of exotic plants for her garden. In the following year Calcraft took an adjacent farm, and started a dairy herd with six Alderney cows and a bull, so that the estate should be self-supporting.

Holwood had formerly been a hunting-box and boasted an extensive range of stabling. Georgiane looked forward to indulging more often the fondness for riding which she had developed since her first essay at horsemanship in the Welsh mountains some years before. Calcraft, who said that he wanted to see her well mounted, asked a military friend of his to find a good horse for her. This friend said that he himself possessed one of the finest mares that was ever mounted, but that she was so spirited that he himself could not at times hold her in, and he was sure no woman could manage her. Calcraft, having a great opinion of Georgiane's skill in riding, or, as she suggests, secretly wishing that her neck might be broken in the attempt, laid a considerable wager that she could not only ride the mare, but also completely manage her. And at dinner one evening he told her that he had bought for her the most beautiful mare that was ever seen.

Next day the mare was brought down to Holwood. Although Georgiane had no mean opinion of her own capability as a horsewoman, it was with difficulty that she could be persuaded to mount her. She confessed that she had a presentiment that she would have an accident, and, even if she was not aware of the former owner's opinion of his mare, it is surely neither surprising nor to her discredit that she should have realised that the task would be beyond her powers. But, in the end, she did consent to make the attempt and set out with a party. As they were entering a field the spirited mare was frightened by the glitter of a hedging-implement held by a labourer who was opening the gate for them and bolted with her. Georgiane did her utmost to pull her in, but her left hand was nearly pulled out of joint in the effort. The mare made straight for a stone quarry, and though Georgiane managed to throw herself off just before they reached it, she was so near the edge that she toppled over it. It was a bad fall. Her shoulder was dislocated, both bones in her left arm were broken, and her hand hung limply from it. Fortunately, an army officer who happened to be of the party was able to administer first aid, but some hours passed before the arrival of Mr. Adair, the surgeon, who was sent for from London to attend her. And he was not wholly successful in setting her arm, for her left hand was stiff ever after.

This accident must have taken place in the summer of 1755, for it was while she was still confined to bed during her convalescence that Calcraft brought her the sad news that their friend, General Braddock, had been killed on July 9th. At this time news from America took about six weeks to reach England.

One day Calcraft came into her room in great excitement crying: "Your fortune is made, your fortune is made." He showed her an announcement in the paper to the effect that a Mr. Thomas Sykes had died in the south of France and had left his fortune to "Miss Bellamy, belonging to one of the theatres". The notice had been inserted by Mr. Loyd, Garden Court, the Temple. At first Georgiane could not remember who Mr. Sykes might be, and then she remembered the kindly old gentleman she had met several years before when she was staying with the Crawfords at Watford. Calcraft hastened off to Mr. Loyd, who told him that the will had, indeed, been brought to him several months before for his inspection and showed him a copy of it. He thought that the will itself had either been in Mr. Sykes's own possession when he died, or was with Mr. Crawford, who had chambers in the Temple, but might be at his house near Watford. Failing to find Crawford in London, Calcraft proceeded at once to Watford, where Crawford told him that Mr. Sykes, when last in England, had enquired much about Miss Bellamy. His servant was daily expected in England with the will and the body of Mr. Sykes, who had expressed a desire to be buried at St. Margaret's,

Westminster. He thought that the fortune would amount to about £50,000. But, alas for Georgiane's high expectations—if, indeed, there is any truth at all in this story—Mr. Sykes's servant embezzled all the property of his late master's that was ready to hand and disappeared. Neither the will nor Mr. Sykes's body ever reached England, and, since no legal claimant ever appeared, the whole of the estate and personal property passed to the States of Holland.

Georgiane, who always liked to make much of her illnesses, was rather annoyed because Rich pressed her to come back to Covent Garden long before she thought she was fit enough, but at length she consented to do so and made her re-appearance as Rutland in the *Unhappy Favourite* on October 11th. In the mad scene, when she had to throw herself on the floor, she deliberately fell on the right side instead of her left in order not to risk her injured arm, and Kitty Clive, who was seated in the boxes, cried out in consternation: "Oh, she has broken her other arm." The audience was greatly concerned and called out for the curtain to be dropped, but Georgiane rose with great agility and finished the scene with more applause than she had ever received before, chiefly, she admits, owing to the kindly solicitude of Mrs. Clive, whose good humour was better than her recollection.

In November Barry returned to Covent Garden, with Miss Nossiter still in tow. He made his first appearance in *Hamlet* on November 12th, but Miss Nossiter did not perform until a month later, when she appeared as Monimia. She had not had a great success in Ireland, not so much because of her own want of merit, as because Barry's wife was well-loved in Dublin, and the interloper was resented. At Covent Garden there seems now to have been an amicable arrangement between Mrs. Bellamy and Miss Nossiter to share the principal parts. Both actresses made frequent appearances with Barry, Georgiane as Juliet, Belvidera, Athanais, Indiana, and Almeria, Miss Nossiter as Cordelia, Eudocia, and Lady Townley, all parts which were usually allotted to Georgiane, and as Mandane in

Busiris, which Barry insisted upon reviving, but which was not successful and was not repeated.

Rich seemed to be delighted when Barry and Georgiane at last appeared together in *Romeo and Juliet*. "I have the Juliet now as well as the Romeo," he said with pride. But when Georgiane herself ventured to remark to him on the play's success, he took the major part of the credit to himself. Taking a pinch of snuff, he replied shortly: "Yes, Mistress, but it is owing to the procession." As a counter-attraction to Rich's procession, Garrick provided a most sonorous bell for the funeral scene in the Drury Lane production, in which Mrs. Cibber now played Juliet to his Romeo; but the Covent Garden version had the greater success this season. It is pleasant to record, however, that the intense rivalry between the two theatres did not prevent their helping each other out in any emergency. On April 8th, 1756, a note on the Drury Lane playbill stated that, since Mrs. Cibber's illness prevented her playing the part of Sigismunda as advertised, Mr. Rich had obligingly allowed Mrs. Bellamy to play the part, which she as obligingly did.

On January 15th, 1756, Rich revived Lee's famous play *Alexander*, more generally known by its alternative title, the *Rival Queens*. It had been suggested to him that Barry would be admirable as Alexander, while the parts of the two queens, Roxana and Statira, seemed eminently suitable for Mrs. Woffington and Mrs. Bellamy. Georgiane was quite determined to outshine her rival on this occasion and commissioned Madam Montête, the wife of the fashionable hairdresser, who was going to Paris, to bring her back the two most elegant tragedy dresses she could procure there. Madame Montête did not fail her, and Georgiane says that in these "robes de cour" taste and elegance were never so happily blended. Rich had bought a cast-off dress that had belonged to the Princess Dowager of Wales for Mrs. Woffington to wear as Roxana. It was beautiful by daylight, but being of a delicate straw-colour looked a dirty white by candlelight. Nothing could have pleased Georgiane better, for the dress she proposed to wear was of a deep yellow which would make her rival's costume look even more insipid. Over it she wore a regal robe of purple.

When she entered the Green Room in all her finery, Mrs. Woffington glared at her in rage and amazement. Then drawing herself up haughtily, she said: "I desire, Madam, you will never more, upon any account, wear those clothes in the piece we perform tonight." Georgiane replied with spirit: "I know not, Madam, by what right you take upon you to dictate to me what I shall wear. And I assure you, Madam, you must ask it in a very different manner, before you obtain my compliance." Mrs. Woffington thereupon decided that it might be wiser to be more conciliating; Georgiane gave way to a politer request, and the performance that night passed off smoothly.

Next night, however, Georgiane perversely sported her other dress, which was even more splendid, and Mrs. Woffington, unable to threaten or persuade her into removing it, set about her in good earnest in the scene in which Roxana stabs Statira and made her take refuge from her wrath in the wings. But Georgiane was not yet defeated. As she herself put it: "though I despise revenge, I do not dislike retaliation." So, on the earliest opportunity, she again donned the yellow dress and purple robe which had first aroused Mrs. Woffington's wrath. She considered that her rival's behaviour had absolved her from her undertaking not to wear it again. Mrs. Woffington furiously demanded how she dared to dress again in the manner she had so strictly prohibited. Georgiane did not deign to reply directly to her, but explained to Count von Haslang, who happened to be in the Green Room, her reason for changing her attire. Mrs. Woffington loudly remarked that it was well for Mrs. Bellamy that she had a Minister to supply her with jewels and such paraphernalia. This barbed interpretation of her friendship with the Secretary at War angered Georgiane, who tartly replied that she was sorry that *even half the town* could not furnish Mrs. Woffington a supply equal to the minister she so illiberally hinted at. And with this Parthian shot she made a hasty exit from the Green Room, leaving Count von Haslang to cover her retreat and stop her enraged rival's pursuit. Otherwise, she says, she would have stood a chance of appearing in the next scene with black eyes instead of the blue ones which nature had given her.

After this little incident, the two actresses never again addressed a word to each other off the stage, until some years later on her deathbed Peg Woffington sent for Georgiane to beg her pardon for calumniating her character on another occasion. Georgiane had not previously been aware of this, and it is regrettable to have to record that she on her own confession received the dying actress's apology ungraciously.

Much as they disliked each other, the great success of the *Rival Queens* obliged the two actresses to appear together repeatedly this season, for the piece was often revived and drew crowded houses on each occasion. Georgiane considered it bombastic, and believed that its success, apart from Barry's superb acting, was due almost entirely to Rich's magnificent pageant showing Alexander's triumphal entry into Babylon. No doubt Rich thought so too. The *Rival Queens* seems to have been a somewhat dangerous play, containing, as it did, two female parts of equal importance, which necessarily had to be played by actresses of outstanding ability. In 1678 the great Elizabeth Barry, impelled by much the same motive as was to animate Peg Woffington, had nearly killed the unfortunate Mrs. Boutell in the stabbing scene. The two actresses had had a dispute over a veil which both of them wanted to wear. The story of the quarrel between Mrs. Woffington and Mrs. Bellamy soon got abroad and increased the popularity of the piece. Possibly the audiences hoped to see a real murder on the stage. Nor was the incident soon forgotten; next year, at the Haymarket, Foote produced a farce based on it: *The Green-Room Squabble, or a Battle-Royal Between the Queen of Babylon and the Daughter of Darius*. Foote must have possessed first-hand information on the subject, for he himself had been acting at

Covent Garden at the time, and Georgiane had played with him and created the part of Lucinda in a new farce of his entitled *The Englishman returned from Paris*.

Whatever Peg Woffington may have thought, there is really no reason to suppose that there was ever any harm in Georgiane's friendship with Henry Fox. Doubtless he admired and was amused by the pretty young thing, and while she was living with his assistant, Calcraft, found her useful to him in many ways, but his interest in her seems to have been purely avuncular, while she regarded him, as she regarded a good many other elderly men in her life, as a friend and counsellor upon whom she could lean heavily in the varied crises she was always encountering. But it was perhaps inevitable that others besides Peg Woffington should have put a less indulgent construction on their relationship. And a joking remark of Fox's added colour to this unwarranted supposition. On the evening of her benefit he had been detained by the Duke of Cumberland and, coming late to join his wife at the theatre, found that he had lost his ticket. Laughingly he told the doorkeeper that it was immaterial, as it was *his* benefit. This casual and harmless remark came to the ears of a journalist, who referred to Miss Bellamy as "the great Captain's captain" and insinuated that no commission or place was disposed of in his department except through her recommendation. Georgiane, who maintained that she had never requested any improper favour of Fox, was most indignant. But she was even more apprehensive about the effect this libel might have on Lady Caroline. Fox laughed at her fears. But she was, nevertheless, convinced that never after the publication of this libel did Lady Caroline receive her with the same cordiality she had honoured her with before. And this mattered a great deal to Georgiane. For a time she was so sensitive about having her name associated with that of the Secretary at War and thus antagonising his wife that she refused to go down to Holwood, where Fox at this time often found it convenient to meet his political friends informally. He was reported to be there most Saturdays, greatly to the alarm of both the Lord Chancellor and the Duke of Newcastle, who suspected that he might be intriguing with Pitt, who lived not far away.

Chapter Eleven

By THIS TIME Calcraft was already beginning to build up a large fortune. He was agent to no less than ninety regiments, besides six independent companies; he was contractor for clothing and coal for the colonies, paymaster to the Board of Works, and deputy commissary of the musters. It was said of him that it was in his power to make or mar a military career. Soon the great increase of his business made it necessary for him to move to a much larger house. Georgiane decided that it would be much better to leave the choice of it entirely to him, and announced that she would like to go abroad for a few weeks. Calcraft not only did not demur, but actually encouraged the idea. Tired of her frigidity towards him, he was at this time consoling himself with a lady of the town called Lucy Cooper.

Georgiane's chief object in going to France was to visit her old friends, the Miss Merediths, who were now living at Toulouse. The younger of them was supposed to be dying, and the doctors had advised a warmer climate. Travelling by way of Boulogne, Georgiane took the opportunity to visit the convent of the Ursulines, at which she had been educated, and stayed there four days. In Paris, she found that her friend, the Marquis de Verneuil, was away staying with Voltaire, who was kind enough to send her an invitation to join them at Ferney. Reluctantly she had to refuse, as she was anxious to get to Toulouse. There she was surprised to learn that the elder Miss Meredith, who had not even been ill when she left England, had died a few days before, while the younger was so much better in health, that she accompanied Georgiane back to

Paris. By this time the Marquis de Verneuil had returned from his sojourn with Voltaire, and he entertained them both lavishly and showed them the sights of Paris.

On her return to London, Georgiane found that Calcraft had taken a palatial house in Parliament Street. This was conveniently near the various Government departments with which he was concerned, and his office, in which he now employed as many as fourteen or fifteen clerks, was in the same building. It was already quite clear that they were going to live in much more expensive style. More servants were engaged, and Georgiane's maid, Clifford, was promoted to be her 'woman', which sounded more impressive.

Calcraft said he would now allow her £2,500 a year for housekeeping. Concluding from this that he must have realised that the expenditure of the household had already increased, Georgiane was certain that he would not cavil at paying the £1,200 debt she had incurred for their expenses at Brewer Street, and she also, less reasonably, expected him to let her have the £600 she had borrowed from Miss Meredith during her stay abroad. Accordingly, she collected all her bills and submitted them to him.

To her astonishment, Calcraft replied that he could not pay them. Since she herself had been making a good income at the theatre, she ought to have been able to manage on the £400 a year he had been allowing her. What, for instance, had she done with that windfall of £1,000, of which he now revealed himself to have been the anonymous donor? He disclosed that he had also been responsible for the fifty-pound banknote she had found on the chimney-piece at Frith Street on the occasion of their first meeting. At the time Georgiane accepted both these statements, but afterwards said that she still believed that the £1,000 came from Lord Downe.

She was altogether shattered by his refusal. But Calcraft flatly, and, it must be admitted, with some reason, declared that it was obvious that she simply did not know the value of money. When she could convince him that she did, he would give her a thousand pounds for every hundred she was now asking from him. For the present he would only give her some £300, which, with the £1,050 he had already presented to her, would make up exactly the amount she owed. With this small amount of money she could not make any headway, so she borrowed £400 from the comedian, Sparks, and continued to borrow from Miss Meredith until her debt to her amounted to £1,200.

When Georgiane told Fox about the financial discussion she had had with Calcraft, he expressed his surprise that Calcraft did not publicly own her as his wife. Georgiane, who at this time still believed the tale Calcraft had told her of Fox's disapproval of his marrying an actress, burst into tears and asked him whether he himself had not been, and still was, the bar to such a union. Greatly surprised, Fox said that he had never opposed it; in fact, both he and Lady Caroline had always supposed that they were secretly married. Georgiane then told him the whole story of what had happened at Donyland Hall. Fox was amazed at this revelation of Calcraft's duplicity. But, with worldly wisdom, he advised her not to tell Calcraft yet that she had discovered the truth, as it would inevitably produce a violent quarrel which might be dangerous for her in her present condition—she was at this time several months gone with child. She thanked him for his advice and said that she would take it. But from this time forward she really hated Calcraft.

Although Fox strongly deprecated Georgiane's refusal to go to Holwood, Calcraft soon had good reason to be grateful for it, for one Sunday morning she was awoken by her maid, who told her that a fire had broken out in a baker's shop in Cannon Row directly opposite his offices, where all the regimental accounts were lodged. And there was an imminent danger of the fire spreading, as the adjoining buildings were highly inflammable, one being a coal and wood merchant's yard and the other the premises of a retailer of spirituous liquors. Georgiane leapt out of bed and went down in an under-petticoat and slippers. She knew that there was nobody in the house to help her; Calcraft's clerks did not come on Sundays, and the servants were all at Holwood. But she sent the porter to collect all the chairmen he could find and had all the books carried down into the pay office. It was not until a gentleman suggested that she was running the risk of catching cold that she recollected how she was dressed. She now found that she had continued for four hours, just as she had leaped frightened from her bed, in the midst of upwards of a hundred spectators.

She had scarcely got her clothes on when Calcraft, who had been sent for from Holwood, arrived "raving like a bedlamite that he was ruined and undone". But when he discovered that everything was safe and that, even if the fire had spread, he would have lost nothing, he called Georgiane his "Dear Preserver" and loaded her with praises. But though she had been the means of preserving his fortune, he showed no disposition to show his gratitude by helping her in her own difficulties. Georgiane now decided that she must try to do something about them herself. Through Furtado, a Jewish moneylender, she got into contact with a man called Morris, who purchased annuities for Mr. Davy, a wealthy silk-throwster in Spital-fields. This man advanced her £500 on condition that she paid £100 a year for the rest of her life out of the annuity of £120 settled upon her by Calcraft. But she could redeem this debt at any time on the repayment of the money with an additional £50 by way of premium. She had borrowed this sum of £500 expressly to repay Sparks what she owed him, but instead of going to him with it, she waited for him to claim it from her, making herself quite easy in her mind because she had it ready. But ready money in Georgiane's hands was a dangerous possession, and so it proved on this occasion. She received a call from her cousin, Crawford, who told her that he needed the sum of £400 for three months to complete an important purchase he had agreed to make. Always willing to oblige, and having, so she says, no doubt of his honesty and capability, as he was thought to be well off, she told him that she could let him have £200, and she would lend him a pair of diamond ear-rings on which he could easily raise the other £200 he required. He expressed his gratitude and gave her his note for £400 payable in three months time. But when the time for repayment came, he informed her that he could not pay her. If, however, she would like to have her ear-rings back, a Mr. Smith of the Exchequer would advance sufficient money to redeem them on their joint bond. Incredible as it may seem, Georgiane agreed and, moreover, signed a bond he had brought with him without giving it more than a casual glance. Crawford went off and was to return immediately with the ear-rings. He did not come back. And when she sent to him for the ear-rings a few days later, she was told that he had fled to France. His affairs had been in a desperate situation, and he had taken in all his friends in order to provide money for his flight. "I blush when I recall my imprudence on this occasion." Georgiane confesses, as well she might.

By this time Fox had managed to persuade her to go down to Holwood again, and she was there when on September 4th, 1756 she fell into labour, and, before her doctor could arrive from London, gave birth to a son, afterwards christened Henry Fox Calcraft. Four or five days later Calcraft came into her room, where she was conversing with a lady who had come to see her, and told her that he had received a letter from Davy requesting the payment of her annuity. This had annoyed him a good deal, for so far he had not paid any of it, and had secretly hoped that she had forgotten all about it. Georgiane did not feel at all like discussing finance, and she told him to go away, pay the money, and fulfil his contract. If he did not, she would force him to do so when she was up and about again. And she revealed to him that she was now aware that he had deceived her in telling her that it was Fox's disapproval that had prevented him from marrying her in the first place. Calcraft departed, muttering something about her extravagance. Within the next few moments the full extent of his duplicity was revealed to her. After he had gone, she complained to her visitor of his brutality in troubling her about such a trifle at a time like this, since he knew that she spent all she earned at the theatre on entertaining his friends and supplying his brother and sister when he failed to do so. That was why she was in debt. Her visitor then told her that Calcraft would never marry her, for the simple reason that, even before he knew her, he had been married for some years to a young woman at Grantham, who was still living there with an aunt of his. Georgiane was so mad with rage and shock at this revelation that she leapt out of bed and fell senseless to the floor.

When she came to, she felt terribly ill, with a severe pain in her side. Her physician, Dr. Hunter, and the surgeon, Mr. Adair, were sent for, but could not account for her condition. She became so ill that she was thought to be dying, and Father D'Arcy, an Irish priest, came to hear her confession and administer the last sacrament to her. In her *Apology* Georgiane draws a very transparent veil over this event: "And the business being settled, for which he came, I was wholly resigned, and waited my visitation with the longing of a bride." But she did not die, though she did not seem to get better. Several weeks later she was removed to London, where more doctors were called in for consultation, but were equally puzzled, some suggesting an adhesion, others an imposthume. This congeries of medical disagreement, Calcraft said afterwards, cost him £900.

Shortly before Christmas all the doctors gave up her case, except the persistent Mr. Adair, who by stealth brought in a certain Irish physician—a curious sidelight on the height to which political passions were carried in those days. Georgiane explains that his political views were so different from their own, that his introduction in their house was deemed reprehensible. But Dr. Lucas's Tory principles apparently did not prevent him from making a correct diagnosis of the Whig lady's illness, and he pronounced her to be suffering from a confirmed abscess in her lung. After giving her some pre-

liminary treatment, he sent her off to the hot wells at Bristol.
Mrs. Sparks, the wife of the comedian, accompanied her to
look after her. She was so weak that she could not walk and
had to be carried everywhere. Dr. Ford, who had charge of her
case at Bristol, prescribed port and punch, both of which she
had never tasted before and disliked intensely, and bled her
frequently and profusely. Then, one day when she was out for
an airing, the abscess broke. Ford, who was hastily summoned,
ordered her to be taken straightway to the pump-room, where
she was drenched with the hot mineral water and then put
into bed between well-warmed blankets and given burnt
brandy. For the first time for many weeks, she was able to lie
down and soon fell into a profound sleep. When she awoke
eighteen hours later, she was able not only to stand, but even
to walk into the next room. Thenceforth her recovery was
rapid.

Soon she was well enough to go back to London. But she
had formed a determination not to return to Calcraft, and she
wrote to her mother, who had taken his old house in Brewer
Street, asking if she might come there. Her mother wrote
back consenting to receive her and telling her that the house
would be made ready for her. But when he heard of her plans,
Calcraft went nearly mad with apprehension, fearing that she
might reveal the reason why she had left him. Letter after
letter came beseeching her to come back to him, and he wrote
repeatedly to Mrs. Sparks, begging her to intercede with
Georgiane on his behalf. In the meantime Georgiane had
written to Quin, explaining the whole position and asking for
his advice. Quin replied that he would not advise her to make
the rupture public or to leave Parliament Street until the
whole of her debts were discharged, and, even then, not to stir
till her future was amply provided for. Mrs. Sparks at length
prevailed upon her to read one of Calcraft's letters, in which he
besought her for the sake of humanity, for her children's sake,
and for her own, to return to him. He swore that he would pay
all her debts within three months, and concluded with urging

the violence of his passion for her. Georgiane was not in the least moved by these impassioned pleas, but she had been impressed by Quin's sage advice, and she finally consented to return on two conditions: first, that Calcraft would pay all her debts, and second, that he would never attempt to see or speak with her alone.

It may seem strange that Calcraft should have bowed to such onerous conditions, but it soon appeared that his sole purpose in getting her back was to prevent inconvenient revelations and save appearances. He adhered strictly to his promise not to attempt to see her alone, and, in fact, carefully avoided her, fearing her reproaches. As for his promise to pay her debts, he thought he could safely forget that, for nobody but Mrs. Sparks knew he had made it.

For the time being Georgiane was not worried, as she had just received a legacy from her friend, Miss Meredith, who had returned to France and died there. In her will she had forgiven Georgiane the £1,200 she owed her and had left her, in addition, a legacy of £500, her jewels, which were valued at about £2,000, and all her best laces.

A contributory cause of poor Miss Meredith's death had been her unrequited passion for the Duke of Kingston, who had encouraged her for some time and then transferred his affections elsewhere. As a last reproachful token of her regard, she had left him a gold box with her miniature on the lid, and Georgiane was entrusted with the duty of delivering it to him. This, she confessed, was a little awkward for her, since the Duke had once been an admirer of her own, "though not an *honourable* one, as my friend had fondly hoped he would have been to her." But she wrote to him, and he called on her to receive the box. When she handed it to him, she remarked that she wished there had been two portraits, that she also might have the likeness of her friend. But she was profoundly shocked when the Duke calmly took out his penknife, and, cutting the portrait from the lid, gave it to her.

Her long illness had prevented Georgiane from appearing at

all at Covent Garden this season, and all her accustomed parts had been played by Miss Nossiter. But in return for Mrs. Sparks's great kindness to her, she consented to appear as Almeria in the *Mourning Bride* at Sparks's benefit on March 31st, 1757, this being, as the playbill announced, "the first time of her performing since her late indisposition." She did all in her power to render the benefit a success and disposed of nearly two hundred gold tickets among her friends. Her public had missed her, and she had a great reception on her re-appearance.

About this time Lord Tyrawley came back from Gibraltar. Since he had disapproved so strongly of her association with Metham, Georgiane could not suppose that he would be more likely to approve of her present entanglement, and was rather embarrassed by his return. But as it was generally believed that she was married to Calcraft, she decided to let her father think so too. He accepted the situation as it appeared to be and visited them at the house in Parliament Street. Georgiane was even able to persuade him to give Calcraft the agency for his regiment, the Coldstream Guards. Calcraft undertook to give her the emoluments of this agency, but she says that she never received a single guinea of them from him.

She had now disclosed the truth about her relationship with Calcraft to Lady Tyrawley, who however, regarded Calcraft's promise to marry her as giving some sort of sanction to the arrangement, and did not scruple to hint to Lady Powerscourt and Lady Dillon, to whom she introduced her, that she was really married.

Her brother, Frank, too, made one of his comparatively rare appearances in Georgiane's life. Only recently she had got him out of very serious trouble. Happening to be at Gibraltar, when Lord Tyrawley was Governor there, he had incurred his father's wrath very deservedly by an inconceivably cruel and crassly stupid jest. Lord Tyrawley was very lame from one of the many wounds received in his numerous battles, and his son had followed him up the ballroom at an assembly in Gibraltar imitating his limp. Lord Tyrawley had not forgiven this insult. Shortly afterwards, Lieutenant O'Hara, in temporary command of his ship while the captain was ill ashore, had distinguished himself in an engagement with an enemy vessel, and, on the captain's death a little later, had confidently expected to succeed him in the command. But Lord Tyrawley had intervened and persuaded the Admiral not to promote him. Furious with rage, O'Hara had promptly sent his commission to the Lords of the Admiralty, "desiring that they would offer it up, with their next sacrifice, to the goddess Cloacina." For some reason he escaped a court martial—possibly his father, thinking he had been punished enough already, had secretly intervened in his favour—but he was not given further employment.

Georgiane had done everything in her power to procure his reinstatement and had eventually succeeded through the good offices of one of the most zealous admirers of her acting, Mr. Yorke, whom she persuaded to introduce her to his sister, Lady Anson, wife of the great Admiral who was then First Lord of the Admiralty. And now Frank, whom she seldom saw or heard of, unless he was in trouble of some kind or in need of money, sent her a note informing her that he was confined in a sheriff's officer's house in Stanhope Street, Clare Market, for a debt of £60, which Lord Tyrawley refused to pay for him. For once Calcraft acted with real generosity. He went immediately to Stanhope Street, discharged the debt, and brought Frank home with him. He must have been in an unusually good humour that day, for Georgiane says that he gave her a most amusing description of the scene in the sponging-house where he had discovered Frank carousing with a trollop.

After a visit to some friends at Malmesbury, Georgiane was about to go on to Bristol when she received an express asking her to go at once to Windsor, where Fox was engaged in a bye-election as a result of his acceptance of the office of Paymaster General. His opponent, a Mr. Bowles, had proved unexpectedly formidable, having the support of the powerful

Beauclerk interest; Fox needed every vote he could muster, and he thought that Georgiane might be useful, since she had several friends in the neighbourhood who possessed influence with voters.

It was a very lively election, and there was great excitement in the town. Georgiane was standing at the door of an inn with Fox's elder son, Stephen, who had come over from Eton, when a rough fellow came up with a bludgeon and aimed a savage blow at them, crying out "No Foxes! No Doxies!" He was promptly knocked down by a bystander; but the boy was so affected by the shock of the incident that he developed a nervous tic which lasted for several years. Georgiane relates that one day next season he and his brother, Charles James, who had just joined him at Eton, came to visit her at the theatre and asked her to persuade Rich to put on the *Rival Queens* the following night, as the younger boy had heard great accounts of it. They waited in her dressing-room while she sent a message to Rich, but for some reason the manager sent back a refusal, and the vexation and disappointment so upset Master Fox that he had one of his attacks and nearly frightened Georgiane out of her wits.

When the election, which Fox won with a substantial majority, was over, Georgiane decided not to go to Bristol after all. Hoping to find some congenial company at Holwood, she went straight there from Windsor, but was disappointed to find nobody in residence but Dr. Francis, who was an over-frequent guest and almost a household familiar. Having promised to visit Foote, who was then living in one of the houses Sir John Vanbrugh had built at Blackheath, she proposed to the doctor that they should ride over there next morning. Unfortunately the two of them had a rather heated altercation over some literary matter at breakfast, and Dr. Francis, who never suffered contradiction easily at the best of times, was rather disgruntled and remained ill-humoured on the way to Blackheath. They found Murphy, the actor, and Cleland, the author, with Foote, who proposed that they should all go for a

ride before dinner.* Georgiane was already in the saddle when
Murphy came out of the house laughing and told her that Dr.
Francis had decided that it was inconsistent with his sacerdotal
dignity to appear with an actress in public and had refused to
accompany them. Since he did not scruple to live in her house
and was always glad to accept of a place in her box at the
theatre, Georgiane found it difficult to account for this sudden
whim on the part of a man whose respect for her had nearly
bordered on servility. She could only imagine that it was
because she had had the temerity to praise another author.
They set off without him and, when they returned, found that
he had gone back to Holwood without waiting for his hostess
or his dinner. Georgiane retaliated by sending for her chaise
and driving straight to London, leaving Dr. Francis to nurse
his grievances in the solitude of Holwood.

On arriving back in Parliament Street, Georgiane found that
there had been serious trouble in the Calcraft family. Calcraft
had heard that his young sister, Christian, had become involved
in an undesirable love-affair and had gone off to Grantham to
fetch her. His clerk, Willis, also told her that Captain Calcraft
had got himself into a serious scrape. While at Huntingdon on
a recruiting party, he had visited a noble peer in the neighbourhood who loved gambling more than propriety and persuaded
him to play cards with him. The young man had lost £200,
and had paid his "debt of honour" out of regimental funds,
giving a draft on his wealthy brother for the amount. Calcraft
had refused to honour the draft and had sent it back before he
left for Grantham. Realising that this would mean a court
martial for his brother, Georgiane determined to avert it at all
costs. It was true that she had not the money herself, but she
could borrow it.

* Here is a typical instance of Mrs. Bellamy's eccentric chronology. She says
they were going over to the sale of the furniture belonging to the Duchess of
Bolton, who had just died. The Duchess died in 1760. But she places the
incident immediately after the Windsor election, which was in July, 1757. It is,
of course, possible that there might have been a sale at the house in 1757.

A more serious problem was to get Calcraft's dangerous letter out of the post office. Fortunately, she recollected that her milliner, Mrs. Jordan, happened to be related to the Secretary of the post office, so, having borrowed the money and obtained a bank-bill for the requisite amount, she prevailed upon Mrs. Jordan to go to the post office, break open Calcraft's letter and substitute the bank-bill for the rejected draft.

The letter was re-sealed with her own seal, which, she says, was very similar to Calcraft's, though the only similarity appears to have been that they both contained lions. She asserts that Calcraft had appropriated Lord Tyrawley's "three black lions" and had further added the greyhound crest from General Braddock's arms on the plate he had left them. But the lions used by Calcraft—to which he was not then entitled— though they were certainly black, were *passant guardant in pale* like the leopards in the royal arms of England, whereas the solitary black lion of the O'Haras, which she herself had unwarrantably adopted, was *rampant*. More than ten years later Calcraft applied to the College of Heralds for a grant of the arms, which he stated that he and his ancestors had been using—*per fesse argent and ermine, three lions passant guardant in pale sable*—and for a suitable crest. The arms were duly granted to him with the addition of a crest: *on a wreath of the colours, a greyhound courant sable, charged with a cross crosslet or*, so there may be some foundation for Georgiane's assertion that he had taken a fancy to the greyhound, which does, in fact, figure in the arms of Braddock. At the same time, he obtained for certain of his illegitimate children, though not for the two he had by Georgiane, a grant of the same arms *within a bordure wavy azure for difference*, the crest being differenced with a *palet wavy or*.*

Calcraft was extremely surprised when he received an effusive letter of thanks from his brother, and concluded that

---

* The original grant of these arms, dated December 8th, 1770, is preserved at Rempstone, as is the hatchment displayed on Calcraft's death. There is no crest above the arms on the seal affixed to one of the codicils atttached to his Will at Somerset House.

it was meant to be ironical. And when he became aware of Georgiane's intervention, he was at first much annoyed, but later relented, not, she believed, so much out of affection for his brother, as because she had averted a disgrace which would inevitably have reflected upon himself. At any rate he thanked her for what she had done and returned the money she had advanced.

He had brought his young sister back to London with him and asked Georgiane to find a place where she could board and lodge until he could settle her with some family in the country. Presumably the reason why he would not have her in his own house was because he regarded her as being in disgrace. The obliging Mrs. Jordan consented to take her as a temporary boarder and later found her a situation as companion to a widow in Essex. But Calcraft refused to give the poor girl any money at all, and she would have made but an indifferent appearance if Georgiane had not taken care of her wardrobe.

Calcraft had no objection to spending money on his own clothes. About this time he decided that his rising position in the world demanded that he should make an appearance at Court. He consulted Georgiane about the clothes he should wear on this important occasion, and she suggested a plain suit of brown rateen, a cloth then fashionable, with a white silk lining and gold buttons. This sober garb, she thought, would become his standing as a financier. But Calcraft had quite other ideas and appeared in a milk-white coat trimmed with blue velvet and fastened with embroidered silver frogs, and a waistcoat and breeches of the same. When he entered the room in this gorgeous costume, Lady Rochford, who happened to be sitting with Georgiane, gazed at him in astonishment and exclaimed, rather rudely but at least in French, "*Ah! quelle figure!*" Georgiane could scarce restrain her laughter. Calcraft was most disconcerted at his failure to dazzle the ladies, and Georgiane never knew whether he did, in fact, wear this suit at Court, for he appeared at dinner that day in a plain blue frock. But he afterwards presented her with a miniature of himself in his white suit, framed, economically, with rose-diamonds, which meant that she would not be able to raise money on it.

For some reason the season of 1757–58 started off rather tamely at Covent Garden. There were no big names among the performers. The principal male parts were undertaken by the comparatively inexperienced Ross, who had transferred his allegiance from Garrick to Rich, and Smith, who, Georgiane says, was not then as good as he later became, while the leading women's parts were shared by Mrs. Hamilton and Mrs. Vincent. It was not until the production of *King Lear* on December 5th that either Barry or Mrs. Bellamy appeared. But they followed with *Romeo and Juliet*, *Macbeth*, in which Georgiane played Lady Macbeth for the first time, and *Othello*. And this season Georgiane played several more parts that were new to her, Mariamne, in the tragedy of that name, Anna Bullen in Banks's *Virtue Betrayed*, and Lady Randolph, in Home's *Douglas*. This famous tragedy had first been produced in Edinburgh in December, 1756, and had caused a sensation. But Garrick, to whom it was offered, refused it—some said because he thought he would be overshadowed in it by Mrs. Cibber—and the earliest London production had been at Covent Garden in March, 1757, with Barry as Norval and Peg Woffington, most unsuitably, as Lady Randolph. Georgiane also at last had the opportunity to play in London two parts she had played long ago in Dublin, Cleopatra in *All For Love*, which she played at her own benefit, with Mrs. Elmy in her more usual part of Octavia, and Constance in *King John*, a part for which she was now more suited than in the days when she had quarrelled with Garrick about it. But she is reported to have "cathedralised the unhappy princess offensively".

While in Gibraltar Lord Tyrawley had spent considerable sums of money on repairing and improving the fortifications there, and his alleged extravagance in this respect came to the notice of Lord George Sackville, Lieutenant-General of the Ordnance, who, at the end of March, 1758, instigated certain members of Parliament to censure his conduct in the House of

Commons. Papers and plans relating to the works carried on at Gibraltar between July, 1756, and November, 1757, were laid before the House. On hearing of this, Tyrawley, who had little reverence for Parliament, remarked that he did not even know where the House of Commons was, but later, to the surprise and consternation of his critics, he demanded to be heard at the bar of the House in his own defence. This privilege could not be denied to him, and a day was fixed for him to appear before a Committee of the whole House.

Tyrawley proceeded to draw up a memorial, which he proposed to read to the House, and was so highly delighted with it that he read it first to everybody he met. It was a racy composition and contained some particularly pungent, if entirely irrelevant, remarks about Lord George Sackville's peculiar agility in avoiding all foreign command. Sackville took alarm when he realised what a tiger he had stirred from its lair and succeeded in getting the day of hearing adjourned for a fortnight until April 13th, 1758, in the hope that the matter might be dropped altogether. But Tyrawley was determined to vindicate himself, and nothing would induce him to recede.

At the very last minute Lord George attempted to spring a surprise on his adversary by bringing before the House, without mentioning what it was and without warning Lord Tyrawley, the confidential report of Colonel Skinner, who had been Chief Engineer of the works at Gibraltar. Fox immediately rose to protest against this underhand proceeding and to lay open what he called "the unhandsome darkness of this conduct". But Tyrawley did not really need his advocacy; he was quite capable of looking after himself. With an airy contempt for the forms and formalities of the House he refused the chair that was offered to him and, nonchalantly leaning on the bar itself, he proceeded to bombard the luckless Skinner "with such arrogant humour that the very lawyers thought themselves outdone in their own style of worrying a culprit". Then, with great art and frankness, he read his memorial, the terms of which he had judiciously modified from their pristine vigour. He claimed that the truth was that he deserved great credit for doing that for which he was being blamed. If he had spent too much money in achieving it, his plea was that, as he had never been an economist of his own money, but made use of it when occasion required, he had laid out the public money whenever he judged it to be necessary.

"Such tough game tempted few hunters," as Horace Walpole put it, and no members rising to pursue the ex-Governor with criticisms, the House decided to accept his explanations. It was only then that Tyrawley drew from his pocket a letter from the King himself, wholeheartedly approving of his conduct and thanking him for having taken "such needful precautions to secure a place of so great consequence". When asked why he had not produced this letter before in his vindication, he said that he considered His Majesty's approval to be a sufficient exculpation of his conduct, but that, in order to show that he was worthy of so great a happiness, he wished to be exculpated by the nation likewise, whose soldier he was.

Perhaps his greatest triumph was that, in spite of his utter defeat on this occasion, Lord George Sackville was so much impressed by Tyrawley's integrity, that, when, more than a year later, he himself was to be tried by a court martial for his alleged disobedience in refusing to order the cavalry to charge at the battle of Minden, he said that, being convinced of his innocence, he would be perfectly willing to accept Tyrawley as President of the court, even though he knew he had been the foremost in abusing his conduct. But Tyrawley wisely refused to act. He said that it was well known that he would not be partial even to his own son; but that the general opinion seemed so much against the accused man that he was probably guilty and that therefore the adverse vote he would be obliged to give "might possibly induce illiberal persons to attribute his decision to what he was incapable of—retaliation". General Sir Charles Howard was appointed instead.

Lord Tyrawley had always had expensive tastes, but he had never been a wealthy man and was consequently in perennial need of money to gratify them. He now wrote to his wife suggesting that she should help him by cutting off the entail of the Blessington property. On succeeding to their mother's estates in 1745, her brother had been created Earl of Blessington, but in 1754 he had lost his only son and heir, Viscount Mountjoy, who had died of small-pox in Paris at the age of nineteen. Upon his own death the estates would now devolve upon Lady Tyrawley as his only sister.

Lady Tyrawley wrote to Georgiane, who happened at the time to be at Holwood, asking for her advice. Georgiane replied that she ought to give Lord Tyrawley a positive denial. She pointed out that her only income now was an allowance of £800 a year from him, and that, if he died, she would have nothing to live on but her pension as a General's widow. The estates in which he now wished her to sell her rights would be a good reserve to her. Lady Tyrawley followed this advice, which Georgiane acknowledges she gave chiefly because Lady Tyrawley had often said that she proposed to leave everything of which she died possessed to her and her children. But Lord Tyrawley conceived a shrewd suspicion that it was Georgiane who had advised his usually tractable wife to refuse his request, thereby thwarting his schemes, and from this time forward he never treated her with his old affection.

This summer, accompanied by Mrs. Walker, Georgiane went to the Continent for several months, leaving a letter for Calcraft reminding him of his promise to settle her debts before her return. She had hoped that the Marquis de Verneuil would take her to pay the visit to the great Voltaire that she had had to defer two years before, but unfortunately the Marquis was now dead, having blown himself up in one of the alchemical experiments to which he was addicted. She went instead to Brussels, where she spent some time, and then went on to Antwerp in the hope of making some enquiries about the late Mr. Thomas Sykes from his brother who lived there. But Mr.

Sykes was away in Paris, and she was told that in any case the
States General of Holland had taken possession of all his
brother's property at the Hague, so that she had nothing
further to hope for from that quarter.

While in Antwerp she received a letter requesting her to be
back in England in time for the opening of the theatre in
September. She was most reluctant to return, because it meant
going back to Calcraft and a home that had become hateful to
her. She would have liked to retire also from the stage, but she
felt that she had no choice so long as her affairs were so involved, and she engaged again with Rich. Calcraft was away in
Marlborough when she got back, but she found that he had
not kept his promise to pay her debts and was obliged to insert
in the papers a public announcement of her engagement at the
theatre in order to allay the growing apprehensions of her
creditors. She hastened to Somerset House to consult Lady
Tyrawley, who advised her to leave Calcraft, if she could not
come to some arrangement with him about her debts.

On his return to London Calcraft pretended to be ill and
refused to talk about money matters, but Georgiane pursued
him into his office and insisted upon a full discussion, threaten-
ing to leave the house immediately if her demand were not
complied with. Calcraft pleaded that he himself was really
distressed for money at the moment. He had just bought two
estates which had absorbed a great deal of his capital, and he
had had to lay out a considerable amount of money for Lord
Granby. Moreover, he had recently had serious losses. He
had hoped that Miss Meredith's legacy would have enabled her
to set her affairs in order, since it amounted to £1,700 without
the jewels. Georgiane reminded him that £1,200 had to be
deducted from this, since it merely represented a debt she had
already owed to Miss Meredith. She told him that she believed
she now owed rather more than £3,000, but that her woman,
Clifford, had a better knowledge of the details than she had and
could furnish him with an exact list. She must insist upon
these debts being paid, if she were to remain with him.

Calcraft shook his head and said that it was a large sum she was asking for. But if she could put off the payment until her benefit at the end of the season, when she could herself contribute, he would undertake to see her clear on condition that she would promise never to incur any more debts. Georgiane told him that she disliked conditions, but she would be willing to consent, provided that he would take over the necessary expenses for his own brother and sister. She said that he ought to recognise that they must have money. A young officer in the Guards could not possibly live on his pay alone, and a young woman, "who was obliged to appear as a gentlewoman," could not subsist on £50 a year. She concluded by handing him a large bill for wine, telling him that she had not engaged to pay for his wine out of the household expenses. This he settled at once, but for the rest she had to remain content with promises.

Evidently she did not consider that her undertaking not to incur any more debts should take effect until Calcraft had paid off the existing ones. About this time she was presented with a beautiful set of carriage horses. Calcraft flatly refused to pay for their keep; he said he had enough of his own to keep already. So she was obliged to defray the cost herself, and this added sensibly to her expenses.

Chapter Twelve

GEORGIANE'S FIRST APPEARANCE in the following season (1758–59) was as Indiana on October 2nd. And later in the same month she played Monimia, Sigismunda, and Desdemona. On November 1st there was a special performance of *Romeo and Juliet* "bespoke by some persons of quality". Georgiane played Juliet, with Ross as Romeo. The stage box on this occasion was occupied by a fashionable party which included the beautiful Countess of Coventry, who as Maria Gunning had been befriended by Georgiane in Ireland. But the only occasion on which they had met since those days was when the penniless Miss Gunning, a few days before her brilliant marriage, had come to crave a small loan from her actress friend. As Georgiane was speaking the famous soliloquy before Juliet drinks the poison on awakening in the tomb, the stillness was suddenly interrupted by a loud laugh from Lady Coventry. Georgiane was so disconcerted that she stopped abruptly and was unable to proceed. She had to come forward and beg the audience's leave to retire till she could collect herself. The audience was so angry at this ill-bred interruption that they insisted that Lady Coventry's party should leave the theatre.

Georgiane's brother, Captain O'Hara, happened to be in one of the side boxes near Lady Coventry, and, indignant at the insult offered to his sister, reproached her with her rudeness, to which she replied that she could not bear Mrs. Bellamy since she had seen Mrs. Cibber. Her whole party then left the theatre, with the exception of the courtly Lord Eglinton, who hastened round to the Green Room to make an apology for the unmannerliness of his friends. He assured Georgiane that no offence had been intended to her. Lady Coventry had been twirling an orange on her finger, and her laughter had been caused by some ridiculous thing that was said upon the occasion. Georgiane graciously accepted the apology and returned to the stage to finish the play, amid the acclamations of a sympathetic audience.

The story of this incident does not rest upon Georgiane's account alone. Tate Wilkinson recorded it also to make the point that the audience is all-powerful in keeping order or creating disorder in the theatre. "On an uproar, when Lady Coventry and several other persons of quality were obliged to quit the stage box, on account of a supposed affront given to Miss Bellamy in Juliet, it was the audience and not any other force compelled these disturbers to leave the theatre."

Georgiane had thought to regard the incident as closed, but when next morning her brother repeated to her what Lady Coventry had said to him, her resentment was rekindled, and she determined to take her revenge. She accordingly hunted out the note Miss Maria Gunning had insisted upon giving her for the money she had borrowed just before her marriage, and sent a servant with it to Lord Coventry's house, requesting repayment. She says that hitherto she had never expected or wanted to get the money back and had never intended to ask for it. The servant waited at the house until her ladyship returned from riding and then presented the note to her. Lady Coventry glanced at it and returned it to him, remarking disdainfully, "What! is it Mrs. Bellamy, the *actress*?" Georgiane's servant answered that it was, and that Mrs. Bellamy expected the money to be paid. "If she is impertinent," cried Lady Coventry, "I will have her hissed off the stage." The man replied with dignity that continuing on the stage was a matter of indifference to his mistress; but if she chose to perform, it was not in her ladyship's power to prevent it. But as he saw little prospect of getting the money, he left the house. He was speedily followed by one of the Countess's servants, who assured him that the money would be sent shortly. But from that hour Georgiane never heard anything more from Lady Coventry concerning the money.

This autumn Calcraft was suffering very severely from gout in the head, and, although by this time Georgiane's indifference towards him had turned to active dislike, she could not be insensible to the pain he was undergoing and did all that she could for him. She says that she attended him with the same assiduity and tenderness as if she had really been his wife. And Calcraft was appreciative of her attentions; he would not allow anyone else to apply to his eyes the poultices composed of bags of seeds which his doctor had prescribed for him. As soon as he was sufficiently recovered, he was ordered to Bath to complete his cure, and came back very much better. But Georgiane's disgust for him returned with his returning health.

The outstanding event of the theatrical season of 1758–59 at Covent Garden was the production of Robert Dodsley's *Cleone* on December 2nd. This play had been written as long ago as 1740 but had never been acted. Recently Dodsley had offered it to Garrick, who had declined it and had been confirmed in his adverse opinion by Mrs. Cibber. But Rich saw in it an excellent part for Mrs. Bellamy and accepted it. Georgiane decided that she would play the part simply and quietly in consonance with the simplicity of the language. She would not rave and rant after the accepted manner in the culminating scene when the heroine goes mad. In her opinion, this was "an effort worth trying; as from its novelty I should, at least, have the merit of its being all my own".

But her conception of the part was far from impressing Dodsley's many literary friends who attended the rehearsals, and even Lord Lyttelton, in spite of his partiality for Georgiane herself, told the author he thought she had totally misconceived the character. She felt bound to admit that she did not do justice to her own rendering at these rehearsals, for the nursing of Calcraft during the past weeks had been a great strain on her; she was feeling far from well and would have liked, had it been possible, to have the production deferred until she was feeling stronger.

At the final rehearsal she was further disconcerted by the sudden reappearance of George Metham, whom she had not seen since their separation. At some time in the interval he appears to have renounced the faith in which he had been brought up; in 1756 he had been High Sheriff of Yorkshire, and he was now Member of Parliament for Kingston-upon-Hull, neither of which offices he could have held, had he still been a Roman Catholic. He had been knighted in April, 1756, and was now known as Sir George Montgomery Metham. It is possible that he became an Anglican about 1754, for in May of that year he presented a patten to the parish church of North Cave, of which he was lay rector and patron.

The nonchalant insolence of Sir George's bearing towards Georgiane did not help to calm her anxious nerves. Taking a pinch of snuff in a careless manner, he walked up to her and wished her joy, regretting that he had not had an opportunity of doing so before. He told her that she looked more angelic than ever. Then, turning to a bystander, he remarked: "I certainly am the happiest being in the universe, in having been blest with the affection of two of the first actresses, and most accomplished women in Europe." The scarcely veiled effrontery of this back-handed compliment upset Georgiane, and her acting became more feeble and flaccid than ever. When she spoke the line "Thou shalt not murder", Dr. Johnson caught her "somewhat too briskly" by the arm and adjured her in his gruffest manner: "It is a commandment, and must be spoken 'Thou shalt *not* murder!'"

Dr. Johnson's bullying combined with Metham's insolence had upset her so much that she ended the rehearsal in a state of prostration, and kind friends advised her not to appear next day in so trying a part. But her name had been announced and she felt that it was her duty not to disappoint the public. She therefore determined to go on, whatever might be the consequences, and she would alter nothing. "I was likewise resolved," she says, "to play the character agreeable to my own conception, though against the united opinion of all the literati."

Next evening, when she arrived at the theatre to dress for the opening performance, the author himself came up to her and told her that all his friends, as well as himself, considered that she was not forcible enough in the mad scene. But Georgiane's nerves were by this time overwrought, and she answered him with a petulance of which she was afterwards ashamed. She told him that she had a reputation to lose as an actress, but, as for his piece, Mr. Garrick had anticipated the damnation of it, publicly, the preceding evening, at the Bedford Coffee House, where he had declared that it could not pass muster, as it was the very worst piece ever exhibited. With this she left him. Dodsley told her afterwards that at the time he greatly regretted having chosen her as his heroine.

Georgiane's notion of simplicity had been carried out even as far as her costume, and for the first time on the eighteenth-century stage she appeared in a straight clinging robe without the hoop which was then fashionable and which was worn by all the Roman empresses, Eastern princesses, abbesses, Juliets, and Lady Macbeths.

The gamble came off. Her success was immediate, outstanding, and undeniable. The applause was so great and continuous that at first she could scarcely believe that it *was* applause. Then she heard the stentorian voice of Dr. Johnson himself shouting in the pit: "I will write a copy of verses upon her myself." And when she appeared to speak the epiloque, she had leisure to practise all the curtsies taught her by her dancing master over and over again, so favourable was the reception she met with from the audience.

The play caught on, and was acted for sixteen nights in succession. Ross played Cleone's husband, Sifroy, and the cast also included Sparks, Ridout, Dyer, and Clarke in important parts. The only other woman's part, that of Cleone's com-

panion, Isabella, was played by Georgiane's old friend, Mrs.
Elmy. But there can be no doubt that the success of the play
was due almost entirely to Georgiane. It was her triumph. In
the preface to the printed version of the play it is stated: "Mrs.
Bellamy sustained the trying character of the principal, and in
the conclusive scenes of maternal agony over her murdered
child harrowed the hearts of the audience with powers then at
their height, and by many conceived of the highest excellence."

Georgiane was so exhausted when she got home that night
that she could not bring herself to go to Calcraft's apartment to
give him an account of the evening, as she customarily did.
Dr. Francis had told him of the unfavourable opinions of her
acting that had been expressed at the rehearsals, and, as he
knew also that she was not feeling at all well, he concluded that
her failure to come to report to him must be the effect of
chagrin at her disappointment, and rose from his bed of sick-
ness to come along to see her. She had just assured him that her
reception had been "well enough", when Dr. Francis ran in,
almost breathless, and cried out: "Oh, Calcraft! it is beyond
description. I have hastened, as fast as I could, wishing to be
the first to acquaint you of the uncommon applause and
deserved success she has met with."

Next morning the house in Parliament Street was thronged
with friends who came to congratulate her, among them Lord
Lyttelton and Sir Charles Hanbury Williams. Lyttelton handsomely acknowledged that he had been wrong in his opinion
about her subdued playing of the mad scene. Georgiane then
turned to Sir Charles and asked him whether he thought that
violent madness would have had the desired effect. Sir Charles
did not answer, but stared wildly at her, and looked as if he
was going to lay hold of her. Observing this, Lyttelton hastily
pulled her away, and only just in time, for Sir Charles snatched
up a knife which lay on the breakfast table and vowed he would
murder her. His friend, Mr. Harris, who was sitting beside
him on the sofa, had to hold him down while Georgiane made
her escape. The strange thing is that, until that moment, Sir

Charles had shown no previous sign of insanity, and only a few minutes before he had been congratulating her warmly on her performance. His mental collapse was complete. He never recovered, and died shortly afterwards by his own hand, persisting to the end in his wish to destroy Mrs. Bellamy.

What pleased Georgiane almost more than anything else about her success was to receive a letter of congratulation from the generous-hearted Kitty Clive. "It was the more flattering to me," she says, "as her sincerity could never be doubted." The run of *Cleone* could have lasted even longer, if she had felt strong enough to continue. But she found the emotional strain of the part very exhausting. Her friend, Mrs. Cibber, told her that she "pranced her galloping nags too fast, for she went beyond the post and consequently was jockeyed".

Georgiane's success in *Cleone* raised her prestige considerably and she was in great favour with the public at this time. The failure of a new version of *Cymbeline* was attributed to her refusal to take the part of Imogen, which had to be played by Mrs. Vincent.

It had been arranged that Georgiane's benefit this season (1758–59) should take place on March 19th, but as this happened to be the evening Mrs. Cibber had fixed for her benefit at Drury Lane and as many of the same people would wish to attend both performances, Georgiane wisely decided to defer hers and asked Mrs. Hamilton to exchange dates with her. The credit of having the first benefit of the season appealed to Mrs. Hamilton, who chose as her play the *Rival Queens*, in which she would play Roxana. Mrs. Bellamy readily agreed to play Statira with her.

Mrs. Hamilton's following came chiefly from the less expensive parts of the house, and a large concourse of her supporters attended. When the gallery was overflowing, Mrs. Hamilton invited her friends to occupy the boxes and the places on the stage usually reserved for the more fashionable members of the audience, "wisely preferring their two shillings apiece to empty benches." It had been a very rainy afternoon, and, according to Georgiane, "the heat of the house occasioned the wet clothes of the dripping audience to send forth odours not quite so sweet as those of Arabia." But still it was not very well-mannered of her to drench her handkerchief with lavender water and ostentatiously hold it to her face even while she was on the stage. Ross, who was playing Alexander, and happened that night to be in a good mood for acting, was rather annoyed that she would not face him and asked why she kept turning her head away. She confessed that she did it because she was just suffocated with the stench; the people, she said, smelled so of tripe that they were horribly offensive.

At the earliest opportunity Ross hastened to tell Mrs. Hamilton that Mrs. Bellamy had said that her audience stunk; but Mrs. Hamilton, though deeply offended, decided to bide her time before taking her revenge. She waited until half-past six on the very evening of Mrs. Bellamy's own benefit a few days later, and then, just before the curtain was due to rise on the *Careless Husband*, sent to inform her that she would not play the part of Lady Graveairs, for which she had been announced. It was, therefore, necessary that an apology should be made to the audience for the delay in starting. This should have been done by Ross, who was playing Sir Charles Easy, but he flatly refused to do it. He loved mischief like a schoolboy and was thoroughly enjoying the situation. Smith, who was playing Lord Foppington, was too frightened to face the audience with such an announcement, so Georgiane herself had to appear before the curtain in the flounces and furbelows of Lady Betty Modish and request the audience's patience until Mrs. Vincent could dress for the part which Mrs. Hamilton was to have performed.

The audience rather unjustly sided with Mrs. Bellamy, and two nights later expressed their disapproval of Mrs. Hamilton with hisses when she appeared in the *Spanish Friar* as the Queen, all bedizened with the flashy false jewels of which she was so inordinately fond that Colley Cibber had once compared her head to a furze bush stuck round with glow-worms. But Mrs. Hamilton was not easily cowed by such demonstrations; she came down stage and thus addressed the audience: "Gemmen and ladies! I suppose as how you hiss me, because I did not play at Mrs. Bellamy's benefit. I would have performed, but she said as how my audience stunk, and were all tripe people." The audience were delighted by her frankness, loudly encored her and cried out: "Well said, Tripe!" And the name stuck to her ever after. Georgiane was playing the part of Elvira for the first time that evening.

After a whole year's absence from the stage Miss Nossiter had come back to Covent Garden for this season, making her first appearance as Dorinda in the *Beaux Stratagem*. Her friendship with Georgiane had now grown into an intimacy, and they liked to appear as often as possible in the same play. Both the *Rival Queens* and the *Mourning Bride* were suited to this purpose, and were therefore often repeated during this season. When *Jane Shore* was revived for Miss Nossiter's benefit on April 5th, Georgiane resigned her usual part of Alicia to her friend, and herself played Jane Shore, a part which had less appeal for her. Georgiane found Miss Nossiter even more agreeable off the stage, and invited her to spend all her spare time with her at Parliament Street.

Being convinced that Calcraft really was going to pay off her debts at the end of the season, Georgiane proposed to go away for a short visit to Holland. But he was to disappoint her once again. He went to Lady Tyrawley and asked her to intercede with Georgiane to have patience for another year, since a very great loss had put it out of his power to pay them now. At this time Georgiane imagined that he had received a full list of the debts from Clifford, but she found out afterwards that he had never even asked for one, which convinced her that even then he never had the slightest intention of paying them. In the circumstances she thought she had better try to do something about them herself. She borrowed £2,000 on her jewels from Bibby, the pawnbroker, of Stanhope Street, Clare Market, and, adding this to the money she had received at her benefit, paid her creditors as far as it would go, reserving £200 for her journey to Holland, where she stayed for some weeks at Amsterdam and the Hague.

On her return to England, Rich approached her with a view to an engagement at Covent Garden for the following season. But the prospect did not appeal to her. Except for the production of *Cleone*, Covent Garden had not been very successful last season and there had been no leading actor worthy to take the place of Barry, who had returned to Ireland and had launched a new theatrical venture at the Crow Street Theatre in Dublin in partnership with Woodward, who had left Drury Lane after a disagreement with Garrick. It was Woodward who was putting up the money for the project, for Barry had not a penny and was deeply in debt. But Barry was silver-tongued off the stage as well as on it—Rich had said of him that he was "capable of wheedling a bird from the tree and then squeezing it to death in his hand"—and he had had little difficulty in extracting the money out of the usually hard-headed Woodward. The venture appeared to be going well, and Georgiane was rather attracted by the idea of joining the new company, when Woodward wrote asking her to do so. But she did not want to make a decision so many months ahead, and wrote to him that, if she did decide to come to Ireland, she would give him the preference over anyone else.

She had come back from Holland in the best of health, but feeling very gloomy and depressed. Though living in the same house, she and Calcraft rarely met except now and then at dinner. If she were not entertaining at home, she invariably went out. On New Year's Day she gave her customary concert and ball, and on this occasion the ball was opened by Count de Bathmore, the Danish Minister, with the Countess of Harrington. Calcraft was not present, but rather surprised her by sending her a hundred guineas by the House Steward as a contribution to the expense of the entertainment. When she went to her apartment after the ball, her woman, Clifford, wished her joy of the hundred guineas and told her that Mr. Calcraft had been very much afraid that she would not have her usual entertainment that day, as it would have prevented him from keeping his assignation with his paramour.

For some time past Clifford had been hinting to Georgiane that he was having an intrigue with a married woman who was one of her most intimate friends. Georgiane had refused to believe this, but now she began to think that there might be something in it, and she consented to go one evening with Clifford and "convince herself by ocular demonstration that her female friend was one of the most worthless of women". She surprised them *in flagrante delicto* together at a house in Leicester Square. As soon as she had left them, Calcraft hurried after her to persuade her not to give him away, as he feared he might be prosecuted by the deceived husband for criminal conversation with his wife. Georgiane consented, but this incident was the last straw, and she made up her mind to leave him the moment he had redeemed his promise to pay her debts, as he had undertaken to do at the end of the season, which would be in about three months time. During these three months they did not meet more than twice.

When the time of the promised settlement was due, Georgiane went again to consult Lady Tyrawley, who advised her to have the whole thing out with Calcraft, and, if he did not consent to what she asked, though she was sure he would, to leave his house immediately. This Georgiane determined to do and, even though she must have known that it would be imprudent to leave Parliament Street before her affairs were settled, she decided to speak to Calcraft that very evening, and to set out next morning for Bristol, if he continued to prevaricate. And so, on returning from Somerset House, she instructed Clifford to seal up the receipts for the jewellery she had bought from Lazarus, Maisonneuve, and Deard, and for which she had paid some £6,000. She had pledged them all with Bibby, retaining only the jewels left to her by Miss Meredith. She also told Clifford to order her chaise and four to be ready at six o'clock next morning and to do the packing necessary for her journey.

She dined alone with Calcraft that evening. It was rare for her to do so. But Mrs. Walker, whom she had warned of her intentions, purposely absented herself. She too was getting ready to leave with Georgiane, since neither of them shared Lady Tyrawley's sanguine belief that Calcraft would keep his promise. At last Georgiane brought herself to broach the difficult subject; she told Calcraft frankly that she was over-whelmed with debt, and that he had deceived her beyond a possibility of reparation. Calcraft remarked that late hours had affected her health and consequently made her low-spirited. Did she not enjoy every pleasure that the world could afford? He then commented on her extravagance. As for her debts, he would be satisfied that she had some regard for him before he parted with so large a sum.

Georgiane replied hotly that, considering the terms they had been on since she had discovered the cruel deception he had made use of to ruin her, he had no possible right to censure her conduct. And, as to showing any regard for him, she neither had professed, nor ever could profess that she had any. What she now required from him was simply the performance of a promise which she claimed as a debt from him. He ought to consider such a promise as binding, even if her debts had not been largely incurred on keeping up his household. But as he knew that they had been, it rendered the obligation still stronger. And she demanded an immediate and positive answer. Calcraft returned an unhesitating refusal.

Georgiane had been fully prepared for this. She now fell back on her alternative proposal. If he would not keep his promise to pay her debts, would he lend her £2,400 on the jewels she had pledged for £2,000? She had added the £400, as the interest had accumulated in the meantime, and she had no ready money for her journey to Bristol. Calcraft said that he would give her £2,000, but demurred at the extra £400. She flatly refused to take less, and in the end he gave in and produced the money. In exchange she handed over to him the receipts for the jewellery, which proved their value, requesting him to dispose of them as soon as he could, and, after repaying himself the money he was now advancing, to let her have the remainder to pay her creditors. To this he agreed.

Calcraft was there when the chaise came to the door at the appointed time. Since their little daughter was to return to her school at Campden House that day, he affected to believe that the carriage was there for that purpose, but observed that it seemed unnecessary to have four horses for so short a way. Georgiane retorted that she was going a great way, for she proposed to lie at Reading that night. And, since the horses were her own, she presumed she had a right to make use of them. Calcraft turned as pale as death, though he had actually been informed by Mrs. Walker of Georgiane's intention to leave him. But it was "with the most calm and apparently unaffected indifference" that he handed her into the carriage. Georgiane bade farewell to him, adding that they would never, she hoped, meet again.

At Salt Hill, on the Road to Maidenhead, she encountered Henry Fox and told him all that had happened. He blamed her for leaving the house before her affairs were settled, and earnestly begged her to return before it was too late. He said, moreover, that Calcraft had been hinting that she "entertained a partiality" for a certain noble earl—the Earl of Harrington— and that her leaving his house so suddenly would tend to confirm his suspicions. But Georgiane was feeling as if she had at last escaped after a long imprisonment, and she drove on into the West.

Chapter Thirteen

WHILE SHE WAS IN BRISTOL Georgiane received a letter from Mossop making her very advantageous offers to appear in Dublin. Much to the disgust of Barry and Woodward, he had deserted them and was about to launch out on management on his own. He was hoping to initiate a successful venture at the Smock Alley Theatre, which he had had re-decorated and provided with new scenery and a new wardrobe, and he thought that his fortune would be made if he could persuade a fashionable actress of Mrs. Bellamy's status and reputation to appear with him, even if at first it were to cost him more than he could well afford. Superficially, he had good reason for taking this view. Georgiane's fame still endured in Dublin, where on her former visit she had had a great success socially as well as in the theatre and was remembered as having been a very promising actress and a beautiful and charming girl. And since then she had made a great name for herself playing leading parts with brilliant success in both the great London theatres. No doubt Mossop was also influenced by the thought that this seemed a very propitious moment to approach her, for he had heard that her financial embarrassment was such that, for the time being at least, she could not safely appear on the stage in London. He could, therefore, put a very tempting offer before her.

In her reply, Georgiane frankly informed him of the promise she had already made to Woodward that she would join his company if she did come to Ireland. She also wrote to tell Woodward of the offer Mossop had made her, and said that she would still give him and Barry the preference, if they would agree to her terms, which would be a thousand guineas for the season with two benefits. And when, after a reasonable time had elapsed, she had received no reply from him, she closed with Mossop's offer on the same terms, with the additional proviso that she should act only what she pleased. Mossop himself hastened down to Bristol to bring her the agreement to sign.

The Irish manager was so elated with his success in engaging Georgiane that, on his return to London, he boasted of it everywhere, and the news soon reached Calcraft. He was so perturbed by it that he wrote to Lord Tyrawley, who was then at Bath, begging him to go over to Bristol and try to persuade Georgiane to return to him on whatever terms she pleased. Her father at once went over to see her, accompanied by Quin and General Honeywood. Both Tyrawley and Quin did their utmost to dissuade her from this Irish adventure and make her go back to Calcraft in her own interests, but she remained inflexible in her determination. She did not tell her father that one of the chief causes of her obstinacy was that, if she broke her agreement with Mossop, she would have to pay him £2,000, and that she was perfectly certain that Calcraft would never pay it for her. But she declares that, in any case, nothing now would have induced her to return to Calcraft because of his meanness and his refusal to pay her debts after repeatedly promising to do so. Her dislike and contempt for him had become ineradicable. When her visitors were leaving, Quin rallyingly bet her a hundred guineas that she would not go to Ireland after all. And she says that, when she did go, he sent her the money without being reminded of it, together with a letter assuring her of his unalterable friendship.

Shortly afterwards Georgiane set out for Ireland. She had a very disagreeable and uncomfortable journey over bad roads across country from Bristol to Chester, where she was met by her servants with her baggage, plate, theatrical wardrobe, and, in fact, everything she required except the money she was expecting Calcraft to send her from the sale of her jewels after he had deducted the £2,000 he had advanced to her. There was, however, a very odd letter from Calcraft himself. "Christ Jesus God," he wrote, "why do you keep me in this torment? If you will not write, tell me so, and make me completely miserable. I have had a letter from my Lord, and have seen that to your maid; by which I find you are unalterable in your resolution. I hate Holwood, and every place which reminds me how happy I have been in your company. Caroline has almost broke my heart with shewing me the sweet letter which accompanied your fairing. Every body is made happy but me; but vexation and the gout will soon relieve you from the man you hate. I have ordered the plate, your new sedan, and books to be sent you. I have sent you the parchment I have found, which I suppose is the counterpart of your annuity; but depend upon it, I shall not think it sufficient for your support. For God's sake write to me, and be assured whilst I have breath, I am affectionately yours.

"JOHN CALCRAFT."

The parchment he alludes to was not the counterpart of her annuity, but the document given to her by Mr. Davy when he had lent her the £500. It showed that she had sold her annuity conditionally, and she was certain that Calcraft would have examined it and must have known perfectly well that it was not what he professed to think it was, for it was marked in large letters on the back "Counterpart of the deed of annuity assigned to—Morris in trust for Mr. Davy".

At Parkgate she found that the packet was not ready to sail, and, as she was afraid of infringing her agreement by arriving in Dublin too late for the opening of the theatrical season, she decided to press on to Holyhead and sail from there. In the drooping state of her spirits the journey was a melancholy progress, and at the inns where she spent the night there always seemed to be someone playing the Welsh harp, which depressed her still further, for the ditties they played seemed to suit all too well the gloomy temperature of her mind. The weather was wild and stormy, and at Conway the wind was too high for the ferry-boat to venture the crossing, so that she was obliged to spend the night at the ferry-house. But this proved to be an unexpectedly pleasant interlude. It was true that all the people who had been detained had to spend the evening together in one not very large room, and there were a great many of them, besides her own party, which consisted of a guide, two postillions, two footmen, and three maids; but she was surprised to be given one of the best suppers she had ever sat down to at an inn, and later she was accommodated for the night in a very good bed in a small neat bedroom.

When she reached Holyhead, Georgiane sent her coach and horses with the postillions and footmen back to London. The weather was wilder than ever, and the sea so rough that, although the packet was ready to sail, few of the many people waiting to go over to Ireland were prepared to venture the crossing. But to Georgiane in her present mood of dejection the state of the sea was a matter of indifference, and she decided to embark. She had cause to regret it later; a storm began to rage, the crossing took four days instead of a few hours, and she was so excruciatingly sea-sick, that, when the packet at last made Dunleary, she had to be carried ashore. A coach, sent from Dublin, was fortunately waiting to convey her to a friend's house on College Green.

Owing to her former reputation for beauty and elegance and the trumpeting that had heralded her return to Dublin, a crowd of students had gathered at the front door of the house "in expectation of beholding a wonder". The reality was a dismal disappointment to them, as Georgiane herself was the first to admit. "At length I stepped out of the coach. The long-expected phænomenon now made her appearance. But, oh, how different a figure from what their imagination had depicted! Fashion to yourself the idea of a little dirty creature, bent nearly double, enfeebled by fatigue, her countenance tinged with the jaundice, and in every respect the reverse of a person who could make the least pretensions to beauty. Such was I, when I presented myself to the sight of the gazing crowd. And so great and natural was their surprise and disappointment, that they immediately vanished, and let me crawl into the house, without admiration or molestation." But by the evening she had recovered sufficiently from her weariness and the effects of the sea-sickness to attend a reception at the Parliament House, where she met many of the senior members of Trinity College and the Provost himself. Many others, having heard of the disappointment her appearance had caused in the morning, came out of curiosity to see her, but were agreeably surprised, for, as she herself says, "nothing is so favourable to an object as exaggerated dispraise," and, now that she had had time to bath and rest and attire herself with her usual elegant simplicity, she was able to make a more favourable impression than could have been expected.

Next morning Mossop came to congratulate her on her safe arrival. He had a rather disturbing piece of news to tell her. It appeared that, when Woodward had heard that she had engaged herself with Mossop, he had been laid up with a fever in Cork where he had gone to open a theatre he and Barry were starting there. He had been very angry and had sent Barry her letter promising them the preference, and Barry had promptly posted it up in one of the principal coffee-houses in Dublin. The implication that she had played them a shabby trick could not fail to do her harm, whatever explanations might be forthcoming.

The haste with which she had made her journey to Ireland proved to have been unnecessary, for on October 25th King George II died, and the theatres remained closed for several weeks. In the meantime Georgiane took a furnished house in Frederick Street, and, while waiting for the season to begin, enterained with the lavishness to which of late years she had become accustomed. She had also become accustomed to not paying her bills, and she obtained her wine and other supplies on credit through her old admirer, Mr. Crump, who had eagerly waited upon her immediately after her arrival.

The theatres opened on November 17th, but Georgiane was not due to make her first appearance for another fortnight. There was great rivalry between the two theatres, each of which was favoured by a section of Dublin high society. The principal patronesses of the Smock Alley Theatre were the influential countesses of Kildare, and Powerscourt. Their support was very necessary, for Georgiane herself considered that the Smock Alley company was greatly inferior to that at the Crow Street Theatre, which besides the famous and popular Barry and the accomplished comedian, Woodward, included Mrs. Abington, Mrs. Fitzhenry, and a promising newcomer, Mrs. Dancer, who was later to become Barry's wife and to acquire fame for herself as Anne Spranger Barry. The Smock Alley Company, on the other hand, reminded Georgiane of "Sir John Falstaff's ragged regiment, a part of which he had robbed the gibbets of".

Mrs. Bellamy had been billed to make her first appearance as Belvidera in *Venice Preserved* on the night of December 1st. Great expectations had been aroused, and, as was often the case in those days, the rival house tried to take some of the wind out of her sails by staging the same play on the same night. But Mrs. Bellamy's return to the scene of her former triumphs had aroused such eager curiosity that the Smock Alley Theatre was given the preference by the public that night; the house was crowded to capacity, and the audience was waiting on tenter-hooks for her first appearance. A celebrated account of the performance was recorded by the actor, Tate Wilkinson, who, it must be remembered, was not himself present at it. "On speaking her first line behind the scenes—'Lead me, ye virgins, lead me to that kind voice'—it struck the ears of the audience as uncouth and unmusical; yet she was received as was prepared and determined by all who were her or Mr. Mossop's friends, and the public at large, with repeated plaudits on her entrée. But the roses were fled! the young, the once lovely Bellamy was turned haggard! and her eyes that used to charm all hearts appeared sunk, large, hollow, and ghastly. O time! time! thy glass should be often consulted! for before the short first scene had elapsed, disappointment chagrin, and pity sat on every eye and countenance. . . . By the end of the third act, they were all (like Bobadil) planet-struck; the other two acts were hobbled through. Mossop was cut to the heart, and never played Pierre (one of his best parts) so indifferently as on that night. The curtain dropped, and poor Bellamy never after drew a single house there. . . . What a change from the days of her youth! and, as an actress of note, her name never more ranked in any theatre, nor did she ever again rise in public estimation."

Now while there seems to be no sort of doubt that Georgiane's appearance on this occasion did cause great disappointment and possibly did mark the beginning of the gradual failure of her powers as an actress, in this account, which he must have heard at second-hand on a visit to Dublin some time later and which, in any event, was written many years after Mrs. Bellamy's final eclipse, Tate Wilkinson does seem to have let himself be carried into exaggeration by the drama of a story he obviously enjoyed writing so much that he forgot for the moment that Mrs. Bellamy appeared regularly and with great success the following season at Covent Garden and that two years later he himself played with her in Edinburgh, where he stated that she was in great beauty and reputation and was "a tower of strength" in the company.

Georgiane herself admitted that she was by no means so well received at the beginning of the season as she formerly had been, and that it hurt her greatly. But she attributed her lack of success to the fact that she was at first almost single-handed to face the competition from the rival company, which was so strong that it would have done credit to a London theatre. But the Smock Alley company was shortly afterwards reinforced by a capable comic actor, Brown, and by West Digges, who was already a great favourite in Dublin, especially among the ladies. With their coming, the standard of acting in the company improved, and henceforth they had more than their share of public favour. And it is quite untrue that Georgiane herself never afterwards drew a single house in Dublin; notably she scored a personal triumph in *Cleone*, the part which she had first created and in which she was acknowledged to be unrivalled.

West Digges, whom Georgiane had not encountered before, was a man of high aristocratic connections to whom the call of the theatre had proved an irresistible vocation. His father came of a good old Kentish family, and his mother was a sister of the first Earl de la Warr. He had started his career in the army as an Ensign in the 44th (Lee's) regiment of Foot, but his extravagant habits had speedily got him into trouble, and his uncle, Lord de la Warr, had requested the War Office to transfer him to garrison duty in Gibraltar or Minorca, where he might have less scope for spending. But Digges had preferred the stage to exile and in 1749 had made his theatrical début at this very theatre in Dublin as Jaffier in *Venice Preserved*.

He had always remained very much the fine gentleman, and was admired everywhere for the elegance of his appearance and dress and the ease of his bearing and manners. James Boswell, who knew him well, admired him so much that he aspired to model himself on him. "Talk gently and Digges-like. Acquire an easy dignity and black liveliness of behaviour like him," he adjured himself in one of his memoranda. What he meant by "black liveliness" he explains in a passage in his *London Journl*, in which he expatiates on Digges's exquisite manners: "Indeed, I must say Digges has more or as much of the deportment of a man of fashion as anybody I ever saw; and he keeps up this so much that he never once lessened upon me even on an intimate acquaintance, although he is now and then somewhat melancholy, under which it is very difficult to preserve dignity; and this I think is particularly to be admired in Mr. Digges. Indeed, he and I never came to familiarity, which is justly said to beget contempt."

Georgiane and West Digges did, unfortunately for both of them, come to familiarity, and it did in the end beget mutual contempt. But this was not to happen yet. At first, having been warned that he was a plausible and dangerous Don Juan, Georgiane decided to keep him at arm's length. She was free to admit that he was handsome and talented and possessed the art of persuading those with whom he conversed that he was the best of men, but as his character was universally known to be that of a man of gallantry and she did not want any more entanglements of that nature, she declined to receive him as a visitor in her own house.

Mossop decided to put on *The Orphan of China*, with Mrs. Bellamy as Mandane. This adaptation by Murphy of Voltaire's play had been a great success during the previous season at Drury Lane. More appropriate dressing for plays had recently become the fashion, and the magnificent costumes to be worn by Mossop and Mrs. Bellamy were ordered from London. But there was some difficulty in providing costumes for the rest of the cast, since Mossop had quarrelled with the tailor, Tracey, who flatly refused to give him credit—and credit in the present state of his finances was essential to him. The matter was very urgent, because the other house had also announced the piece and had already published glowing accounts of the clothes and decorations they were expecting from London, so that it was imperative to get in ahead of them. Georgiane undertook to mollify Tracey and was so successful in her cajolements that in the end he consented not only to make the dresses and expedite the making of them, but also to find the materials. By dint of rehearsing three times a day the Smock Alley company got the piece ready in a week and were able to give eight performances before large audiences and to skim all the cream before the costumes for the other house arrived from London.

Georgiane rarely if ever replied to the letters she continued to receive from Calcraft, who seems at first to have thought that she had merely left him in a tantrum and would eventually return to him. On January 17th, 1761, he wrote to her in desperation:

"MY DEAREST GEORGIANE,

"Packet after packet arrives from Ireland without a letter from you: why won't you write, and fully? I never am so well pleased as when I hear fully from you; nor ever so uneasy as when I do not. The children are both well, and charming ones. I have been with my brother to Poole this week, and have secured his election, I hope, without opposition. Pray do write. You don't know the distress your neglect occasions to

"Yours ever and ever,

"J.C."

But Georgiane regarded the break as final and had no intention of going back to him. This letter, like the others, remained unanswered.

In the meantime, West Digges had fallen a victim to Georgiane's charms and had resolved upon her conquest. In view of her aloof attitude towards him, this experienced philanderer, conversant with all the wiles whereby a woman's heart may be softened, determined to proceed very warily; he sighed at a distance and treated her always with such profound respect that at last she began to think that the character she had been given of him was much exaggerated.

Presently she allowed herself to be persuaded by a lady of their mutual acquaintance to admit him into her house as a visitor. She continued to find him most polite and respectful, and thought him a most entertaining companion. Nor did he ever venture to declare his passion until he fell ill—or pretended to do so, when he started to write her the most affecting letters telling her that his unrequited love for her was the sole cause of his malady. She began to soften towards him, and, to use her own words, "a circumstance soon after happened, which helped to forward the attainment of his wishes".

Her reckless extravagance was once more getting her into trouble. Although she received fifty guineas a week, being the only member of the company who was regularly paid, she never had any ready money to hand owing to what she airily

called her own thoughtlessness together with the wastefulness
of her servants, over whose expenditure she never attempted to
keep any sort of control. Her account with Mr. Crump for
wine and other supplies had now amounted to £400. She paid
half and proposed to pay the rest after her benefit, which she
thought would be in good time. And so, when she heard that
her friend, Mr. Crump, had failed and that a business associate
of his, one Hosea Cotes, had taken possession of his effects and
books, she was only faintly perturbed. Mr. Cotes would surely
be willing to wait a week or two for payment. But she did not
know that Mr. Cotes happened to be a shareholder of the Crow
Street Theatre, and for this reason had no cause to feel indulgent towards any members of the rival company and, most
of all, their leading lady, who was a formidable menace to his
own interests.

One day, shortly after she had heard the news of Crump's
failure, Georgiane noticed that a mean-looking fellow seemed
to be following her about everywhere she went in the magnificent sedan-chair which she had brought over with her and in
which she was always carried abroad. He was running beside
the chair when she went in the morning to a rehearsal of
Coriolanus, he loitered about outside the house when she went
to pay a call on a friend, and he was still accompanying her
when she returned home to dine. She thought little of it and
attributed his presence to curiosity about her sedan, which was
in the very latest fashion, and was always an object of great
admiration in Dublin. But on setting out rather later than
usual for the theatre after dinner that evening, she was
astonished to find that he was still dancing attendance on her.
At last, just as her chairmen were entering Damask Street, he
revealed the purpose of his presence. He knocked at the front
window of the sedan, and, when she let down the glass to ask
what he wanted, displayed a paper which he informed her was a
writ for the £200 she owed to Mr. Cotes, as Crump's
successor. He told her that he was instructed to attach her
person and must insist upon her accompanying him. She

promised him that he should have the money forthwith and a handsome present for himself in addition if he would go to the theatre, but he peremptorily refused, on the ground that he had particular orders to the contrary from the plaintiff. Georgiane realised that she had no alternative but to comply and suffered herself to be taken to a sponging-house in Skinner Row. She immediately sent for Cotes, but he was nowhere to be found, and the man who had arrested her now told her quite candidly that the reason why they had waited until the evening to take her was to prevent her from appearing at the theatre that night. Cotes's little scheme had been very effective; there had to be a scratch performance at Smock Alley, and Mrs. Bellamy's part had to be read by another actress, Mrs. Usher.

As soon as the performance was over, Mossop hastened to try to get her released, but Cotes, who had given strict instructions that the affair was to be settled by nobody but himself, took good care to keep out of the way and was not run to earth till two o'clock in the morning, when he had the impudence to admit that he knew he could easily have got the money by applying to the theatre, but had determined to prevent Mrs. Bellamy from playing that night. "Everything," he said, "is fair, where interests clash."

Mossop was exceedingly angry and was eager to chastise the insolent Cotes, but West Digges, constituting himself Georgiane's champion, insisted upon taking this congenial task upon himself and performed it so efficaciously that, for fear of being prosecuted for assault and battery, he found it expedient to leave Dublin in a hurry. And in any case his own debts made it convenient for him to do so.

Before he left, he wrote to Georgiane, earnestly requesting a last interview with her. She consented. It proved to be a fatal mistake, for his attractions coupled with her gratitude for his chivalry induced her to enter into what she calls a "serious connection" with him, which "though not binding to a person of her religious persuasion, was notwithstanding valid to all intents and purposes".

What the exact nature of this mysterious connection was and whether any kind of matrimonial ceremony was involved in it have never transpired; but, in any event, any such ceremony would not have been valid, for, whether she knew it or not, West Digges at this time was already married. And quite apart from this, he always appeared to have regarded their union as less binding than she professed to do, for during one of the quarrels about each other's extravagance which frequently arose between them while they were together, he is reputed to have said: "Madam, I give you leave to treat me like a foot-pad; rob me and let me go, but don't tie me neck and heels."

About this time Georgiane received a letter from Alderman Cracroft, to whom she had entrusted the management of her affairs in London during her absence, informing her that Mr. Davy's attorney had been instructed to sue her for the arrears due on her annuity, unless she would send over a power of attorney enabling him to claim directly from Calcraft, who had refused to pay it. Georgiane, who imagined—or, at any rate, says she imagined—that the annuity had been regularly paid, immediately and indignantly signed the power of attorney and sent it back to the Alderman. She heard later that Calcraft had treated the person sent to make the demand upon him so cavalierly that he himself had been arrested, and, furious at such an indignity being offered to a man of his great consequence, had thrown the cause into Chancery, where it remained in suspense during Davy's life, that gentleman being too wealthy and indolent to pursue it.

The Smock Alley theatre closed down early in June, 1761, but Georgiane, probably not without the insistent persuasion of her Dublin creditors, remained on in Ireland until the middle of the summer. Since Mossop was unable to pay her all he owed her, she was obliged to borrow £400 to settle her affairs before she could leave. She pawned her jewellery and all her valuables, including a gold and enamel snuff-box recently given to her by Lady Kildare.

Being far from well, she found the long journey back to

England beyond her strength, and at Chester was taken so ill that she had to remain there for several days. On her recovery two ladies, who had travelled with her from Ireland and had kindly delayed their own journey so that they might see her safely to London, persuaded her to go to a concert in Chester, where she encountered Mr. Crump. As she had heard nothing of or from him since the unpleasant incident of her arrest in Dublin, she supposed he knew all about it and had consented to the action taken by Cotes, but, to her great surprise, he came up to her and saluted her with his usual cordiality as if nothing untoward had interfered with their relationship. Explanations followed, and she discovered that he was utterly ignorant of the whole affair.

On hearing from her what had happened, he left the concert abruptly and she afterwards heard that he had gone straight off to Ireland to reckon with Cotes, who, however, heard of his coming and hastily betook himself to England to escape his wrath. The unfortunate and much injured Mr. Crump who, it appears, had for some time been showing traces of insanity, shortly afterwards died raving mad. It is, perhaps, a little surprising that others who were caught up in the tortuous and chaotic tangle of Mrs. Bellamy's financial affairs did not undergo the same fate.

Chapter Fourteen

ON HER ARRIVAL IN LONDON Georgiane went to her former lodgings in Chelsea and wrote to Alderman Cracroft saying she would wait upon him in a few days time in order to discuss her affairs. It was imperative that something should be done to settle them, but she could not hope to do so while she was openly living with West Digges, as those persons who would be willing to assist her would not care to do so while he was with her. Fortunately, he had accepted an invitation to return to act in Edinburgh, where his reputation as an actor stood very high.

When she went to see the Alderman, his first question was whether she had any engagement at the theatre. She told him that she had not and that she could not make one until her affairs were settled. To her astonishment he told her that this was going to be very difficult, since the amount that she owed was considerably more than she had given him to suppose. This again astonished her—or at any rate she said it did. She had imagined that Calcraft would have used the overplus from the sale of her jewels for the payment of her debts. Since they had cost her some £6,000, and she had given Calcraft all the receipts for them to prove this, she had thought that they would realise at least £4,000, and that therefore, after he had repaid himself the £2,000 he had advanced her, ample funds would have been available to pay off everything she owed. But the Alderman told her that Calcraft had delivered all her jewels to Mr. Jeffries, a sword-cutler in the Strand, who, by his orders, had broken them up, and that they had fetched only £1,100. According to her account, they included a windmill which, upon being wound up, went for three hours, and a "cap, set in a style peculiarly elegant". She requested the Alderman to write to Calcraft for an explanation. But her astonishment and embarrassment were only increased by Calcraft's reply, in which he stated that, after her departure for Ireland, he had received a complete list of her debts from her maid, Clifford, who had left her to get married, and that they amounted to no less than £10,300. On the receipt of this news, she says that her courage entirely forsook her—and no wonder.

The Alderman now tentatively suggested that she might take the benefit of a recent Act of Insolvency and go bankrupt, but she replied that she was incapable of such a thought. In her, she said, it would be the blackest fraud, for hers were debts which she admitted had been contracted from extravagant thoughtlessness, and not like those of the fair trader, which were generally the consequences of losses and misfortunes. She would prefer to throw herself on the mercy of her creditors, to whom, if they would allow her time, she would appropriate the whole of her theatrical salary, reserving only the proceeds of her benefit for her own support. The Alderman applauded her resolution and undertook to draw up for her a letter of licence, which he thought all her creditors, as well as himself, would be willing to sign. He was as good as his word and, with his usual generosity, also advanced her some money for her present needs.

The letter of licence drawn up by Cracroft was duly signed by all her creditors, except one, who said that she never signed any document of this kind on principle, but that she would never proceed to any violent measure for the recovery of her debt. This creditor was her lace woman, but also dealt in "every other article necessary for a lady's toilet", and the amount owing to her was considerable. But Georgiane was not worried, for it seemed at this time that she would have no difficulty in keeping her side of the bargain; Rich received her with open arms and at once engaged her for the forthcoming season at Covent Garden.

Shortly afterwards she discovered that she had been deceived about the fate of her jewellery. One evening, on a visit to Lady St. Leger, she saw a lady wearing a pair of her bracelets. She could not possibly be mistaken about them, as they had on them her initials in diamonds and also in blue enamel set around with brilliants. On enquiry she found that Calcraft himself had made a present of them to the lady who was wearing them. And later Lady Harrington told her that he had presented her successor in his favours with her best diamond ear-rings which had cost her £570, and several other valuable pieces of her jewellery, including the pink diamond ring she had inherited from her aunt, Miss O'Hara. She was no longer at a loss to know how her jewels could have been disposed of for as little as £1,100, and at once ordered a suit to be commenced against Calcraft for the whole value of them. This suit was 'amicably settled' the following March, but nothing, in Georgiane's eyes, could compensate her for the insult and injury.

At the beginning of the theatrical season she took a house in Jermyn Street. She intimates that "by a most fortunate *political* event" she was enabled to live in a degree of elegance little inferior to what she had been accustomed to but does not explain in her *Apology* what this "political event" was. She does, however, let fall certain hints in her suppressed letter to Calcraft. It seems that a number of political personalities, among whom was a certain Lord H., were willing to pay handsomely for the privilege of using her house as a convenient place where they could meet for political juntos without giving the impression that such was the purpose of their meeting. The supposed hostess was rarely if ever present. "Indeed, the visitors only paid me short *How d'yes* before they met. And I can with truth affirm, I was never of the company but that once; as I declined having any knowledge of their politics or holding any conversation with persons in that line." There seems good reason to conclude that her visitors were certain members of the Tory Party, who at this time were beginning to abandon their old opposition to the Hanoverian dynasty and to enter the political area as loyal supporters of the young King, George III. They had already gained a foothold at Court; six Tories had been appointed Grooms of the Bedchamber, and the Tory Earl of Huntingdon, who had been Master of the Horse to the King when Prince of Wales, had been promoted on April 3rd from being Master of the Horse to the King to the more important political office of Groom of the Stole and First Lord of the Bedchamber. There can be no doubt that he was the mysterious Lord H., though Calcraft, who was well aware of the fact, maliciously made mischief for Georgiane by informing Lady Harrington that the Lord H., whose name was being coupled with that of Georgiane, was her own husband. As a consequence of this slander Lady Harrington had withdrawn her favour from her. Georgiane indignantly denies that she ever had any sort of intrigue with Harrington, for whom she had the utmost respect, or, for that matter, with the "noble earl at the Stable-yard" (Huntingdon's official residence). And at this time in particular, she affected to regard herself as a respectable married woman. But she was concealing her association with Digges from the world, and her living alone did subject her to a number of offers to afford her a somewhat equivocal protection. She boasts that one gentleman offered her £10,000 to be admitted as a favoured lover. But, she says, notwithstanding ill nature or envy might have suggested insinuations to the contrary, she never, even in thought, deviated from the duty she owed *as she imagined*, to Mr. Digges, whilst the *union* between them existed.

Georgiane made her first appearance this season on September 25th as Juliet, with David Ross as her Romeo. Thereafter she appeared regularly in most of her accustomed parts— Monimia, Athanais, Estifania, Cleone, Desdemona, Zara, Imoinda, Sigismunda, Almeria, Rutland, and Alicia. Whatever Dublin audiences may have thought of her, there was certainly as yet no sign of the falling-off of her popularity with the London public.

On November 13th Rich introduced into his production o *Henry V* a pageant of the procession from the Abbey at the Coronation, doubtless in honour of the Coronation of King George III, which had taken place two months before. In order to prevent the principal performers from refusing to appear in it, for few of them had much sympathy with his passion for pure spectacle, Rich himself proposed to walk in the procession as the Queen's chamberlain. Unfortunately, he was taken ill at the final rehearsal, and never even had the pleasure of seeing this last and most magnificent spectacle of his devising. He died on November 26th. Georgiane, who was playing Katherine, took part in the procession every night. The play was acted no less than twenty-three times in succession and it must have gratified Rich as he lay dying to know that it was mainly to his pageant that the success was due. No great regard can have been paid to accuracy in the costumes, for the same procession was later introduced into all the other historical plays of Shakespeare staged that season—*Henry IV, Part II, Richard III* and *King John*.

The only part not already familiar to her which Georgiane played this winter was that of Miss Grantham in *The Liar*, first produced on January 12th, 1762. This was supposed to be an entirely new play, never acted before, but the truth was that it was an adaptation by Foote of Steele's adaptation of Corneille's version of the original Spanish play by Lope de Vega. It was given four performances.

Georgiane carefully avoided meeting Calcraft after her return from Ireland, and she refused even to see her children if she could only see them in his presence. But one evening in the autumn he attended a performance of *Zara* at Covent Garden, and the very sight of her seems to have revived his passion for her. He began by writing letters to her proposing a reconciliation, but they remained unanswered. Then, one Sunday in January, he accosted her in Derby Court and begged her to grant him half an hour's conversation. She refused to listen to him and went home, whereupon he betook himself to a tavern, the Prince of Orange's Head, at the corner of York Street and Jermyn Street, and from there he proceeded to pester her with notes. In a short space of time she received no less than twenty. When she took no notice of them, he forced his way into her house, and, on her refusal to have anything more to do with him, drew his sword and threatened to run himself through with it. Quite unperturbed, Georgiane requested him to refrain from doing so until she could call some witnesses to the tragedy, as she deemed it a crime that such an exalted character should make his exit from life with only one spectator. Furious at having his bluff called, Calcraft returned his sword to its scabbard and took his departure.

His final effort was to send Nurse Carter, who had brought up their children and was now his housekeeper, to try to persuade Georgiane, if she would not become reconciled and return to him, at least to listen to proposals he had to make about the settlement of her debts. Nurse Carter did her best as mediator, and in the end Georgiane said that, if Mr. Calcraft would write to her or send his attorney to her with his proposals, she would be willing to consider them, and to consult Alderman Cracroft on the propriety of her accepting them. Presently one of Calcraft's clerks brought her the proposals, which were to the following effect: he would give her the money to pay off Mr. Sparks's bond of £400; he would compromise all her debts with her creditors if she would consent either to retire to his house in Dorsetshire—a proposition which she rejected out of hand—or to go abroad and remain there for the time being, since none of her creditors would accept less than the full amount of their debts so long as she remained within their reach; and, finally, he would give her an additional annuity of £100, which, with what she was already receiving from him—presumably he meant the annuity which she had assigned to Davy and which he had never paid— would enable her to live in France or Holland until everything had been satisfactorily settled.

Alderman Cracroft advised her to accept these proposals,

and she was the more inclined to do so since an additional reason for taking refuge abroad had also arisen in the meantime. In February the one creditor who had refused to sign her letter of licence had called on her and asked her to give a bond and judgment for the money she owed her. The woman had pointed out that it was a large sum and that, in the event of Mrs. Bellamy's death, her furniture, plate, and other personal effects would secure it for her. Georgiane consented to sign the bond on condition that the security might be given for not less a period than a year, and a few days later she carelessly and unsuspectingly signed the bond without taking the trouble to read it through. But very soon after the woman wrote to her to say that she must insist upon immediate payment of the whole sum owing, otherwise she would put the judgment in force against her. It appeared that, while the bond was for a year, the judgment was only for a month. Fearful of being arrested, Georgiane packed up all her plate, which she deposited with Alderman Cracroft as security for her debt to him, and herself took refuge at her mother's house in Brewer Street. But even there her situation was precarious, and to fly the country at once seemed to be the only wise course to pursue. And so, on the evening of the day she had signed the documents agreeing to Calcraft's proposals, she set off secretly for Harwich with the intention of going to Holland.

As companions on her journey she had Miss Betty Cibber, a granddaughter of Colley Cibber's who was a little weak in the head, and a young man called Smith, for whom she had obtained an appointment as surgeon to a regiment. On their arrival at Harwich, they found that contrary winds would prevent them from sailing, and Georgiane, being afraid that she might be pursued, decided to go and stay in the less conspicuous environment of Manningtree until the wind should change. While they were seated at supper that evening, they heard the clatter of a chaise arriving in the inn yard, and a few minutes later, to her great surprise, West Digges made his appearance, and in a masterful, not to say truculent mood. He told her that he would not be deserted in this manner, and, having ordered her companions to return to London, he insisted upon carrying her off in his chaise. Georgiane was so terrified by the violence of his temper that she meekly obeyed his injunctions, although she was utterly unprepared for any sort of journey. Her baggage was all at Harwich, and she had no clothes with her but a few shifts, her night-dress, and the travelling habit she was wearing. But Digges was inexorable and, though Georgiane protested that nothing would induce her to go to Edinburgh, insisted upon driving north.

Before they reached the border the little money they had with them was nearly exhausted, so it was agreed that Digges should go on to Edinburgh to raise money and should then send for her to join him somewhere in Scotland. Two days after he left her, a post-chaise arrived, and the driver told her that Mr. Digges had instructed him to take her to the Grass Market, which she says she supposed to be the name of a town. On her arrival in the dark at an inn, she was greeted by a slatternly creature who gave the name of Molly Kershaw, and said that she was a particular friend of Mr. Digges, and had been sent by him to conduct her to the lodgings that had been engaged for her. After they had partaken of a particularly nasty dinner at the inn, they proceeded to the lodgings. Georgiane was not very favourably impressed by them. They were situated on the third floor over a chandler's shop, and she was astonished to be greeted with the sound of music from near by. On her enquiring whence it came, they told her that it was from the theatre in the Canongate, which was directly opposite, and where Mr. Digges was performing that evening in the *Beggar's Opera*. With a shock she realised that, through her ignorance of geography, she had enabled Digges to decoy her to Edinburgh. She was so angry that she forthwith seized a pair of scissors and cut off her hair quite close to her head, so that it would be impossible for her to appear on the stage. Beyond saying that she had somehow taken an unconquerable aversion to Edinburgh, but without being able to assign any reason for it, she gives no explanation of her reluctance to appear there; but the probability is that she considered it beneath the dignity of a leading actress from Covent Garden and Drury Lane to perform in what was, after all, a provincial theatre in the Playhouse Close, a narrow and gloomy alley off the Canongate, which had been opened in 1747 by David Ross, and was at that time the only theatre in Scotland. Its capacity was very limited, and, as the prices of seats were much lower than in London—two shillings and sixpence, one shilling and sixpence, and one shilling—a night's takings, even with a full house, would amount to no more than seventy or eighty pounds.

Next day Digges informed her that the managers of the theatre, Mr. Bates and Mr. Dowson, had acquainted him that it would be useless to open the doors unless he could induce Mrs. Bellamy to appear, since her arrival in Edinburgh was no secret. She could not imagine how this could have happened, since it was not supposed to be known that Digges had brought her there, and, to avert suspicion, it had been arranged that he should continue to live at his own lodgings. They were now faced with a difficult situation. Georgiane had very little money left, and Digges still less, and her letters of credit for Holland were, of course, of no use to her in Scotland. There was no alternative but for her to comply with the managers' wishes. It was very unfortunate that she had cut off her hair, but she overcame this difficulty by having recourse to a wig.

Accordingly, on May 1st, 1762, the following advertisement appeared in the *Edinburgh Courant*:

The following Four PLAYS only will be performed at the Theatre, Canongate,

> *Tancred and Sigismunda*
> *Rule a Wife and Have a Wife*
> *Jane Shore*
> and *The Provoked Husband*

in which a gentlewoman will appear for the first time on the stage of this kingdom.

Tancred and *Sigismunda*, the first play on Wednesday, May 5, to begin at 7. Occasional prologue by Mr. Digges.

The succeeding plays will immediately follow on Thursday, Friday, and Saturday. As these performances will be conducted with the utmost regularity and decorum, no person whatever will be admitted behind the scenes.

The Prologue spoken by Digges on the first night was specially composed for the occasion by the Scottish poet, John Cunningham, who was a member of the company. Georgiane had already met him on her first visit to Dublin, where he had played with her at the Smock Alley Theatre and had distinguished himself less as an actor than as the author of an amiable and successful little farce called *Love in a Mist*. He had been a fervent admirer of hers, and, while in Dublin, had written several poems to her, including one in which he had addressed her as "Enchanting Bellamy".

Although her name was never mentioned in the bills this season, it was an open secret that the anonymous 'gentle-woman' was the celebrated Mrs. Bellamy, and she was received with the acclamation due to her reputation. The *Courant*, though always ready to print advertisements of forthcoming theatrical attractions for payment, rarely noticed the performances themselves, but on this occasion it departed from its usual practice and printed the following paragraph as an item of news: "The expectation of the public was never so highly raised, nor its pleasure so truly gratified, as they have been for some nights at the theatre. The house has been generally filled by five o'clock, and crowds turned away for want of room."

Only four performances had been advertised, but Georgiane had been engaged for eight, and on May 10th another advertisement appeared in the *Courant*: "Many people having been turned from the doors of the Theatre last week for want of room, to satisfy public curiosity, and in obedience to the request of several persons of distinction, the house will continue open one week longer." One of these persons of distinction was the Duchess of Hamilton, and it was by her "particular desires" that, on May 11th, Mrs. Bellamy appeared in *The Provoked Wife*, with Digges as Sir John Brute, a part he had apparently not played before, at any rate in Scotland. *The Orphan*, with Digges as Chamont, followed on May 12th, and *Romeo and Juliet* on May 13th. The parts of Georgiane's youthful lovers were played by a young Scottish actor called John Jackson, who, unfortunately for himself, incurred her displeasure by approaching too near her in the balcony scene of *Romeo and Juliet* and thus screening her from the audience. She was not mollified by his flattering plea that it was impossible for him to refrain from even scaling the wall, if accessible, when so charming an object was in view, and she saw to it that he was not engaged for the next season.

On the morning of the day when her last performance was due, Georgiane was arrested at the instance of her one unrelenting creditor, who had succeeded in discovering her whereabouts. But the arrest proved to be against the laws of Scotland, which allowed some days notice to debtors before they could be taken, so she was released at once and was able to appear that evening as Lady Macbeth. The case later came to trial and was skilfully handled for her by Mr., afterwards Chief Baron, Montgomery, who produced in Court a letter from her creditor, in which the woman admitted that she had deliberately inserted the provision that the judgment should be for a month though the bond was for a year, which showed that the security had been obtained by very dubious methods. The Court made her consent to receive her debt by instalments of £200 a year.

Elated by Georgiane's great success at the theatre, Digges advertised three more plays, but he omitted to consult Georgiane before doing so, and she flatly refused to appear in them, so that he was obliged to announce that there had been a mistake. She did, however, condescend to appear as Cleone for her own benefit on May 22nd; but that was her last appearance this season, which closed on May 29th with the *Beggar's Opera*, in which Digges played his favourite part of Macheath.

Georgiane always maintained that at this time she believed herself to be united to West Digges, but she was never very explicit about the exact nature of the union, nor did she ever state where and when the marriage ceremony, if any, took place. It was true that, in certain circumstances, cohabitation did constitute a legal marriage in Scotland, and, if she was really unaware that he already had a wife, she may have thought that the mere fact of their openly setting up house together made them married by Scottish Law. But, if this was so, why did she not take his name, instead of letting him take hers? Perhaps Digges's temporary adoption of the name of Bellamy in 1762 was an ingenious expedient on his part to avoid the risk of a prosecution for bigamy while he was openly living with Georgiane in Scotland. However, that may be, when, in the autumn of 1762, the name of Mrs. Bellamy appeared for the first time in the bills of the Edinburgh theatre, West Digges also made his bow as 'Mr. Bellamy' after a discreet announcement in the *Courant* that "For family reasons a gentleman of the theatre has been obliged to alter his name in the public bills". With his accustomed courtesy he invariably gave precedence to the name of his alleged spouse. "And let that lady perform whatever character she would," says Tate Wilkinson, "she was always placed at the head of the bill; as, for instance: 'This day *Romeo and Juliet*: Juliet, Mrs. Bellamy: Romeo, Mr. Bellamy.'"

Digges's assumption of the name seems to have been generally accepted; in the *Scots Magazine* for March, 1763, there appeared a poem addressed "To Mr. Bellamy on his perform-ance of the character of Sir John Falstaff, on the Edinburgh Theatre". For this season of 1762–63 it was agreed that Mrs. Bellamy was to have a third of the profits, with two benefits, while Digges was to be on a weekly salary.

As soon as Georgiane had made up her mind that she was

going to remain in Scotland, she had sent to her mother for her theatrical wardrobe and paraphernalia. With them came a young woman named Mary Wordley, who had stage aspirations and, in the elder Mrs. Bellamy's opinion at least, showed promise. She was an intelligent girl and had been well educated by her father, who was steward to the Earl of Powys. Georgiane immediately took a fancy to this lively and high-spirited little creature, who soon became known in the company as the Goddess of Nonsense.

Since Edinburgh was always crowded for race week at the beginning of September, it was decided to open the theatre for a number of performances before the autumn season proper should begin. The little theatre, which had been repainted and redecorated during the summer, opened on Saturday, September 4th, 1762, with the *Provoked Husband*. The next attraction was "*Macbeth*, as written by Shakespeare".

On September 8th an open letter to Digges, quite probably written by himself, or, at least, by an obliging friend, appeared in the *Courant*, asking why "when you have so very capital an actress now on your stage, you chose to neglect gratifying your audience of this city with a tragedy which never failed drawing full houses, and receiving uncommon applause, I mean the favourite tragedy of *Douglas*. You were original in the character of the young man in that excellent piece, and as we must certainly see Lady Randolph excellently played, let me hope you will oblige many of your friends." In response to this appeal, Georgiane appeared as Lady Randolph on September 15th, with Digges in his old part of Norval, which he had created at the first performance six years before. It was announced with great pride that the music and dresses would all be 'Scotch'. This brief preliminary season ended on September 18th with *Rule a Wife and Have a Wife*. The theatre was then closed for a few weeks, but re-opened on November 10th with the *Beggar's Opera*.

In the summer Georgiane and Digges had taken a small country house at Bonnington, then still only a small village on the banks of the Water of Leith. Here for the next two years "Mr. and Mrs. Bellamy" lived together as man and wife. Little Miss Wordley lived with them, and they had a constant flow of other guests and entertained profusely. On the whole, they seem to have got on very well together, though quarrels between them were frequent, and it was rumoured that, after a particularly violent row one winter's night, Digges removed most of his clothes with the avowed intention of going to drown himself in a duck pond near by. Why he should have thought it necessary to undress for this purpose is not quite clear, but possibly he was not entirely sober. Georgiane calmly let him go and then fastened the street door behind him, so that when the cold air had dissipated his rage and damped his resolution he was obliged to eat humble-pie before he was re-admitted

Most of these quarrels were about money. Georgiane admits that Digges was always kind to her and did everything possible to make her happy, but she says that her temper was so much soured by the continual demands for the payment of debts he had contracted before they were together that she could not relish any enjoyment or behave towards him with that complacency she could have wished. Digges, on the other hand, blamed her for her extravagance, and no doubt with equally good reason. Years later, in a letter to Tate Wilkinson, dated January 21st, 1777, he wrote that he was about to take the benefit of the Scottish Act of Insolvency: "This crisis will relieve me of many untoward straits in which two large bail-bonds which I signed for Mrs. Bellamy (who I shall ever mention with respect and compassion) continually involved me..' The truth is there was little to choose between the two of them in the matter of improvidence, extravagance, and financial unreliability in general.

About the middle of the season Digges went off to London to see his brother, a captain in the army who had just returned from foreign service. As usual he was short of money, but Mr. Still, the Treasurer of the theatre, advanced him his expenses for the journey, and he economised in London by staying with Georgiane's mother. In the meantime the theatre had to manage as well as it could without him. The strain on Georgiane as the leading actress was considerable, especially as she was not feeling at all well. The sudden death of Mrs. Aickin, who had been her chief support, still further affected her health, so she was obliged to look for some other actress of quality who could relieve her from having to appear constantly, and she accounted herself very fortunate when an old acquaintance, Mrs. Kennedy, arrived in Edinburgh. This lady was that same Miss Orpheur, whom she had known in Dublin on her first visit there, and who had played Prince Arthur in *King John* when she had refused to do so on that memorable occasion of her quarrel with Garrick about her desire to play Constance. Mrs. Kennedy, her husband, and her son were now all engaged, on Georgiane's insistence, at a salary the managers protested they could not afford. But they were obliged to give in; Georgiane could not reasonably be expected to play every night, and no actress could well supply her place unless she had acquired some standing and reputation.

Unfortunately, this engagement proved disastrous, for Mrs. Kennedy was taken ill soon after her arrival, and, as a disfiguring eruption appeared on her face, she was able to appear only four times in the whole season. On one occasion, when she was feeling better, she sent word that she would be able to play Zara in *The Mourning Bride* for a benefit in which she was particularly interested. But at four o'clock in the afternoon she was again taken so ill that it was quite impossible for her to appear. It was too late to change the play, which, moreover, was being put on ''by particular desire'', and Georgiane herself could not take her place, as she was to play Almeria. In this quandary Mrs. Kennedy's sister, Mrs. Farrel, offered to come to the rescue. She was some twenty years older than Mrs. Kennedy and usually played old nurses and the like. But in the past she had played Zara, and she remembered the lines. Her elderly appearance in this youthful role astonished the audience, who rudely expressed marks of disapprobation throughout the play and gave vent to hoots of derision when she died. Mrs. Farrell thereupon rose from the dead with great dignity and, coming down to the front of the stage, informed the audience that she was concerned she could not acquit herself so as to give satisfaction, but as good nature had induced her to take the part, merely to serve the person whose benefit it was, she hoped they would excuse it. She then retired and laid herself out again, and the mutes covered her face with her veil.

On his return from London Digges presented Georgiane with a huge silver repeater, which she had seen in an Edinburgh shop and had long desired to have, in order that she might know the times at which she ought to take the various potions and medicaments with which she continually dosed herself. This repeater was to play a leading part in a very awkward incident which occurred later.

Although Calcraft regularly paid the annuity he had promised her, in spite of the fact that she had not kept her side of the bargain by living abroad—Georgiane declares that he seems to have thought that Scotland *was* abroad—and although their success at the theatre was such that they ought to have been able at least to pay their way, Georgiane and Digges were so reckless in their expenditure that they were always up to their ears in debt and perenially short of ready money. According to Georgiane, at the beginning of the ensuing season and just before the Edinburgh race week, it again became necessary for Digges to travel to London, this time because his mother had died leaving him £4,000 on condition that he would assume her maiden name of West and quit the stage altogether.*
Somehow money had to be raised for the journey, so Georgiane persuaded the long-suffering Mr. Still to advance seventeen guineas on the security of her repeater and agreed that Digges might take another ten or fifteen guineas from the office. More

---

* It is characteristic of Digges that he accepted the conditions, and, as soon as the money was spent, reverted to his old name, his old profession, and his old ways.

could not be spared, because one of the instalments of the £200 she had contracted to pay her inflexible creditor was due in a few days time.

In point of fact it was not until two years later that Mrs. Digges died; but presumably Georgiane thought it necessary in her *Apology* to find some plausible explanation of her financial embarrassment at this time. Only very rarely does she impute her troubles to her own extravagance and improvidence; usually she puts the blame on ill fortune—or somebody else. And on this occasion it was Digges. Her story is that, when she sent to Mr. Still for the £200 at the end of the week, he replied that he had not a shilling in the treasury. Digges had taken everything and owed him more than £200. Fortunately for her, her creditor's attorney, Mr. Ferguson, "possessed the most liberal mind and was an honour to his profession." In other words, he allowed himself to be wheedled by little Miss Wordley—Georgiane herself being too distressed, as she says, to explain the circumstances to him—and he generously took the debt on himself, sent the money to his client, and allowed Georgiane three months in which to repay him. Georgiane mentions with regret that Mr. Ferguson was one of the five persons buried in the débris when the newly-constructed North Bridge in Edinburgh collapsed on August 3rd, 1760, but she does not say if she ever repaid him her debt. It is just possible that he did get his money back, for shortly after he had advanced it to her, she received an unexpected gift of exactly £200 from a Mr. Hearne, who had just returned from the East Indies, and, on making enquiries for her, had casually heard of her distress. This gift, she explains, was a token of gratitude. Several years before she had started him on his prosperous career by recommending him to Calcraft as a clerk because of his remarkably fine handwriting.

In February, 1764, the young actor, Tate Wilkinson, arrived in Edinburgh. He had not been engaged for the theatre and, on his own confession, had come there "at haphazard, merely from his own whim and inclination". But he was highly delighted to find there his old friend, Mrs Bellamy, with whom he had not only dined frequently when she was living with Calcraft in Parliament Street, but also had been on an intimacy for years by seeing her constantly at Lady Tyrawley's, whose apartments at Somerset House he had frequented. Georgiane made him very welcome and insisted that he should make a home of her house at Bonnington during his stay in Edinburgh. She invited him to the Green Room at the theatre, where he was pleased to discover another old acquaintance in Mrs. Mozeen, who had played Desdemona to his Othello at Portsmouth a few years before.

Wilkinson was, of course, hoping to be asked to join the company and was very gratified when, on his third day in Edinburgh, he was invited to sup at a tavern by Dowson and Bates, the managers of the theatre. His hopes began to rise still further when they asked him what terms he would want for eight or ten performances. But then they went on to explain that they could not afford to pay him much, as he had come uninvited and at the height of the season, when they did not really need any additions to the company. Besides, Mr. Dowson added, Mr. and Mrs. Bellamy were towers of strength. Wilkinson admits that this was true, which is a little inconsistent with his description of Mrs. Bellamy's final and irretrievable eclipse as an actress in Dublin several years before.

The young actor soon perceived that, though the managers meant to be polite and friendly and would like to avail themselves of his services, they were determined not to engage him if it were going to cost them too much. And they had the whip-hand, for he acknowledged that he had only himself to blame for having, as he himself expressed it, undertaken "an expensive tedious journey, merely on speculation" when he could have stayed on in Ireland with Barry, who had pressed him to do so. At the end of the evening he and the managers parted amiably, but he no longer thought much of his prospects of obtaining an engagement with them.

At dinner with the Bellamies at Bonnington on the following day he told them what had passed and declared that it had determined him to quit Scotland immediately. Georgiane said that what the managers had told him was the exact state of affairs as they then stood. "And," she continued, "as Mr. Bellamy and myself are concerned in the profits in one interest, and as we settle all the plays, we do not want you, Mr. Wilkinson, as it is evident you have thrown yourself into their power if you play at all; and, if not, you have no alternative but to depart and make better use of your time, as you certainly can; for Bates and Dowson undoubtedly think, as you are on the spot, you will not neglect any decent engagement." This was true, if scarcely encouraging. But it soon transpired that Mrs. Bellamy had merely been explaining how the situation must appear to the managers. "My friend Tate," she now went on, "you are sure I wish you well from my long knowledge of you; and if you will for once depend upon my advice, and stay over Saturday or Monday next, a wonderful change may happen in the movements of the theatrical machine that will astonish Bates and Dowson, and you may command your own terms; at present they are sure they can do without you, but Sunday will cause a contrary opinion."

Wilkinson was much surprised at this mysterious turn in the conversation and begged Mrs. Bellamy to be more explicit. And so, having assured him that she was relying on his secrecy, she proceeded to explain that Mr. Bellamy, or Mr. Digges, was deeply involved in debt and could not remain in Edinburgh any longer without loss of liberty. Unfortunately, there was a law in force in Scotland that, if any person in debt was known to be quitting the kingdom, he could be arrested, even on a Sunday, if an information were sworn against him. It would, therefore, be necessary for Mr. Digges to make a clandestine departure. On Saturday night he would, on some pretext, get all the cash he could from Mr. Still, the Treasurer. She was careful to point out that the rest of the company would not suffer thereby, for Mr. Dowson was well off and would have to pay them. By Sunday night Digges would have been secretly and securely conveyed out of the reach of his creditors and would be safe on the other side of the Tweed in England. On Monday Bates and Dowson would be in the utmost consternation, and their only relief would be to call on Wilkinson to come to their rescue.

Tate Wilkinson seems to have had no scruples whatever about falling in with this somewhat equivocal scheme, and everything turned out exactly as Mrs. Bellamy had prophesied. On the Monday the managers, suddenly deprived of their leading actor, were obliged to approach Wilkinson hat in hand with the offer of most favourable terms, including two clear benefits. Wilkinson accepted with alacrity and for the remainder of the season took Digges's place. But he does not mention any of the parts he played, except those of Trim in the *Funeral* and Zamti in the *Orphan of China*, which were played on the nights of Mrs. Bellamy's two benefits. The performance of the latter play was marred by the non-appearance of Collins, the actor who was to have played Zamet. He was suddenly taken ill—or said he was—and as nobody else knew the part, it had to be read by an actor called Creswick. Mrs. Bellamy evidently believed that Collins's illness was deliberately feigned to spite her, for Wilkinson says that she represented to the audience in an acrimonious apology and manner that Mr. Collins purposely distressed the representation and that nought but malevolence and ill-behaviour was the true cause of the disappointment.

About this time, owing to the debts which both she and Digges had accumulated, an execution was levied in the house at Bonnington, and Georgiane was obliged to return into the city itself. She says that the great historian, David Hume, lent her his lodging in the Canongate. If this is so, it must have been his apartment in a mansion known as Jack's Land. But, wherever she was, she could not refrain from keeping open house. Tate Wilkinson records that, whenever he was not otherwise occupied, he could always be certain of a warm welcome and an agreeable party at her house. Though by no means a handsome man and rather lacking in the elegance which was so much admired at this time, he had a good presence and a most agreeable manner, and he had deputised for the absent Digges with such success that Mrs. Bellamy asked him to stay on for the short season the company was about to play in Glasgow. But he had had enough of Scotland for the time being, and, pleading ill-health, he bade her farewell at the end of the season and went to York instead. He always remained a good, if candid, friend to her, and at the end of her career she summed him up thus: "Justly admired as an actor, beloved as a man, and esteemed as a friend."

Mrs. Bellamy's great success in Edinburgh had aroused the interest of certain citizens of Glasgow, and they had offered to build a theatre there, if she would come and play in it. It was a bold venture on their part, for Glasgow had been hostile to the theatre ever since the days of John Knox. A wooden theatre had been erected there as recently as 1752, but the popular feeling against it had been so strong that the audiences had to attend it under military guard, and in the following year it had been destroyed by a hostile mob, inflamed by Whitefield's preaching against it as the Devil's house.

Even now the five broadminded merchants who had combined to subscribe the cost for the erection of a new theatre experienced some difficulty in obtaining a site for it, since nobody seemed to be willing to sell land for so profane a purpose. But in the end they had found a maltman, one John Miller of Westerton, whose desire for money transcended his religious principles and who had agreed to sell them a site in the village of Grahamston, without the confines of the city, though, doubtless to salve his conscience, he assured them that, as it was intended for a temple of Belial, he would expect an exorbitant and extraordinary sum for the purpose. It was now completed and ready for Mrs. Bellamy to open her season there at the beginning of May, 1764.

At the very last moment, when she was about to set out, and

the chaises she had ordered to transport her and her household were already expected, she found that she had not enough money to pay for the journey. In a desperate effort to raise the necessary cash, she sent one of her servants, by name Anne Waterstone, to a watchmaker's in the High Street to dispose of the silver repeater Digges had given her. Hours passed; the chaises were already at the door, but Anne Waterstone had not come back. At about four o'clock in the afternoon a man dressed as a beadle came and informed Mrs. Bellamy that a woman supposed to be in her employment had been detained about a watch she had tried to sell. Georgiane dismissed the chaises and sent Mr. Still to find out what had happened and to try to get Anne Waterstone released. The watchmaker explained that it was from him that Mr. Digges had purchased the repeater. Although it was invaluable because of its workmanship, its great size had rendered it not easily saleable, and he had let Mr. Digges have it at a very reasonable price, on his written promise to pay for it at the end of the season. But since he understood that Mr. Digges had left Edinburgh and did not intend to come back, and since the watch, which had not yet been paid for, had been offered to him for sale, he had been suspicious that it had not been honestly come by, especially as the woman who brought it refused to say who had sent her. In these embarrassing circumstances the best that Mr. Still could do was to compromise the matter by surrendering the repeater to its original and rightful owner upon his agreeing to give up Mr. Digges's note of hand and literate Mrs. Bellamy's servant. Anne Waterstone bore no malice for this rather unpleasant experience. She lived on in Edinburgh to a great age and continued to the last to adore the memory of her former mistress. In fact, she was "from this cause, a zealous friend of all players, and would never allow a slighting remark upon them to pass unreproved".

By some means or other Mr. Still managed to raise enough money to pay for half the expenses of the journey, and Georgiane herself was able to borrow the remainder. And so they were able, after all, to set forth next morning. Georgiane's party consisted of herself, Miss Wordley, and three servants. She insisted upon taking her favourite singing-birds with her wherever she went, but for fear that they might suffer by the jolting of the carriage on the rough Scottish roads she paid a porter to carry them on foot all the way from Edinburgh to Glasgow. It is scarcely surprising that the thrifty Scots "wondered to hear of ten guineas being expended for such a purpose".

On the journey to Glasgow Georgiane's drooping spirits were revived by the gaiety and good humour of Mary Wordley, but they were soon to be downcast again. On reaching Glasgow at noon they were greeted with the news that a mob set on by a fanatical Methodist preacher had invaded the theatre the night before and set fire to the stage. The main structure of the theatre itself had been saved, but the whole company's theatrical wardrobe and properties, which had been sent on ahead and had been piled up on the stage, had been completely destroyed. Georgiane computed her own loss at as much as £900. Poor Miss Wordley had lost her little all.

Mrs. Bellamy promptly made a public announcement that, unless she could appear next night as had been arranged, she would not appear on the Glasgow stage at all. This firm statement had the most excellent effects. One of the merchants who had been responsible for the building of the theatre came forward immediately with an offer of financial help and, further, met Mrs. Bellamy's objection that she could not appear for want of clothes by undertaking that suitable ladies' clothes for the players would be available in time, if they on their part would undertake to get the stage repaired. The manager, Mr. Bates, hired some industrious carpenters who nailed down boards for a temporary stage and covered it with carpets. And by six o'clock in the evening the promised dresses were also forthcoming. The *Glasgow Mercury* of May 11th announced: "The ladies of Glasgow presented Mrs. Bellamy with forty silk gowns to replenish her wardrobe destroyed by the mob."

Some of these dresses, Georgiane says, were almost new, "nor did the ladies confine themselves to outward garments only," and so she did not have to resort to any odd shifts. She had not, of course, expected that the sort of robes then considered appropriate for wearing in tragedy would be provided from private sources and had wisely decided to open with Murphy's contemporary comedy, *The Citizen*, followed by the *Mock Doctor* as the farce. These pieces were played punctually at the hour advertised and were received with great enthusiasm by the audience. At the end of the performance a lady rose from her seat in the boxes and announced that, in case any personal attack upon the players were contemplated, none of the audience would stir until all the performers and their servants had got safely away from the theatre and had been escorted into the city by the town guard.

Even without the support of Digges or Tate Wilkinson the brief season in Glasgow was a triumphant success. Reddish was Mrs. Bellamy's principal tragedian, while the chief comedy parts were entrusted to Aickin. There were crowded houses every single night. Both *Macbeth* and *Douglas* were called for by the patriotic audience, but Mrs. Bellamy at first declined to put them on until the proper costumes could be made and brought from Edinburgh. In the end she amusedly consented to play Lady Macbeth in white satin instead of the usual black velvet, when it was represented to her that it was in white satin that the ghost of Lady Macbeth walked every night at the castle of Dunsinane, as she could ascertain for herself if she were willing to pass a night there.

Soon after her return to Edinburgh Georgiane decided to bring her stay in Scotland to a close. Her own explanation of this decision was that Mr. Bates had entered into an engagement with Sheridan to appear in Edinburgh without her knowledge and consent and contrary to his agreement with her. That was the real reason why she declined to appear any more in Edinburgh and resolved to return to London. But she discloses that it was about this time that she first discovered the awkward fact that she was not really married to West Digges and that he already had a wife living. She appeased her outraged vanity and virtue by affecting to believe that Digges had acted in good faith towards her in the belief that his wife was dead, she having herself announced her death in the papers in order to save herself from being molested by him.

On July 25th, 1764, the following advertisement appeared in the *Edinburgh Courant*: "As Mrs. Bellamy is not to appear any more on the Edinburgh stage, she begs leave to return her thanks to the public in general, and to those friends who have done her the honour to patronise her in particular, for the favours she has received during her residence in Scotland, of which she will ever retain the most grateful sense." In her *Apology* she prints a rather longer and more flowery version of this advertisement and asserts that she continued it every day for a month, which is quite untrue. Nor is it true that she appended to it a note requesting her creditors to send in their accounts in order that they might be paid. On the contrary, she was being dunned on all sides, and this is far more likely to have been the real reason why she left Scotland at this time. She did, however, manage to pay off some of her more pressing debts with the aid of a timely loan of £200 from her generous friend, Mr. Hearne, and a remittance from Sir George Metham, to whom also she had written to request his assistance. Sir George added an invitation to spend some days with him in his Yorkshire home at North Cave on her way to London, since their son George, now aged fifteen, was then at home for the holidays from Eton.

Chapter Fifteen

Sir George Metham had kindly invited Georgiane to bring her little friend, Miss Wordley, with her, and they set forth for Yorkshire at the beginning of August. On the first day they did not get very far, for many of their Edinburgh friends had insisted upon escorting them on the first stage of their journey, and they all ended up by spending a last convivial evening together at Haddington.

Metham had intimated that he would send his chaise to meet them at York, but it was not there on their arrival at the post-house, and as an enquiry at the various inns produced no news of it, they were obliged to spend the night at York. Georgiane took advantage of the delay to pay a sentimental visit to the convent at Micklegate Bar. She was sad to find that Father Blunt was dead and that very few of the nuns she had known were surviving. The next morning there was still no news of Sir George's chaise, and they were obliged to hire one. At a village some twenty miles from York, Georgiane decided to leave Miss Wordley at the inn and go on alone. She had begun to wonder if the invitation had been sincerely meant and wished to be certain of a kind reception before she introduced her friend.

As she approached the house, she perceived Sir George Metham himself in the distance. He came to meet the chaise, since the road led only to his house and he knew that the visitor must be going there. He seemed greatly surprised to see Georgiane alone and in a strange carriage, and cried out as he approached her: "My dear Pop! how comes it that you are by yourself and in a hack? My chaise has been waiting for you several days at York. I began to be alarmed at your stay, and sent George, and my nephew, and some others, yesterday, to make enquiries about you. But where is Miss Wordley? I hoped to have had the pleasure of her company."

Georgiane explained what had happened, and Metham immediately sent the hired chaise back to the inn to fetch her friend, while he took her to the house, where she was welcomed by his old valet, Sherrad, who shed tears of joy on her hand as he kissed it. It was not long before Miss Wordley made a triumphal appearance, escorted by the cavalcade of young gentlemen, who had by chance discovered her at the inn on their way back from their fruitless journey to York. It afterwards transpired that the coachman who had been sent in charge of Sir George's chaise had lingered at a favourite tavern of his, where he had soon become oblivious of his mission.

After tea Sir George asked if he might have the pleasure of showing Georgiane to her apartment, as he had something particular to say to her. This proved to be a grave and pompous statement that, when they had parted, he had rashly bound himself by the most sacred vows never more to have any tender connexion with her, and he wished her to understand this. But he was not best pleased when Georgiane, who could scarcely forbear laughing at his solemnity, assured him that it was not necessary to make such an apology, as she would certainly not have accepted any invitation to renew her former relations with him. But though it was obvious that her complete indifference had hurt his vanity, by the time they rejoined the company he had reassumed his customary good humour and politeness. And this continued throughout the three months of her stay at North Cave.

Much as she was enjoying Metham's generous hospitality, Georgiane knew that it was imperative that she should return to London and seek an engagement. Her financial affairs were much embarrassed, and she still owed more than £4,000. Metham expressed himself anxious to do all that he could to help her in spite of his own difficulties. For this purpose he proposed to sell one of his estates, and he commissioned her to

approach her friend, Alderman Cracroft, to find a purchaser.
In the meantime, until he himself came to town, which would
be soon, he would give her an allowance of seven guineas a
week. And to help her to obtain an engagement, he would
write to his cousin, Lord Eglinton, asking him to use his
influence with Mr. Beard, who was now acting manager at
Covent Garden.

Lord Eglinton's reply was very disappointing to Georgiane.
Beard had informed him that he could not possibly reinstate Mrs.
Bellamy in her former position; her old parts had been divided
between Mrs. Ward and Miss Macklin, and there was consequently no room for another tragic actress, especially as
musical pieces were now the staple at Covent Garden. In spite
of this rebuff, which Georgiane characteristically attributed
merely to the manager's desire to save so heavy a salary as hers,
she determined to go back to London, and set off accompanied
by Miss Wordley and young George Metham, who was due to
return to Eton.

On her arrival in London she went to her mother's house in
Brewer Street. Mrs. Bellamy usually let it to augment her
income, but fortunately it happened to be empty now, and her
mother consented to let her have the first floor and undertook
to pay her incidental expenses out of the money Sir George
Metham was to allow her. But as Mrs. Bellamy, from bitter
experience, did not trust too much to Metham's promises and,
besides, was convinced that it was now too late for Georgiane
to get an engagement at either of the theatres, she would not
let her keep Miss Wordley with her to cause additional expense,
and a lodging was found for her near by.

Next day Georgiane took her son back to Eton. She had
grown very fond of the boy during the three months they had
spent together at North Cave, and was delighted by the
solicitude he showed for her. He had given an example of this
on the very night of their arrival in London. Greatly shocked
when tallow candles had been brought into the drawing-room,
he had immediately gone out to buy a supply of wax ones, and

had enticed his mother out of the room while they were being changed.

One of her first acts on returning to London was to make quite certain that West Digges should understand that their former connexion was now at an end. She wrote to him telling him that they must never meet again, and, in fact, they did only meet each other casually three or four times after that. Probably he was quite as relieved as she was; the extravagance of each, when added to the other's, could lead only to disaster for both of them.

Alderman Cracroft gladly agreed to try to find a purchaser for Sir George Metham's estate. He told Georgiane that he had managed to keep her various creditors at bay during her absence, but now she really must provide more money to satisfy them. When he asked her if she had any hope of obtaining an engagement, she had to confess that she had not yet secured one, but said that she would try to get one, even if it were only for a few nights, which would entitle her to a benefit. She had always been able to rely upon her benefits bringing in a large sum. She begged him, therefore, to get her letter of licence renewed, and to raise money on the plate she had deposited with him. He was to pay himself back out of the proceeds and let her have the rest to support her until Metham came to London.

In order to secure her debt to himself, the Alderman now suggested that she should insure her life, and it was the enquiries made by the Insurance Office on this occasion that first revealed to her that she had really been christened by the names of George Anne. In the sixth volume of her *Apology* she printed the following certificate:

Declaration of George Anne Bellamy's Register; that the said George Anne Bellamy is of the age of thirty-three years, and was born at Fingal in kingdom of Ireland, upon the twenty-third day of April, in the year one thousand, seven hundred, and thirty-one.

Henceforth she elected to be known both professionally and in private life by the names which had been given to her at her baptism.

In her desperate anxiety to secure an engagement she bethought herself of Metham's old friend, James Brudenell, son of Lord Cardigan, who had dropped her acquaintance when she had broken with his friend. Now that she was again in favour with Metham, she thought he might be willing to help her. She accordingly wrote to him, asking him to use his influence with the proprietors of the theatre. Brudenell did not disappoint her; he called on her the very next day, promised to exert what interest he had in her favour, and assured her that the ladies of his family would continue their patronage of her.

Two days later, when she was lying late abed, little Miss Wordley came running into the room and told her that she must make haste and get up as Johnny Beard was coming to see her. George Anne, as she must now be called, concluded that she must mean Mr. Baird, a Glasgow admirer of hers, for she could not imagine that the manager of Covent Garden Theatre would demean himself by coming to call in person on a performer whom he had so lately rejected. But to her very great surprise, the visitor proved to be Mr. Beard himself. He told her that he had been deputed by the proprietors to engage her and added that it was necessary that the engagement should be signed that very evening. He then went on to explain, with wry amusement, that Colonel Brudenell, Mr. James Brudenell's younger brother, had peremptorily demanded that Mrs. Bellamy should be engaged within twenty-four hours, or else he would be "obliged to compel them to a compliance". Colonel Brudenell was a friend of royalty, and his favour was important, so that the proprietors thought it wiser not to run the risk of offending him. Moreover, he had the reputation of being a resolute man, and they knew that he could easily carry out his threats, having great influence with certain young men of fashion who would be only too pleased if they were given an opportunity of breaking chandeliers and pulling up benches in the theatre. It was, of course, mortifying for an actress of Mrs. Bellamy's standing to be thus forced on the management of a theatre by the threat of a riot, but she was not in a position to refuse an engagement, however obtained, and she had to swallow her pride.

Alderman Cracroft expressed himself very gratified when George Anne told him of her good fortune, but at the same time he had a piece of very unwelcome news to give her. Her inexorable creditor, Mrs. Ray, had bought up two notes of hers in order to make her own debt up to over £1,000 and thus prevent her from taking the benefit of any Act of Insolvency. And this in spite of the facts that so far she had regularly paid the instalments of £200 a year fixed by the Scottish Court, and that she had never shown any signs of taking advantage of the Act, but had, indeed, refused to do so when she owed more than twice the amount she did now.

In this new difficulty Cracroft advised her to apply to her great friend, Count von Haslang, to afford her the protection of diplomatic immunity by engaging her as his housekeeper and thereby securing her from the liability of arrest for debt. Haslang readily agreed and furnished her with a paper stating that his housekeeper, Mrs. George Anne Bellamy, having informed him that she had some debts she was anxious to discharge, he had given her leave to accept an engagement at Covent Garden Theatre on condition that she appropriated the whole of her salary to the payment of these debts.

On the next day the papers announced her engagement at Covent Garden and stated that she would appear the following Friday as Cleone. She now imagined that her person at least was secure and that her creditor would not venture to attack her. But she had not yet come to the end of her present troubles In the first place, it transpired that the housekeeper she had employed when she was in Jermyn Street had embezzled nearly all the money she had given her for household expenses, so that her tradesmen's accounts for that period still remained unpaid. This meant that she was £200 more in debt than she had thought she was. She had recourse to her current milch cow, Mr. Hearne, who paid these bills for her.

Next she had a rather awkward claim from Mr. Deard, a jeweller from whom she had been in the habit of borrowing diamonds in her more prosperous days. She still owed him £17, and, on the renewal of her letter of licence, she had written to him asking him to sign it. Instead of doing so, Mr. Deard called upon her on the morning of December 7th, the very day she was to make her reappearance at the theatre. She declined to see him, but he insisted. He told her that he had a demand on her for over £100 for a pair of ear-rings which he had lent her and which, instead of being returned to him, had been pledged at another jeweller's. George Anne was horrified. With her usual carelessness she had given them to a friend to return to Mr. Deard before she left London for Scotland, and it appeared that this person, who was now dead, had been dishonest enough to pawn them. That, at least, was her story. Mr. Deard was quite willing to believe that she knew nothing about this transaction, but he firmly pointed out that this did not exonerate her from being accountable for articles which had been entrusted to her personally. Once again the obliging Mr. Hearne came to the rescue.

George Anne had been so upset by Deard's visit that she was very nervous that night, but she had an excellent reception in *Cleone*. As James Brudenell had promised, the ladies of his family attended, and there was a brilliant audience. But as all her friends had rallied round her that night to welcome her back, the piece was poorly attended when it was repeated, against her advice, on the following evening. One most gratifying result of her re-appearance in this part was that Dodsley, the bookseller, brother of the deceased author of the piece, sent her a receipted bill for the amount she owed him for books. Probably he realised that he would never be paid in any case, but none the less he adopted a most graceful way of showing it.

One evening Beard informed her that *Coriolanus* had been commanded by His Majesty for the following Thursday and that she was to play Veturia. She had not played this part since she was last in London and told him that she could not possibly recover it in one day, but he replied that she must, since she had been expressly named. Flattering as this may have been, it did not make her task any easier, and she was conscious that she gave one of the worst performances of her life that evening. "Indeed, to speak the truth," she says, "I verily believe, that no performer, entitled to the least merit, could so completely have massacred a Roman matron, as I unfortunately did that night."

Neither George Anne herself nor Count von Haslang intended her appointment as his housekeeper to be a mere blind, and he required her attendance daily. For this reason she did not mind that she was not called upon to appear very regularly at the theatre. As Beard had warned her, most of her parts in tragedy had been taken over by Mrs. Ward and Miss Macklin, though Miss Macklin had the generosity to restore Juliet and one of two others to her. In the course of the season she played Constance, Cordelia, Desdemona, Marcia, Eudocia, and Cleopatra in *All For Love*.

Miss Elliott, whom she describes as "a very beautiful young woman, and who had great talents", had been given most of her usual parts in comedy, except Lady Townley, which did not benefit her, since the *Provoked Husband* was not in the repertory this season. But Miss Elliot was very delicate and was often too ill to appear, so that George Anne was occasionally called upon to play some of the parts she had lost to her—Millamant, Berinthia, and Lady Fanciful. But Miss Elliot was well enough to play Millament at her own benefit on March 23rd, 1765. In *Comus* they played together, George Anne as the Lady, and Miss Elliot as Termagant.

Having lost all his money in his disastrous partnership with Barry in Ireland, Henry Woodward was now at Covent Garden playing the principal parts in comedy and endeavouring

with some success to recoup his fortunes. He had been George
Anne's professed admirer when she first appeared on the stage,
and, although they had quarrelled since about her failure to
join his company in Dublin, he had forgiven her for that and
now treated her with an affection that caused many to think
that his former passion had revived. Unfortunately, he and
Beard did not get on at all well together, and his partiality for
George Anne did not commend her to the manager, who was
already resentful of her inclusion in the company. Moreover, his
growing dislike of her was fanned by his wife, a daughter of
Rich's, who had once been one of George Anne's best friends,
but with whom she had broken at Calcraft's request because of
some excessive indiscretion on her part. George Anne and
Beard came to high words when she insisted upon her young
friend, Miss Wordley, being given the chance to play the part
of the maid, Tag, in *Miss in Her Teens*, which was to be given as
the afterpiece following *Romeo and Juliet* on the occasion of her
benefit. Beard did not consider Miss Wordley good enough to
appear on the London stage, especially in a part in which the
great Kitty Clive had shone. George Anne had her way, but
thereafter the manager became openly hostile to her.

By this time Sir George Metham had at last come to town.
But Alderman Cracroft had been unable to find a purchaser for
his estate at anything like the price he was asking, so that his
plan to rehabilitate both his own fortunes and George Anne's
had come to nothing. On the day after her benefit he sent to
inform her that their son was ill and asked her to come at once
to his lodging at Palace Yard. She happened to have with her a
visitor who had just arrived from Scotland, and was unable to
go until after dinner. But she was not anxious about young
George, since the servant who had brought the message had
assured her that he had only a slight cold, and so, when she left,
she promised to come back to her guest as soon as possible.

When she arrived at Metham's lodging, she found Macklin,
the veteran actor, with him. Metham informed her that
Macklin had told him she was going to marry Woodward and

challenged her to say if this was true. The idea was, of course, absurd; George Anne herself acknowledged that it could not be supposed that a man of Woodward's age and prudence, who had recently lost a fortune and was trying to build up another, would marry a woman who was so much involved as herself and was "not the best economist in the world". But with that curious perversity which some women cannot resist she laughed and replied: "Yes, to be sure."

After Macklin had left, Metham pressed her to remain with him for the evening, and, when she told him that she could not do so because she had a guest waiting for her at home, he became even more pressing. "And," she says, "in spite of all his usual *nonchalance*, I verily believe, had I been *d'accord*, he would not now have been a rigid observer of those solemn oaths, which had given him so much pain at Cave." The thought that she might be about to marry another had apparently re-awakened his interest in her, and when she persisted in her refusal to stay, he adverted again to the report of her approaching marriage with Woodward. Whether he believed this and was jealous, or whether he seized upon it as an excuse not to fulfil his promises to help her, she was unable to determine; but he showed himself really displeased and parted from her in anger. Years passed before she saw him again.

She could ill afford to do without even such assistance as he might have given her, for she was still up to the neck in debt. One of her creditors had promised in writing that he would sign her letter of licence if she would pay him thirty guineas on account; but on the very day she paid it he served her with a writ for the remainder of what was owing. She was so annoyed that she determined to stand trial, and, on Woodward's recommendation, employed Zachary Stephens, a solicitor in Chancery Lane, to act for her. But somehow, as so often happened with her, the case was bungled, and judgment was given against her by default. In apprehension of being arrested, she fled to France as soon as the theatre closed, and took refuge with a friend, a Mrs. Collier, who lent her the money to settle the debt, so that she was able to return to London in time for the opening of the next season.

Her first appearance was as Cordelia, and she also appeared with success as Juliet. But she was grievously disappointed with her reception as Lady Townley, which she had always considered to be one of her best comedy parts. Like Mrs. Cibber, she had attempted a romantic rendering of the part, and, though some critics had thought her rather insipid, her interpretation had generally been preferred to those of the two great comedy actresses, Peg Woffington, who had been too pert and affected, and Kitty Clive, who had given the impression that Lord Townley had married his kitchen-maid. She attributed her failure to please now, not to any falling off in her own powers, but simply to the fact that, owing to the sudden indisposition of one of the singers, the play was put on hastily on what should have been an opera night.

It was not long before she discovered that a sustained attempt was being made to oust her from the company altogether. Mrs. Rich, who had never liked her from the first, was determined to supplant her by a cousin of her own, Miss Wilford, who had formerly been a dancer in the company, but had made her début as a straight actress at the end of the previous season as Miranda in the *Busybody*. Now she had been announced as Estifania in *Rule a Wife and Have a Wife*, a part which Mrs. Bellamy considered to be hers by rights. She had no objection to Miss Wilford's being given a trial part, for that was quite usual; but she thought that she should have been consulted on the propriety of any other actress's appearing in any part which properly belonged to her. Nevertheless, Miss Wilford appeared as Estifania on October 16th, and was later given several other leading parts which George Anne considered her own. George Anne herself had only one new part this season, that of Portia in *Julius Cæsar*, which had not been acted at Covent Garden for eight years. At her own benefit on March 31st she played Anna Bullen in *Virtue Betrayed*.

Since her mother had now found a tenant for her house in

Brewer Street, George Anne had taken lodgings in Ryder Street, St. James's, where she invited Miss Wordley to live with her. Although she had regularly kept up the payments to Mrs. Ray, that inexorable woman was still persistently pestering her, and, early in the autumn, she kept calling at her house and asking to see her. One day she left a note intimating that, if Mrs. Bellamy would insure her life, she would be perfectly easy regarding her debt. George Anne replied that she would be quite willing to do so, if Mrs. Ray would appoint a proper agent to transact the business, but that she would by no means see or speak with Mrs. Ray herself.

A few days later, Mrs. Ray turned up at the house with a man, and George Anne, concluding that he must be the agent she had asked for, ordered him to be admitted, and began to question him about the proposed insurance. The man, who appeared to be an Italian Jew, looked completely puzzled by her questions, and when she repeated them, informed her in broken English that she was mistaken in his business. He proceeded to explain that his master, the Tripolitanian Ambassador, to whom he was interpreter, had long admired her and had offered to pay off her debt to Mrs. Ray, if Mrs. Ray would effect an introduction to her for a purpose she would have no difficulty in divining. George Anne was furious at this insult to her dignity and moral character and forthwith had him turned out of the house. Foiled in her endeavour to get her debt settled by this simple if not straightforward method, Mrs. Ray at once went off to her attorney and entered up the judgment for the sum of nine hundred pounds, two hundred of which represented the debts she had bought up to accumulate her own.

That evening George Anne had been entertaining Henry Fox, now Lord Holland, to dinner, and when he and her other guests had left, she set forth to go and play cards with Count von Haslang, who was laid up with gout. But in Jermyn Street she was arrested by Mrs. Ray's brother and a sheriff's officer and carried off to a sponging-house in Stanhope Street,

Clare Market, where she remained for six days. The mistress of the house was kind to her, but she was so stunned and bewildered that she remained in a state of something approaching coma, refusing all food and drink. On the sixth day she was informed that the writ was returnable for next day and that she must engage an attorney to procure a *habeas corpus* for her and engage a lodging within the rules of the King's Bench. At this period debtors were confined in the King's Bench prison in the borough of Southwark, but it was possible to purchase permission to live in lodgings 'within the rules', an area of some three miles circumference round the prison.

George Anne did not know what to do. Count von Haslang was far too ill for her to worry him about her affairs; Woodward and all the other friends who might have helped her were out of town, and her mother was also away in Oxfordshire. In her dilemma the only people she could think of were the Stacies. Mr. Stacie was the landlord of the Bedford Head, in Southampton Street, Covent Garden, and she had first known him as the landlord of an inn at Stilton, when she had travelled along the Great North Road with Metham on her way to York. She had consented to be godmother to the child Mrs. Stacie was then carrying, and she had since been godmother to two more children of theirs. Mrs. Stacie came along at once, bringing with her a bill of twenty pounds from her husband for her immediate needs. Miss Wordley, who was then acting at the Richmond Theatre, also arrived and brought all the money she could muster or borrow.

By now Woodward had returned to town, and, as soon as he heard what had happened, sent to ask if he might visit her. She refused to let him come, but asked him to send someone to engage a lodging for her within the rules. He also consented to be one of her sureties. Mr. Stacie had agreed to be the other.

Although she was to have the privilege of living within the rules, she had first to report at the prison itself, and, accompanied by the faithful Miss Wordley, she was conducted there next morning and received most courteously by the Warden,

Mr. Marsden, who entertained her to breakfast and then himself escorted her to the lodging that had been engaged for her at the house belonging to the 'Windmill' in St. George's Fields. It was a vile place, for which she was expected to pay two guineas a week, but it was the best that could be procured at such short notice. Before he left her, Mr. Marsden took out a large purse of gold and offered it to her, with a request that she would make use of it for her present exigencies and return it when convenient. George Anne thanked him, but told him that she was not at present in need of his kind assistance. When he had gone, she commented to Miss Wordley on his "generous politeness". Miss Wordley laughed at her for her simplicity. She had guessed at once that the money must really come from Woodward, who was taking this tactful way of trying to provide George Anne with money which she had refused to accept from him.

That evening Woodward himself came to see her and advised her to write to her friend, Mr. Yorke, the Attorney-General, to consult him upon her case. Miss Wordley took her letter to Yorke next day. He replied at once, saying that he would pay every attention to her affair and would do all in his power to extricate her from it. But nothing could be done until November, and in the meantime he sent her £200, advising her to try to prevail upon her creditor to compromise the debt. If this could not be achieved, she would have to stand trial, but he thought that the verdict would be given in her favour.

George Anne fully realised that the money Yorke had so kindly sent her was intended to go towards paying the debt, and that she must not use it for any other purpose. In the meantime she would have to remain in her present situation. But she could move to more congenial quarters. Miss Wordley found her two rooms adjoining the 'Dog and Duck', a famous tavern of somewhat unsavoury repute. But they were, at least, cleaner, airier, and better furnished. Miss Wordley promised to stay with her every night when she was not playing at Richmond.

George Anne's old friend, Arthur Murphy, had left the stage and become a lawyer, and it was to him that she entrusted her case. He agreed that she ought to take the Attorney-General's advice and try to compromise with her creditor. But if this proved impossible, he would undertake her defence.

She had given up her lodging in town and dismissed her servants, bringing with her only her favourite blackbird and a dog to keep her company. One day the dog, which had been ill for some days and had refused all food, suddenly flew at her and bit her lip. She was terrified of the possible consequences. Woodward, who was himself very worried, did his best to calm her. He took the dog away with him and assured her next morning that, on the way home, it had swum over a piece of water, "an indisputable proof that it was perfectly free from every symptom of the hydrophobia." But she heard afterwards that he had had the dog destroyed. The shock made her very ill, and Miss Wordley nursed her with such devotion and self-sacrifice that she began to pine away herself. Anxiety for her friend made George Anne pull herself together.

Murphy had to inform her that all his efforts to persuade her creditor to accept a compromise had proved unavailing, and that the case would have to come for trial. But her defence would cost her nothing, for Mr. Jennings of Carey Street had offered to act as her voluntary attorney without fee or reward because he was anxious to improve his practice. He pleaded her cause successfully, and the case was decided in her favour. A few days later the relentless Mrs. Ray died. Yorke suggested that this might be a good opportunity to make another attempt to obtain a final settlement of the debt, and, fortunately, Mrs. Ray's executors proved most amenable and agreed to accept £200 down and £200 more at the end of the year.

A free woman once more, Mrs. Bellamy hastened to inform the proprietors of the theatre that she would be able to appear on November 10th; but when she went to the theatre she found that her services were not required, and she did not make her first appearance this season until November 28th, when she played Mary, Queen of Scots, in the *Albion Queens*. All the performers seemed to be delighted that she was free again, and she was warmly welcomed by all at the theatre, except the manager and Mrs. Rich, who were still intent upon superseding her by Miss Wilford. That young lady played Cordelia on January 19th, but her performance did not please the audience, and when *King Lear* was announced again for March 8th, the prompter, Mr. Younger, took it upon himself to obliterate her name from the list of the cast and substitute that of Mrs. Bellamy. But Mrs. Rich and Beard were quite determined that Miss Wilford should play the part. At twelve o'clock on the day of the performance, the deputy-manager, Mr. Gibson, came in great embarrassment to see Mrs. Bellamy and told her that he was afraid there had been a mistake in the billing and he must, therefore, ask her to give up the part to Miss Wilford. The manager would issue hand-bills informing the public that a mistake had been made. George Anne flatly refused. She said that she was an indulged servant of the public, and that, whatever happened, she would play the character. Gibson was aghast and pointed out to her that she would inevitably draw on her the hatred of the Rich family. George Anne replied that she did not care if she did; she neither coveted their favour, nor feared their malice.

In the afternoon she sent her maid to look at the play-bills outside the theatre, and when she came back and told her that they were being changed, she took prompt action and herself had special hand-bills printed and distributed to the audience as they entered the theatre. In these she gave them a simple and straightforward account of what had happened, and concluded by saying that, as she esteemed herself the acknowledged child of their favour, she thought it her duty to be ready in case she should, that evening, be honoured with the preference.

To her great delight, there were loud calls for Mrs. Bellamy on the rise of the curtain, and when Miss Wilford made her first entrance as Cordelia she was received with such outcries that she was obliged to withdraw and give place to Mrs.

Bellamy, who was waiting in the wings ready dressed to come on. A tumult of applause greeted her appearance, and she confessed that she did not recollect ever meeting with more tokens of approbation in so trivial a character during her theatrical career.

Both mortified and furious, Miss Wilford stormed into the Green Room and told George Anne she was surprised that any performer should presume to affront Mrs. Rich. "I could have told her," says George Anne, "that her good cousin affronted the public much more by forcing her then unformed relation upon them; but as I neither dreaded the frowns of the Lady Directress, nor hoped for her favour, I held the little Cordelia's speech in too much contempt to make any reply to it."

While it is true that George Anne had never lacked the courage to stand up for what she believed to be her rights, it is unlikely that she would thus have deliberately defied and affronted the proprietors of the theatre if she had not already been thoroughly convinced that her contract, which was about to expire, would not be renewed in any case.

Chapter Sixteen

In 1767 THERE WAS A CHANGE in the management of Covent Garden. Beard, who since Rich's death had been managing the theatre, decided to retire owing to increasing deafness, and Rich's executors thereupon entered into negotiations for the sale of the Patent to Harris and Rutherford for £60,000. These two, being business men, wished to associate with themselves somebody with theatrical knowledge and experience and approached William Powell, a leading young actor at Drury Lane. Powell refused to join them unless his intimate friend, George Colman, the dramatist, was also included. Harris and Rutherford were not very willing to have a fourth member in the syndicate but eventually consented, and the agreement was signed on May 14th.

The arrangement was that Harris and Rutherford were to have entire control of the financial side, while Colman was to be acting manager of the theatre with very extensive powers. The engagement and dismissal of the performers, the casting, and the choice of plays both old and new were to be left entirely to him. He was, however, to keep the other proprietors informed of his plans and intentions, and they retained a power of veto if their disapproval should prove serious enough for them to think it worth while to express it formally in writing.

Powell was to be principal tragedian. His rise to fame had been very rapid. Born at Hereford in 1735, he had made his first appearance on the stage at Drury Lane in the autumn of 1763, at the rather late age of twenty-eight. Garrick, who was then anxious to make a prolonged tour on the Continent, had coached him to take his place, and his tuition had been rather too successful for his own peace of mind, for Powell had proved a very able substitute and had speedily become very popular.

When Garrick returned in 1765, he had been too fair-minded to resume many of his old parts which Powell had been playing during his absence, but he showed a disposition to drop those plays from the repertory and revive others in which there were suitable parts for himself, so that Powell's appearances became less frequent. In the circumstances Powell thought it would be preferable for all concerned if he transferred himself to Covent Garden, where he thought he would have more scope for his talents. His contract with Drury Lane stipulated that he should forfeit £1,000 if he broke his articles, but Garrick was only too pleased that he wanted to leave. He and Lacy made no difficulty about releasing him, and they all parted good friends.

George Anne's contract had expired at the end of the previous season, and though she at first thought she had a far better chance of being re-engaged by the new management, she had not yet been approached by them. For a long time Colman said nothing to her about renewing her contract, and she began to fear that she was not going to be offered an engagement. But one day Woodward called on her and told her that he had asked Colman whether he proposed to engage her, and that Colman had replied: "Yes, I depend upon her; but multiplicity of business has prevented me from calling upon her; I shall be obliged to you, if you will inform her, that I propose doing myself the pleasure very soon." The next day her articles were renewed for three years, and she was convinced that, being on good terms with Colman, she would be "restored to her former eligible situation in the theatre". It was a great relief to her also from the financial point of view, for she was still acting under licence, and her salary was assigned to her creditors. Alderman Cracroft had by now declined to continue the ungrateful task of receiving her salary and paying it out to her creditors, and it had been taken over by Mr. Powell, of the Pay

Office, who, however, had resigned after one season, on the plea that the job was attended by so much trouble, as it well may have been. But George Anne was very hurt, for she had been the means of introducing him to Fox when he was merely deputy-treasurer of Covent Garden, and she thought it strange and unkind of him to kick down the ladder by which he had climbed. Her long-suffering friend, Woodward, had then agreed to act for her.

As she was preparing to go to the opera one evening early this autumn she was arrested by Sheriff's officers and carried off to a sponging-house at the instance of two wine merchants who had started actions against her. They had repeatedly sent in accounts to her, which she had ignored, because she thought she was not liable for them, the debts having been contracted on behalf of Calcraft when she was living with him in Parliament Street several years before. Woodifield's account, amounting to £80, was for a consignment of red champagne, which, at Calcraft's request—so, at least, she avers—she had ordered to be sent to the Marquess of Granby in Germany. Finmore's was for claret ordered for Calcraft himself. Calcraft had disclaimed both debts. The claret, he said, she had ordered for her own use, which she denied. Finmore had been *his* wine merchant, not hers; she had never dealt with anyone but Tourbeville. Her pride and dignity forbade her entering into any litigation relating to the account for the wine sent to Lord Granby, and she decided to accept liability for this. The Sheriff's officer proved willing to take her word that she would arrange for it to be paid the very next day, and she gave bail for Finmore's account, which she was resolved to contest in order both to expose Calcraft's meanness and duplicity and also to test the validity of the diplomatic immunity conferred upon her by Count von Haslang. She applied for help to her friend, Mr. Hearne, who immediately supplied her with the money. She had already borrowed several sums from him, and he had also redeemed for her the valuables she had left in pawn on her departure from Ireland. Her indebtedness to him now amounted to £640, and she admits in her *Apology* that he got very little of it back.

The theatrical season opened brilliantly. Powell was a great success. George Anne considered him excellent in spite of his comparative inexperience. "There is no doubt but he would have proved an ornament to the stage, had he had time to acquire that knowledge which is requisite to make the profession a science."

Her first appearance with him was in *Venice Preserved* on September 16th, 1767. There had been rumours that he had been anxious that Mrs. Yates, with whom he had acted at Drury Lane, should be engaged as the leading actress to play opposite to him, but he was so extravagant in his praise of George Anne's playing of Belvidera that she thought he had abandoned the idea. A few days later, however, Colman told her that it was absolutely necessary to engage Mrs. Yates to prevent her being engaged at Drury Lane. He promised her that the addition of Mrs. Yates to the company would not injure her in any way. In fact, he said, the effect would be rather the reverse, for many pieces might be revived in which they could shine together. Besides, he undertook that she should retain most of her accustomed characters, if not all of them.

George Anne determined to make the best of a bad job. She admired Mrs. Yates's great talents and did her best to get on with her. But her efforts to be friendly were coldly received by the other lady, and she was deeply hurt at being suspected of being insincere. There was bound to be rivalry between them, for they were of much the same age and aspired to the same parts. Mrs. Yates was given many of the parts that George Anne had been accustomed to play: Calista, Lady Townley, Desdemona, Lady Macbeth, and Cordelia, though Georgiane retained Monimia and Juliet, which she played to Powell's Romeo. But there were, as Colman had said, plays in which they could shine together. Mrs. Yates made her first appearance this season on October 16th as Jane Shore with George Anne as Alicia, and appeared as Hermione in the *Distressed Mother* with George Anne as Andromache.

George Anne had long been anxious to take revenge on Calcraft, and had composed a long letter exposing his treatment of her and vindicating her own conduct, and this she proposed to publish. On October 5th, 1767, the day of the first representation of Colman's play, *The English Merchant*, in which she was to play Lady Alton, she caused the following advertisement to be inserted in all the public papers: "Speedily will be published, a letter from George Anne Bellamy, to John Calcraft, Esq: with this motto:

"So comes the reck'ning when the banquet's o'er,
The dreadful reck'ning, and men smile no more."
GAY.

Just before the piece was about to begin Colman came into her dressing-room and told her that Calcraft had been to see him, vowing vengeance against the theatre if she did not promise to give up all thought of such a publication, which, he said, was at once putting a dagger into his heart, and a pistol to his head. Colman added that he had been very violent and abusive. He had sworn that he would apply to the Lord Chamberlain to have her silenced and would turn her children adrift if she persisted. While Colman admitted that Calcraft had been very rude and that he resented it, he thought that her intention was extremely ill-advised and used all the arguments he could to persuade her out of it. He pointed out that Calcraft did possess considerable influence and could do great damage both to her and to the theatre. She must remember that she was playing under a letter of licence, and consequently, if she persisted in printing this letter, she might greatly injure her creditors. But George Anne was feeling obstinate, and she refused even to listen to the advice of Colonel Calcraft, who tried, in her own interests, to dissuade her from drawing down upon herself his brother's dangerous wrath.

For a long time she withstood all arguments and persuasions, but eventually, not being able to find a single person who agreed with her, she consented to defer publication until the end of the season at least, a promise that she says she never ceased repenting of, for, had she persisted in her intention, she believed she would have vindicated her conduct in respect to Calcraft, and the world would have been clearly convinced of the cruelty with which she had been treated. She made the concession solely out of the esteem and regard she entertained for Mr. Colman, who, she believed, was, in turn, actuated entirely by his friendship for her. It does not seem to have occurred to her that both her contemporaries and posterity might take as poor a view of her financial eccentricities as did Calcraft.

From the very start there had been disagreements between the four new proprietors, mainly between Colman and Harris, though Rutherford always backed Harris, and Powell invariably supported his friend Colman. Harris had insisted upon the engagement of Mrs. Lessingham, a beautiful but quarrelsome woman, and an indifferent but conceited actress, in whom he was interested, and, although he had assured Colman that he did not wish her to be considered with more partiality than any other performer, he had thereafter persistently tried to have her given parts for which Colman thought her unsuited. In particular he wanted her to play Imogen in their proposed new and lavish production of *Cymbeline*. Colman had allotted this part to Miss Ward, and he made strong protests against the change. He had, he said, no animosity against Mrs. Lessingham, but, as her friend, he would advise her never to play a line of tragedy. But eventually, in order to preserve the peace, he gave in to Harris's persistence. On Mrs. Yates's engagement, however, he took it for granted that she would play Imogen, for he could not conceive that, if his partners had the interests of the theatre at heart, they could want anyone else to play a part in which, as George Anne says, she "had long been established and universally admired". But Harris still insisted in putting forward the claims of Mrs. Lessingham, and

Rutherford supported him. In George Anne's opinion, while Mrs. Lessingham's beauty and figure were greatly in her favour, "she could by no means be said to surpass Mrs. Yates, who joined hard-earned science to her other qualifications." There was a violent quarrel, but in the end Colman carried the day. *Cymbeline* was produced on December 28th at a royal command performance, and Mrs. Yates played Imogen. But when Colman announced the play again for December 31st, Harris and Rutherford had recourse to their written veto under the agreement. Colman replied with an ingenious counterstroke. He offered to publish his partners' interdiction as a reason for not performing any play at all that night, but flatly refused to substitute another play. The public would have resented being deprived of their entertainment because of a domestic dispute at the theatre, and it appears that *Cymbeline* was duly performed a second time.

It had come to open war between the proprietors, and for several months their differences were ventilated in the public press. But it cannot be said that Colman had all the right on his side. He was very dictatorial in his methods and seems to have treated Harris and Rutherford with supreme contempt. They complained also, with some justice, that they were made cyphers of by Colman and Powell, who spent so much on clothes and decorations that all the profits were absorbed by their extravagance, although the house was usually crowded. And Colman seems to have been even more addicted than Harris to foisting on the company young ladies who had nothing to commend them but their physical attractions.

Amid all these quarrels George Anne was not at all happy at the theatre, and she went there only when she had to play. She considered that Powell had acted with duplicity in the matter of Mrs. Yates's engagement, and was no longer on good terms with him. In fact, they rarely spoke to each other off the stage. She occupied herself with her duties at Count von Haslang's in Golden Square, and spent as much time as she could with some new friends, Mr. Hoole and his wife. Hoole was the translator of Tasso, Metastasio, and other Italian poets, and George Anne, who had always prided herself inordinately on her culture, found him very congenial company. "A relaxation of this nature," she says, "was necessary to dispel the chagrin I felt that all my visionary theatric castles were tottering."

For her benefit this season she appeared as Mrs. Lovemore in Murphy's play *The Way to Keep Him*, which had not been acted at Covent Garden before. Her last appearance was as Veturia on April 20th, 1768.

On June 4th the theatre closed down, and when, a few days later, Harris and Rutherford went there, they found it barred and bolted against them, and Sarjant, the housekeeper, refused to admit them. They thereupon broke in and removed a considerable portion of the wardrobe, music, and prompt books—enough at any rate to ensure that no play could be put on. They had an exact inventory made of what they took away, and undertook to return it intact when an accommodation should be reached. Sarjant was turned out, and they put in a guard of their own to secure the premises. On legal advice Colman made a formal application to a Westminster magistrate, who ordered that Sarjant should be reinstated in possession of the theatre, and this was done, so honours were about even.

In August, 1768, the young King of Denmark, Christian VII, then only nineteen, came on a visit to England. Shortly after his arrival, he sent word to Garrick of his desire to see a few plays while he was in London. Garrick was most anxious to comply, but it was very difficult for him to get together a company at a few days' notice; it was out of season and most of the London players were either on holiday or away on summer engagements in the provinces. In his dilemma he applied to his old friend, Henry Woodward, and asked him to request Mrs. Bellamy also to come to his aid. She readily agreed to do so. Garrick thereupon announced that a special performance of the *Suspicious Husband* would take place "by particular desire" at Drury Lane on August 18th. He himself played Ranger, with Woodward as Jack Meggot, and Mrs. Bellamy as Clarinda. To her great distress, on her first appearance a solitary hiss was heard. Garrick hastened to assure her that it was apparent malice, as the general opinion was evidently for her, so she composed herself and played as well as she could. The interrupter was just as likely to have been a creditor as a critic.

Shortly afterwards the King expressed a wish to see *Macbeth*, but he asked for it at such very short notice that on September 7th Garrick wrote to Baron Dieda to say that he would do everything possible to entertain the King next night, but he could have wished that he had received longer notice that he might have been better prepared. At one day's notice it was not in his power to produce *Macbeth*, but he would be pleased to do so later on, if His Majesty would fix a suitable date. He proposed instead to regale him with the *Provoked Wife*. Once again he called upon Mrs. Bellamy for her services, and she played Lady Fanciful, with Garrick as Sir John Brute, and Mrs. Stephens as Lady Brute. The young King's longing to see *Macbeth* was duly satisfied on September 22nd, shortly after the season had opened at Drury Lane, when Garrick ventured to convey to him a gentle reproof for his airy assumption that a play of such importance could be put on at a moment's notice. He sent him a message that the role of Macbeth was so exacting that to his great regret he would be unable after the performance to light His Majesty to his coach as both duty and desire would have inclined him to do.

On October 1st the King visited Covent Garden to see *Jane Shore*, in which George Anne was as usual playing Alicia. He was so discourteous as to fall asleep during the performance, so George Anne "unwilling that he should lose the *fine acting* it might be supposed he had come to see," approached his box and shouted the line "O! thou false lord" so loudly into his ear that he awoke with a shock from his slumbers. She was greatly amused afterwards when the Comte de Bathmore, the Danish Ambassador, told her that the King had said that he would not be married to a woman with such a bell voice upon any account, as he should never expect to sleep.

This autumn George Anne experienced an additional chagrin when Colman introduced a young and charming actress called Miss Morris and insisted that she should essay Juliet. This was one of George Anne's favourite parts, and she had already played it this season, on September 26th. It was not customary at this time to take the principal performers' parts from them, except for a person of acknowledged merit, but George Anne admitted that, as the girl's youth and attractions were exactly what Juliet's should be, it would have been absurd to a degree if she had objected to her playing the part. And she was generous in her tribute to Miss Morris, who, in her opinion, might have been another Farren had she lived. But Miss Morris was as fragile as she was beautiful. "This fair flower, like the lily of the valley, reared awhile her head, displayed her beauties to the sun, and diffused around the sweetest odours. But transient as the lily was her fate. Like her lovely emblem surcharged with rain, she soon dropped and charmed no more." She became so ill that she was unable to appear as Juliet at her own benefit on May 9th, 1769, and "at the solicitation of her relations" George Anne readily agreed to play for her. Perhaps she was glad to get her part back, but it was none the less a generous action.

One evening, early in February, 1769, George Anne received a message asking her to go to Somerset House to see Lady Tyrawley. This often happened, and she thought nothing of it, even though she was aware that Lady Tyrawley was ill. Shortly before, Powell had told her that he and Bensley had been dining with Lord Tyrawley and that Miss Nancy O'Hara had remarked that Lady Tyrawley was very ill, and that George Anne might soon expect a considerable legacy. But on this particular evening she had a bad cold and was, moreover, very tired after playing Alicia, so she decided not to go to Somerset House till next morning. At nine o'clock next morning she received a note from Lady Tyrawley's woman, informing her that her mistress had died at three o'clock. His lordship had arrived at five, had locked himself up to examine his wife's

papers, and had then gone away, giving her strict orders not to
have any communication with Mrs. Bellamy, upon pain of his
displeasure. It afterwards transpired that, in rummaging
among the papers, he had found a letter from George Anne,
which had confirmed his suspicions that she had encouraged
his wife to refuse his request to cut off the entail of the
Blessington estate, in the hope that everything would be left to
her. George Anne denied that she had done anything of the
kind. Lady Tyrawley had indeed written to her when she was
at Holwood, enclosing the letter in which her husband had
made this request and informing her that she had decided to
refuse it and leave everything to her, and she had merely
replied, returning the letter and thanking her for her beneficent
intentions. But she had given no advice. Elsewhere in her
Apology she states definitely that she had. Whatever may be the
truth of the matter, it certainly created a final breach between
her and her father. Lady Tyrawley's will, if she ever made one,
was never produced, and George Anne implies that her father
suppressed or destroyed it. She saw him only twice again,
once casually in the Green Room and once in his own house,
when he was first confined during his last and fatal illness.

Unfortunately, her relations with Mrs. Yates had not improved, and their jealousy of each other came to a head on the
approach of George Anne's benefit this season, which was to
take place on March 28th. She had not been feeling well of late
and had therefore decided upon a piece in which she could
appear without much exertion. Her choice had fallen upon *The
Distressed Mother*, which was considered to be one of the
company's strongest pieces, Powell playing Orestes, Mrs.
Yates, Hermione, and George Anne herself, Andromache, a
part in which she displayed considerable merit. But, on this
occasion, she was heedless enough to omit the polite formality
of asking Mrs. Yates if she would appear for her. She excuses
herself rather lamely on the ground that Mrs. Yates had played
the part quite recently, and that it was unusual to request a
performer to play a part in a benefit unless it meant studying a

new one. But when the play was actually announced in the public press, Mrs. Yates flatly refused to appear, and wrote a curt note to Mrs. Bellamy intimating her refusal. George Anne replied not too tactfully, and a few days later their rather acrimonious exchange of notes was printed in the papers.

George Anne's old patroness, the Duchess of Queensberry, consumed with curiosity, sent for her to enquire what the dispute was really about, and George Anne told her that she had no idea, but admitted that she was concerned at the loss of so capital a performer, since, playing as she was under licence, all her regular salary was earmarked for her creditors, and she had nothing for her own support but the produce of her benefit. The Duchess assured her that at least she need have no apprehension about the boxes, since she and her sister, the Duchess of Douglas, intended to take care of them. George Anne discussed possible plays with the two illustrious ladies. She said that she did not feel strong enough to take any of her great parts, Juliet, Belvidera, or Cleone, and eventually they settled on the *Albion Queens*. George Anne played Mary, Queen of Scots, and Queen Elizabeth was played by Mrs. Ward.

The two Duchesses kept their promise to support her, and the benefit was a very grand and fashionable event. George Anne says that the famous Douglas cause was decided in favour of the Douglas family on that very day, and that in consequence there was a great ovation for the Duchess of Douglas. But this is a slight if allowable dramatic licence, though the decision was fairly recent, and this may have been the Duchess's first appearance at the theatre since the event. At any rate the benefit was very lucrative, and the next day George Anne inserted the following advertisement in the papers: "Mrs. Bellamy takes the earliest opportunity of returning her sincere thanks for the numerous and splendid appearance at her benefit yesterday evening."

The theatre sustained a severe loss this year by the death of Powell, who caught cold after playing cricket and died at

Bristol on July 3rd at the early age of thirty-four. The last time he had seen George Anne, he had requested her pardon for the way in which he had treated her and had assured her that he would make amends next season for the injury he had done her in her profession. His place as chief tragic actor at Covent Garden was taken by 'Gentleman' Smith, who had now established himself so firmly as a favourite with the public that he had been able to insert in his contract a clause that he should never be called upon to play on Monday evenings, since it would interfere with the fox-hunting in which he was wont to indulge at week-ends.

On October 7th Covent Garden hastily put on a show in opposition to the Shakespeare pageant Garrick had announced for Drury Lane. A pageant was somewhat incongruously sandwiched into a comedy called *Man and Wife* by Colman. George Anne figured in it as the Tragic Muse. She was rarely called upon to act this season and would rarely have been well enough to do so if she had been. But on October 26th she appeared as Alicia, on November 6th as Arpasia in *Tamerlane*, and, on November 15th, as Lady Alton in the *English Merchant*. On this occasion Mrs. Yates was persuaded, or, as George Anne puts it, over-persuaded to play the youthful Emilia, a character which George Anne considered to be totally unfit for her notwithstanding her beauty. Her own part of Lady Alton would, she thought, have "better become that dignity and figure which she possesses in so eminent a degree". The spice of cattiness contained in this observation does not come too well from an actress who was still playing Juliet, when, at the lowest reckoning—her own—she was nearing forty.

A young actress called Miss Miller had recently joined the company. Like Mrs. Bellamy herself, she had made her first appearance as Monimia, but with considerably less success. In February, Colman insisted that she should appear as Sigismunda, a part which properly belonged to Mrs. Bellamy. George Anne remarks that "this actress had nothing to recommend her but the favour of the acting manager", and she was probably right, for more often than not she contrived to be fair, if not flattering, about her rivals, and Francis Gentleman in his *Dramatic Censor* says that Miss Miller "stumbled upon the part most injudiciously". Nevertheless, before the end of the season she was playing others of Mrs. Bellamy's accustomed parts—Marcia, Imoinda, and Athanais.

George Anne's performances now were few and far between. In the months of February and March she played only Isabella in *Measure for Measure*, Berinthia in Vanbrugh's *Relapse*, which had not been played at Covent Garden for five years, and Roxana in the *Rival Queens*. Hitherto she had always played Statira, but on this occasion that part was played by Mrs. Yates for one night only. At her own benefit on March 31st she played Isabella in Garrick's piece of that name, an adaptation of Southerne's *Fatal Marriage*. Her very last appearance as a regular actress at the theatre seems to have been as Rutland in the *Unhappy Favourite* for Mrs. Ward's benefit. It was fortunate for her that she did not know then that she was not to appear again.

During this season the disputes between the proprietors had reached yet another crisis. Colman came to George Anne and told her that it had become necessary for him to get a paper signed by the performers, expressing their confidence in his management and their willingness to serve under him. He had brought her this paper and requested her to sign it. She told him frankly that, as she was engaged to all four of the proprietors, she did not think, at first sight, that it would be right for her to sign any paper giving one a preference over the others. To this Colman replied that, since by the articles he was only acting manager, he could see no impropriety in her signing a paper which merely related to that right. However, he was so convinced that, after reflection, she would be of his way of thinking, that he would leave the paper with her and would dine with her next day to pick it up.

He had scarcely left her when Rutherford came in with Woodward. Rutherford asked her at once if she had signed the paper. She replied that she had not yet done so, but admitted that it had been left with her for her consideration, and that she probably would do so. Rutherford asked her to show it to him, but this she absolutely refused to do, saying that it would be a breach of trust to do so. Rutherford admitted that, if he had got hold of it, he would have burnt it, as he was sure that two of the principal performers had signed it who would not have done so, if they had known the truth of the matter. But George Anne persisted in her refusal, and he left her in a rage. Woodward remained behind and used every argument to dissuade her from signing it. He pointed out that Colman had treated her badly. Woodward was her best friend, and she owed much to him in every way, so she gave in at last and sent the paper back to Colman with a card saying that she desired to decline signing it, but hoped her refusal would not offend him and he would dine with her as had been arranged. She received no reply at all, and from that moment they became totally estranged. It was a fatal mistake, as it turned out; she had allowed herself, contrary to her own judgment, to be persuaded to take a course which, in the event, proved to be most detrimental to her interests.

About this time she was very much disturbed because of a coolness which arose between Woodward and her friends, the Hooles. This was exceedingly awkward for her owing to her relations with both parties. She was under endless obligations to Woodward, who had been a true friend to her, and she was also indebted to Hoole, not only for £40—which incidentally she never paid back—but also for his kindness towards a nephew of hers. Who this nephew was, if indeed he was a nephew, has never transpired, and she nowhere mentions him by name. She had undertaken his upbringing from an infant, and had had him brought up as a gentleman, believing at the time that she would always be able to maintain him in that state. She had sent him to school at Westminster, but when her financial position began to deteriorate, an alteration in his mode of education became needful, and, while she was in

Scotland, she had sent to her mother requesting her to remove him from Westminster and place him where he could learn arithmetic, with a view to his entering some business house. This was done, and she had regularly sent the money for his schooling. But the boy's pride had been much hurt by this arrangement, and when George Anne informed him that she had found him a place in the City, he had pertly replied that she might have saved herself the trouble, as she had brought him up as a gentleman and ought to support him as such. She suggested that, if he felt so strongly on the subject, he might seek the interest of his schoolfellow, Sir Watkin Williams Wynn, the young Welsh baronet, of whose acquaintance he boasted so much. He had answered that, before he would be a wretched dependent upon any man on earth, he would wait till he was the age to be enlisted and prefer carrying a musket. His spirit had pleased her, and she had determined not to thwart his ambitions. The boy had become friendly with the Hoole family, and it was through Mr. Hoole's good offices that he was given a brevet in the East India Company's service at Bombay. But then there arose the problem of fitting him out. Here Woodward came to her aid, and agreed to advance the money required, some eighty or ninety pounds, on her nephew's own bond, even though he was still a minor. He liked the boy and trusted his character.

This summer George Anne took a small house at the riverside village of Strand-on-the-Green with a view along the Thames to Kew Bridge. It was delightfully rural, but it was conveniently near town, and she still had to attend at Count von Haslang's almost every day. Woodward decided to lodge with her there, and, though he proposed to join Foote in Scotland for the ensuing season, generously insisted upon paying her rent even during his absence. He also sent in a stock of wine and lent her the money to lay in a supply of coal for the whole year. Many believed that at this time and for several years afterwards George Anne was Woodward's mistress. She herself always denied this, maintaining that his former passion for her had mellowed into affection and that they were never more than the best of friends. There seems to be little reason why she should not be believed. She was perfectly frank about the nature of her relationship not only with Metham and Digges, whom she loved, but also with Calcraft, whom she hated. Why should she have troubled to disguise the fact if she had a similar relationship with Woodward, for whom she confessed she felt gratitude and respect as well as a deep and sincere affection?

Before he went to Scotland Woodward had occasion for the forty guineas he had recently lent her, and she tried to procure this money from Count von Haslang, who, however, replied that he had not that sum by him, and referred her to his former housekeeper, now his *gouvernante*, Mrs. Myers, who was so rude to her in front of a crowd of other people that she left the house and refused to resume her duties there.

For some weeks now she remained tranquilly at Strand-on-the-Green, diverting herself with her books and the pet birds with which she always loved to surround herself. She even started to try to write a comedy. But she was attacked a pain in her side, which became so acute that she decided that she must move to London for a while to put herself under the care of Mr. Adair. This was most inconvenient, for her resources were very low at the time. Apart from the remainder of the jewels left to her by Miss Meredith, she had only a few guineas and no prospect of obtaining any more until she received the next instalment of his rent from Woodward. Nevertheless, she wrote to a wealthy friend of hers, Mrs. Moore, who lived in South Audley Street, asking her to engage a lodging in London for herself and her maid for a few weeks. She did this, without considering Mrs. Moore's taste for expense or the contracted state of her own finances.

On his departure for Scotland, Woodward had left in her care his strong-box containing all his papers, and this she thought she must not leave behind. Just before she arrived at Mrs. Moore's she suddenly decided that the wisest course would be to place it in safe custody with a Mr. Colley, in Grosvenor Street. It was fortunate that she did so, for that very night a gang of thieves broke into Mrs. Moore's house, where she was staying the night, frightened the two ladies with threats of violence, and ransacked the whole place in their search for a bag of gold, the presence of which in the house had been incautiously revealed to one of them in a tavern by the callow indiscretion of Mrs. Moore's boastful butler. It was a terrifying experience for George Anne, and she was thankful to remove next day to the lodging that had been taken for her in Leicester Street.

Her future now seemed to be very uncertain. Her three years agreement at Covent Garden had expired, and since her constant friend, Woodward, was not acting there this season, she did not yet know whether she would be engaged again. On the approach of the season a Mr. Cook from the theatre came to her from Colman to inform her that, if she would accept a salary of six pounds a week, he would engage her; if not, he should no longer look upon her as one of the company. It was quite obvious that the offer of a very much reduced salary could only mean that she was to be relegated to minor parts, or, at any rate, to very occasional appearances, and she flatly refused the offer. But Mr. Harris, who came to see her soon after, begged her not to perturb herself and assured her that, as soon as the dispute between the proprietors was settled, she would be reinstated in her old position. And on his frequent visits to her he repeated these assurances, as did also Mr. Leake, who had recently purchased half of Rutherford's share, when he went abroad. Both assured her that no reconciliation could take place in the theatre without her being made a party to it.

Although by this time Count von Haslang had come to her help again, George Anne found her lodgings in Leicester Street very expensive, and, since there was no longer any hope of a theatrical engagement this season, there seemed no point in her remaining in London. Accordingly, as soon as she was feeling so much better that she no longer needed Mr. Adair's constant attention, she returned to Strand-on-the-Green for the winter, and spent Christmas there. In the spring she had a letter from Foote saying that Woodward, whom he had left in Scotland, was well and would be back in a month or six weeks. He said that he had taken a house for him near his own in Little Chelsea, and that Woodward desired that she would go and look at it and get it ready against his coming. Foote added that he hoped to see her soon, as he was proposing to do a short summer season at the Haymarket Theatre and would like to engage her for his company. George Anne went to inspect the house, which she found to be little more than a hovel and very inconvenient. She could not imagine what Woodward could want with such a place, except perhaps, as a cloak to conceal the fact that he was living in the same house as herself. But a petty subterfuge of this sort was so unlike Woodward that she did not believe it. She wrote to Foote declining to have anything to do with the house. At the same time she thanked him for his kind offer of an engagement, but told him that neither her health nor her spirits would permit her to accept it. How, indeed, could she play uproarious comedy or farce in her present mood of dejection?

On his return Woodward came to live with her again at Strand-on-the-Green. He assured her that it had always been his intention to do so, and that he had not commissioned Foote to find him a house. It was just a notion of that crazy and extravagant little man's. He joined Foote for a short season at the Haymarket, which lasted from May to July, and was so lucrative that the two comedians went off together for a tour on the Continent to spend some of their profits. It is not unlikely that Woodward also paid George Anne's expenses for the short trip she made this summer to Boulogne to pay a nostalgic visit to the convent at which she had been brought up.

Chapter Seventeen

ALTHOUGH SHE HAD NOT BEEN ENGAGED LAST YEAR at Covent Garden, George Anne could not reconcile herself to the fact that her theatrical career was over, and she still had hopes that she would be re-engaged for the forthcoming season. This dream was encouraged by Harris, who still assured her that, as the proprietors were on the verge of being reconciled, she could depend upon being included as one of the first articles of the treaty. Foolishly she regarded this as a definite promise, and when Woodward arrived back from his tour abroad, she informed him of the certainty of her re-engagement. Woodward, who had already been in touch with the theatre and apparently had a very different view of the situation, did not reply. But at this moment a servant brought her a letter from her mother, informing her that Mr. Harris had just called at her house and desired to see her there next day, "as very particular business rendered it impossible for him to come to Strand." When she read him this letter, Woodward seemed to be somewhat reassured, though it was obvious that some doubt still lingered in his mind.

Next morning George Anne drove up to her mother's house in Brewer Street. Harris arrived before the hour he had appointed, and she could see at once by his manner that something was wrong. He explained to her that the proprietors were reconciled, but that when he had mentioned an engagement for her, Mr. Leake had not seconded him, as he had expected, and Colman had declared that he would sooner see the theatre in flames and himself in the midst of it than consent to her ever being of the company.

George Anne was very angry and demanded why he wanted to send for her so urgently if it was to communicate to her news of this kind; surely he could have waited till he saw her, or he could have written her a letter. Harris said that the reason why he wished to see her at once was that Colman was very anxious to engage Woodward, and he had sent for her to advise her to prevail upon her friend not to accept an engagement without her. This suggestion made George Anne even more furious. She assured Harris that she had too much spirit to be tacked to the agreement even of the first performer that ever trod the stage, and too much merit to be unemployed and take a salary for nothing. Harris, bowed, said he admired her sentiments, and bade her farewell. They parted, says George Anne, "with as much ceremony and cold good breeding as if they had never met before."

George Anne now could not avoid acknowledging that she would have to abandon all further thoughts of resuming her theatrical career. She did not wish for an engagement unless it meant being reinstated in all her old parts and afforded her due quota of new ones; but, if she could not achieve this on her own merits, she did not want it at all. And above all she reprobated asking such a favour from Woodward, even supposing that he would have been willing to grant it, which she doubted; for she did not think that a person who knew the value of money so well as he did would have consented to have her tacked to him by way of dependent. And at any rate she would not be so unreasonable or so lacking in pride as to make such a request. Nevertheless, she did very much regret having made Colman her enemy, and she knew she had only herself to blame for it. Though she deplored his resentment, she acknowledged the justice of it.

George Anne had formed the habit of giving a small dinner on December 3rd every year in honour of the name-day of her patron and benefactor, Count Franz von Haslang. This year she had invited the Count's secretary and some ladies to dine with her at her mother's house in Brewer Street, where she now always stayed when she came to town from Strand-on-the-Green. On the day before the party her mother was not well but would not let her put it off, and the next day, although she was worse, she would not hear of allowing George Anne to send for the doctor. But she did consent to take to her bed.

The party was very gay; George Anne's guests became very merry, and there was a great deal of laughter. In the midst of it her mother suddenly came in, and, going up to Mrs. Howe, one of the ladies present, desired her not to raise a mob about her door by her immoderate laughing. Since Mrs. Bellamy was well-known as being remarkably polite, the guests realised that there must be some extraordinary cause for this uncommon rudeness on her part, and, indeed, they soon discovered that she had become light-headed. George Anne sent at once for her mother's favourite physician, Dr. Macdonald. He treated her for ten or twelve days, and then, finding that her condition did not improve, called in Dr. Schomberg, who pronounced her to be suffering from a lethargic palsy, and said that nothing could be done for her. For a few days more she lingered on. George Anne was with her when she died.

The landlord of the Brewer Street house had promised never to raise the rent while Mrs. Bellamy or her daughter occupied it, and since the rent was very low George Anne decided to keep it on. As practically everything that her mother possessed had originated from her, and her brother had resigned all claim to her estate, she believed that she was the sole heiress, and thought it needless to take out letters of administration.

One evening, shortly after her mother's death, she was sitting talking to a friend of hers, Mrs. Butler, whom she had invited with her two young daughters to keep her company during her mother's illness and to stay on afterwards. Suddenly they were startled by a loud and violent knocking on the door. She told her servant not to open, but to enquire from the area what the strangers' business might be. The men outside told the girl that, if she did not immediately open the door, it would be broken in, as they had got the broad seal. Not having the remotest idea what the broad seal might be, George Anne herself went to the window and asked what they wanted. They replied that she should be informed when they were let in, and that, if this was not done at once, they had authority to break open the door. As there seemed to be no means of preventing them from doing so, she ordered the door to be opened, and five or six men rushed in and took possession in the name of her cousin, Crawford. After the death of his wife, that gentleman had spent all her money and fallen on evil days, and now, having discovered that George Anne had made no legal claim to her mother's property, he had taken out letters of administration by swearing himself to be her legitimate heir.

Since it was out of term time and it was therefore impossible for her to obtain any immediate legal redress, George Anne found herself forced to quit the house that very night with her friends, though it was already past eleven o'clock and Mrs. Butler's two children were already in bed. She could not imagine where they would find a lodging at this hour of the night, but at last thought of sending to Woodward, who had recently taken a house in Leicester Street. Fortunately, there was plenty of room for them there, since the house was large and, in fact, Woodward had taken it with the idea of letting part of it. He cheerfully consented to accommodate George Anne and her friends for the time being until they could find a suitable lodging.

George Anne had given her mother an expensive funeral in the confident expectation of being able to pay for it out of the estate, so now she sent to the undertaker, Mr. Gordon, to inform him of what had happened and request him to look to the administrator for the expenses of the funeral. But he returned answer that, as she had ordered it, he would expect her to pay for it, adding, somewhat irrelevantly, that it was a very genteel one and that he would defy anybody in the trade to furnish one more elegant for fifty guineas, though he would charge her only forty-two.

George Anne commenced a suit against Crawford as soon as

possible, and he, knowing that it would be discovered that he had obtained the letters of administration under false pretences, decided to fly the country. He got no farther than Gravesend, where, being very drunk, he fell into the river and was drowned. But the thought that her cousin had at last met with a condign retribution for his many misdeeds could scarcely compensate George Anne for the loss of all her mother's possessions, which he had sold for what he could get for them. And, worst of all, his hirelings had destroyed as waste-paper the documents relating to a sum of £700 owing by a Mrs. Holt to the late Mrs. Bellamy, which was to have been repaid on the following Wednesday. Mrs. Holt, the sister of Dr. Warburton, Bishop of Gloucester, was a remarkably greedy woman, and most of the debt she owed to George Anne's mother had been contracted in order to satisfy her inordinate craving for the richer and more costly pleasures of the table. In her haste George Anne had left these papers behind at the house in Brewer Street and she was obliged to inform the Bishop of Gloucester, who was to have paid over the money, that she could not wait upon him to receive it, as the papers were lost. The Bishop replied that he could by no means think of paying the money unless she did produce the papers, as he would still be liable to pay it to those who might find them. And so all that George Anne gained by her mother's death was an addition to her own obligations; she had the funeral to pay for, some small debts of her mother's, and the costs of the suit she had commenced against Crawford, which amounted to £17.

Fortunately, her landlord had stoutly maintained that the house at Brewer Street was his and was let to George Anne herself, so that Crawford had not been able to remove the fixtures as well as the furniture. George Anne sent for her own furniture from Strand-on-the-Green and settled in her mother's old home. Her friends rallied to her aid. Count von Haslang undertook to pay for the furnishing of her first floor, which would come to £120. Woodward presented her with two 'capital basso-relievos' for the door, three handsome girandoles,

a beautiful grate, and other things; all her intimate friends
contributed some ornament, and she delightedly declared that
her house, in appearance was a "little cabinet".

When the day arrived on which Cullen, the upholsterer, was
to be paid for the furnishing of the first floor, she arranged to
settle his account at four o'clock in the afternoon, and sent to
Count von Haslang for the money he had promised her. The
Count's secretary and a friend, Mrs. Tuffnal, were with her
when the answer arrived. It was, she says, "written upon a
quarter sheet of paper and sealed at the corner like a common
note." She opened it and started to read. It began as many of
the Count's letters must have begun: "I wonder you will not
get an engagement——" George Anne read no more and
tossed it into the fire. Soon after, the Count's porter returned
with a message expressing his master's surprise that she had
not condescended to honour him with an answer. George
Anne sent back her compliments and said that she could not
conceive that any answer could be required to a note upon so
disagreeable and hackneyed a subject. Once more the messenger came back; His Excellency thought that, if his letter
required no answer, at least she should have acknowledged the
receipt of the bill. By this time the note and the bill with it
were consumed to ashes, and George Anne screamed: "I am
undone! I am undone! I have burnt it." But for once her
carelessness did not meet with its due retribution. By some
curious chance the Count in an idle moment had noted down
the numbers of the banknotes he had received that morning,
and the Bank was willing to pay, if the note did not turn up by
a certain date. Woodward obligingly advanced the money,
and in due course was reimbursed by the Bank.

Gordon, the undertaker, was now pressing her insistently
for payment, and she arranged to borrow money from a Jewish
moneylender called Cohen in order to pay him. Always un-
businesslike almost to the point of idiocy, upon Cohen's
undertaking to let her have the money within the next day or
two, she handed over to him two notes promising to repay it

with interest, but, when it was not forthcoming and she sent for it, she was told that he had absconded. And she was disconcerted to find that the notes she had so foolishly given him would be presented for payment in due course by the persons to whom he had disposed of them.

In August, 1772, John Calcraft died after a serious illness of several months, leaving behind him a princely fortune, which he had amassed as Army agent and Contractor to the forces. While Fox had held the office of Paymaster General he had had even ampler opportunities of lining his pockets, but in 1763 he had deserted Fox and gone over to Pitt in the well-founded belief that he could do still better in the political as well as the financial arena. In 1768 he achieved a cherished ambition by becoming Member of Parliament for Rochester, which he continued to represent till his death.

His fortune was reputed to amount to more than £250,000, in addition to the great investments in landed property he had made in several parts of the country. His principal seat was Ingress Abbey on the banks of the Thames at Greenhithe, and he had other property in Kent at Leeds, Bromfield, and Northfleet. In 1757, while he was still living with Mrs. Bellamy, he had purchased the estate of Rempstone in the Isle of Purbeck. Ten years later he had become Lord of the Manor of Wareham, and at the time of his death owned most of the town, and had just completed negotiations for further property in Dorset. He also owned estates in Lincolnshire.

About 1764 he had taken as his mistress an eighteen-year-old actress called Elizabeth Bride, a pretty, slender little creature with blue eyes and golden hair, who played small parts in low comedy and farce at Drury Lane. Her father, a scene-shifter and bill-sticker at the theatre, had disapproved of the connexion so much that he had committed suicide, but her mother had been much more amenable and had regarded an annuity of £300 for herself as ample compensation for her share in her daughter's dishonour. Miss Bride had become, as it were, *maîtresse-en-titre* to the great financier, and lived in great luxury,

surrounded by servants in livery and as much bedizened with
jewels as her predecessor, Mrs. Bellamy, had been in her prime.
She had presented Calcraft with four children in appallingly
rapid succession, and at the time of his decease had apparently
just informed him that she was expecting another. In his will
he showed clearly enough that he would have married her, had
it been in his power to do so. She was appointed guardian of
his children with the right to live at Ingress Abbey during her
"widowhood".*

Calcraft, who seems to have had a particular affection for his
Dorset property, left instructions that he was to be buried in a
vault at St. Mary's Church, Wareham, where he now lies. A
tablet was placed on the wall of the church as an affectionate
tribute to his memory "to record the gratitude of his Family,
who owe everything to his Exertions". The sentiment is not
only becoming, but exceptionally veracious. As he had shown
when he was applying in 1770 for the grant of arms to his
illegitimate children by Miss Bride, he was according to them as
full a recognition as it was in his power to bestow, seeing that
he had a legal wife. He was now making his eldest son by her
his chief heir, ignoring the prior claims of Henry, his son by
Mrs. Bellamy, who was nearly ten years older than John. To
Henry and Caroline, his sister, he left only £5,000 apiece on
attaining the age of twenty-one, or, in the girl's case, marriage.
This is understandable in the case of Harry, whom Calcraft had
surrendered to Lord Tyrawley; but he had kept Caroline, who
had proved willing to disown her mother, and at one time had

* To Miss Bride herself Calcraft left £3,000, an annuity of £1,000, and an
additional £500 a year until she married, or the youngest child came of age. Her
eldest son, John, was to inherit the bulk of his property, while £10,000 each, with
certain residuary rights in his landed property in the event of failure of legitimate
issue of his son and heir, John, his brother, Colonel Thomas Calcraft, and his
sister, Mrs. Christian Lucas, who were also beneficiaries under his will, were left
to the other children, Granby, Richard, Catherine, the son who had been born so
recently when he made his will in August, 1771, that he had not yet been named,
and the child (or children), she had told him she was expecting when he added a
codicil just before his death a year later.

even made an attempt to marry her off with a large dowry to the Marquess of Granby, who had recently become a widower. Perhaps it was her unwillingness to oblige her father by marrying a man who was old enough to be her grandfather that lost her his favour. At any rate no more is heard of her, and no guardian was appointed in Calcraft's will for these two children, although both of them were still under age. George Anne asserts that it was announced in the papers that she herself had been left a considerable sum by Calcraft; but that there was not a word of truth in this. Her name was not even mentioned in the will—though she thought it was—as being the mother of Henry and Caroline.*

George Anne had never expected to benefit by Calcraft's death, but not a single penny had been left to Mrs. Calcraft, whose name was not even mentioned in the will, and, as his legal wife, she claimed one third of the estate, which was granted to her by the Court. George Anne was delighted and said that no person received greater pleasure on the occasion than she did. But Mrs. Calcraft's success made her think that perhaps something might still be done about her own annuity, which had not been paid for some time. Mr. Davy's executors also decided to revive the suit relative to the first annuity on which she had borrowed money, but, though she was approached by both sides, she refused to concern herself in this matter.

In regard to her own projected suit, she decided that her best course would be to consult the well-known lawyer, Alexander Wedderburn, about it, but this would cost money, and she had none available, for the rent she was receiving from her tenant was nearly all absorbed in paying the rent for the house. She accordingly wrote to her old acquaintance, Lord Huntingdon, asking for his assistance. Huntingdon readily complied. But a few days after she had received the money from him, she was informed that judgment had been given against her in the suit

* Calcraft's will. Somerset House. The account given in Tooke's edition of Churchill's *Poems* is inaccurate.

brought against her by Gordon, the undertaker, and that if she
did not settle his account immediately, she would be sued for
execution. Several other notes and demands came in at the
same time, including the notes she had given to Cohen, and
which the present holders maintained had been purchased in
good faith by them against a valuable consideration. In these
circumstances she decided that her personal safety was more
important than anything else, so she appropriated to this
purpose the money given to her by Lord Huntingdon for the
prosecution of her suit. Unfortunately for her, she was soon
found out. Lord Huntingdon happened to meet Wedderburn,
and, on asking him how Mrs. Bellamy's suit was progressing,
was surprised to learn that Wedderburn knew nothing whatever of such a suit. Lord Huntingdon was exceedingly annoyed. Yet George Anne declared that she was puzzled at
receiving no answer when she at last did write to Mr. Wedderburn suggesting that she should call upon him. "I suppose,"
she says ingenuously, "this was owing to the multiplicity of
business he was engaged in."

By this time Lord Tyrawley had become so senile that he had
degenerated into idiocy. He had remained in harness for as
long as he had been permitted to do so. In 1762, when he was
over seventy, he had been appointed Plenipotentiary and
Commander-in-Chief of the English troops in Portugal, but to
his intense indignation had soon been superseded as being too
old and replaced by a German, Count von Lippe. He came
home fulminating against his old friends the Portuguese,
declaring that there was really no war there at all, but simply a
combination to get English money, and vowing that he would
eat every man that was killed, if the Portuguese would engage
to roast him. Since his tongue was still rather more active than
his limbs, an attempt was made to appease him by making him
a Field-Marshal and Governor of Portsmouth, but he found it
difficult to reconcile himself to the fact that his career was over
and began to rust away. His old friend, Chesterfield, who was
approaching his end with a rather better grace, once remarked:

"Tyrawley and I have been long dead, but we don't choose to have it known." Chesterfield died in March, 1773, and Tyrawley followed him on July 14th. Since he had had no legitimate children, all his honours became extinct on his death.

George Anne acknowledged that her father's death did not affect her when it happened, "as his lordship's faculties had been so much impaired for a long while before he departed this life, that his dissolution was rather to be wished for than dreaded." She had been completely estranged from him ever since Lady Tyrawley's death, but on hearing that he was gravely ill had thought it her duty to try to become reconciled with him. But when she entered his house at Twickenham and enquired for him, a servant had informed her that Miss O'Hara knew her sensibility to be too great to bear the sight of so conspicuous a character when degenerated into idiocy. Nor could she imagine that Mrs. Bellamy would want to see her, so she would not give her the trouble of an interview with a person to whom she had shown so many marks of dislike and contempt. It seems that the former friendship between the two half-sisters had been broken when George Anne had reproached Miss O'Hara with her partiality for one of the performers during the masquerade in *Man and Wife* in October, 1769. George Anne had refused to accept this delegated rebuff and had forced her way into Lord Tyrawley's apartment. She had had to acknowledge that Miss O'Hara had, at least, not exaggerated his condition, for she had found him "sunk into a state of debility and idiotism". He was sitting up in bed, wrapped in a scarlet gown. His eyes were sunk, his tongue was lolling out of one side of his mouth, and he appeared to be counting his fingers. She had knelt beside his bed, taking one of his hands, bathing it with her tears, and begging his forgiveness. But he had failed to recognise her, and she had had to leave without becoming reconciled to him.

Miss O'Hara sent her formal notice of their father's death and the date of the funeral, and on that day George Anne respectfully dressed herself in mourning. But, several days later, when she was entertaining a company of friends in her drawing-room, they saw from the window a magnificent funeral cortège coming from the undertaker's at the corner of Golden Square. Great was her astonishment when she perceived that the escutcheons on the hearse bore the armorial bearings of the O'Hara family: *Vert, on a pale radiant or, a lion rampant, sable.* On enquiry she learnt that the funeral had been postponed while Miss O'Hara was considering the Government's offer to give the distinguished old soldier a state funeral. Not expecting that such an honour would be accorded to him, Lord Tyrawley in his will had desired that his remains should be privately deposited in Chelsea Hospital among the veterans who had so often fought under his command. Miss O'Hara had in the end declined the Government's offer, on the ground that her father's expressed wishes must be exactly carried out. But George Anne was convinced that the real reason for her refusal was that Lord Tyrawley had desired that half-a-guinea should be given to every old soldier who attended his funeral, and she had meanly interpreted this to apply only to those who had actually seen service with h'm. There were only about twenty-five of them, and, had there been a public funeral, all the pensioners in the hospital would undoubtedly have attended, and she would have had to provide many more half-guineas.

When George Anne had left Calcraft, the children had remained with their father, but later Lord Tyrawley had taken charge of the boy, Harry. As he was living at Blackheath at the time, he had placed the boy in an academy at Greenwich, so that he would be able to see him often. Harry wanted to go to sea, and though the old soldier strongly disapproved, he would not gainsay him, and got him appointed as a midshipman on a man-of-war. But he soon tired of the sea, and, on hearing of his father's death, he decided to abandon a naval career and turn fine gentleman, "a profession", says Georgiane with pride mingled with deprecation, "he was, indeed, much better qualified for than the former." On first coming from sea he stayed with his mother for some months, but he soon got into bad habits, and, having formed a connexion with an undesirable woman, removed to a lodging "where he might take greater liberties than he could at the house of a parent".

Fortunately, at this juncture, her elder son, George Metham, returned from America. He had adopted a military career and was now a Captain, having distinguished himself by his efficiency and intrepidity in the American campaign. Though not as brilliant and intelligent as his young half-brother, George Metham was of a more stable and level-headed disposition, and he took the situation in hand and tried to arrange Harry's affairs. He joined with Harry to borrow money to buy him a commission in his own regiment, which was then in America. Possibly all would have been well, had the younger brother remained thus under the care of the elder; but George Metham received an offer to exchange into another regiment and become Deputy-Governor of Fort Charles in Jamaica. No sooner had George left for the West Indies than Harry's former mistress got hold of him again and persuaded him to sell his commission and accompany her to France, where he not only spent all his money but accumulated debts to the extent of £1,200. He was thrown into prison and remained there until rescued by one of his father's executors.

For some months Woodward had been suffering from a serious and painful disease, and, although he was still acting, he realised that he had not long to live and decided to make his will. He told George Anne that he intended to leave everything to her, with the exception of an annuity to his brother, and asked her to suggest an executor. She proposed a Mr. Townley Ward, who accordingly drew up his will. Some time before this Woodward had compromised his law-suit with Barry over the losses incurred in their Irish theatrical venture and had agreed to accept bonds payable yearly for a term of years at £200 a year. But Barry, who was also playing at Covent Garden, was obviously a dying man. On October 7th,

1776, he had been so ill when playing Jaffier in *Venice Preserved* that, though he had given a magnificent performance, he had returned to the Green Room afterwards in a state of complete collapse. Woodward, therefore, requested Ward to safeguard him by insuring Barry's life, but, through the negligence of a clerk, this was not done, and, when Barry died on January 10th, Woodward was so furious that his instructions had not been obeyed that he tore up his will and had a fresh one made, naming a neighbour of his, Mason Cornish, as executor instead of Ward. By this time he was dying himself. His last appearance on the stage was as Stephano, the drunken butler in the *Tempest*, on January 13th, 1777. He was too ill to act at his own benefit in March.

For several months he lay in bed in his house in Chapel Street, Grosvenor Place, suffering excruciating torments. He would not have anyone but George Anne to attend him, and she was at his bedside night and day. He asked her to name another executor, and she suggested his friend, William Bromfield, the surgeon who was attending him. This was not a very wise choice on her part, for Bromfield had not liked her ever since she had refused to have him as her own doctor when she was living in Parliament Street; but she imagined that he must have been favourably impressed by her devoted attentions to his friend, Woodward, and thought that he was now quite well disposed towards her.

Woodward died early in the morning on April 17th, 1777. He knew he was dying and had just said his last farewell to Bromfield when George Anne came into his room. As she approached his bed to give him his medicine, he took her by the hand and thanked her for all she had done for him. Then, murmuring: "I am going. Lord have mercy on me," he expired.

His will, dated January 20th, 1777, was a simple and not very lengthy document in which the intentions of the testator would seem to the lay mind to be as clear as crystal: "One would imagine," says George Anne—and not without reason

—"that it was next to impossible to counteract the kind intent of it." After the usual provision for the payment of his debts and the customary token legacies to his two executors, he left "to my friend, George Anne Bellamy, my gold watch, chain, and seals. And also my plate, jewels, linen, and china, and the whole of the furniture in the house in Chapel Street aforesaid." He possessed £700 in three per cent Consols. The interest on these was to be paid to his brother, John Woodward, tallow-chandler, of Cripplegate, for life, and then they were to be sold to provide an annuity for Mrs. Bellamy. All the rest of his property was to be realised to purchase an annuity for Mrs. Bellamy, which was to be held in trust and paid to her quarterly. His knowledge of her character made him thus tie it up so that it could not be applied to the payment of her debts or those of any person she might marry.

His assets should have been, and probably were, fairly considerable. The money standing to his credit at Drummond's Bank amounted to some seventeen or eighteen hundred pounds, a large sum was due to him from Covent Garden, and, besides Barry's big debt, Foote and Colonel Calcraft also owed him money, the latter £400. At any rate there should have been more than enough available to carry out his dispositions. But some legal minds abhor the simple and reasonable inter-pretation of the legal document. Mr. Edward Willet, the attorney employed by the executors, quickly discerned ingenious means of complicating the settling of the estate. It appeared that, a long time before, Woodward had lent his brother a fairly large sum of money, which, with the ac-cumulated interest that had never been paid, was very nearly equal to the capital which was to provide his annuity. It was abundantly clear to Mr. Willet that this debt must be recovered before any of the estate could be distributed; Mr. John Wood-ward must repay every penny he owed to his deceased brother before a single penny of his brother's legacy could be paid to him. John Woodward, who had not got the money, refused, and, on Mr. Willet's advice, the executors started an action against him. It may not have been common sense, but it was all immaculately legal—and lucrative for the lawyers.

George Anne was rather bewildered by it all. She did not believe that Henry Woodward had ever expected this loan to be repaid, least of all when he was dead. He had kept John's bond only to prevent his sister-in-law, whom he cordially disliked, from profiting should John predecease him. It seemed obvious to her that, since the will was so recently made, it could not possibly have been Henry Woodward's intention that the legacy should be merely a nominal one, as it would be if so large a sum were deducted from it. Moreover, she herself was the only other legatee and the only person whose interests could be injured by the debt, and she was perfectly willing to cancel it. And, in her ignorance of the law and its workings, she thought that her consent would be a sufficient inducement for the executors to consent to this course. But this view of the matter did not appeal to Mr. Willet, for "the sweets of a suit at law would have been nipped in the bud."

Mr. Willet also found it possible to dissipate a considerable portion of the estate in legal expenses by adopting a peculiarly devious method of attempting to recover the money owed by Barry. The warrants for the bonds given by Barry were held by Mr. Burton of Dublin, and the obvious course would have been to proceed against Barry's executors in Ireland, where, if judgment were obtained against them, execution could be levied on Crow Street Theatre in case of non-payment of the stipulated sums. But Mr. Willet chose to institute the action against them in England, where they possessed no assets. All this would take quite a long time and quite a lot of money. There was a promising legal harvest here, and the legatees would have to be content with the aftermath—if any.

On hearing that she had been left a large legacy by Woodward, George Anne's creditors at once swooped down upon her. And she felt less than ever able to cope with them. She had lost her best friend, adviser, and shield, and she was prostrated by grief. Moreover, she had had no thought of herself during the long months when she had been nursing him, and now her health broke down completely. In all the circumstances she was advised that it would be better to withdraw herself until Woodward's estate was settled and she was receiving her annuity. A lodging was engaged for her at 3, Walcot Place, Lambeth. At this early stage Bromfield was kind to her, and both he and his brother, the apothecary who had been looking after her, visited her there and reassured her landlady, who was apprehensive that her invalid lodger might die upon her hands. They told her that she need not worry about her ability to pay for her lodgings and incidental expenses, since there was money enough. It was also thought better that for the time being Mrs. Bellamy should assume another name, by which she would not be recognised by importunate creditors, and she took that of West. Why not? There had been a time when she was known by it, and West Digges himself no longer used it, having forfeited his right to it by returning to the stage as soon as he had got through his mother's legacy.

Pending the fulfilment of her legitimate expectations under Woodward's will, George Anne had no money at all, but at this very difficult moment she received an unexpected loan of £100 from the celebrated Quaker physician, Dr. Fothergill. She was personally unknown to this great philanthropist, but he had heard of her troubles through Mary Wordley, who, according to George Anne, had now become "a teacher and preacher among the Quakers". This may seem a surprising consummation for a lively actress who had once been styled the Goddess of Nonsense, but Mary Wordley had married and left the stage, and, if her husband was a Quaker and she had adopted his religion, there was nothing to prevent her from rising in the Meeting House to bear witness to her faith and beliefs.

The most unremitting of George Anne's creditors was Solomon, the son-in-law and successor of the jeweller, Lazarus.

Without her knowledge he had obtained judgment against her, and the bailiffs now entered Woodward's house and distrained upon the contents, which had been left to her absolutely. In order to escape the sentence of outlawry, she arranged for the sale of all the furniture at both Woodward's house and her mother's old house in Brewer Street, and with the proceeds she paid off Solomon and also repaid Dr. Fothergill's loan, one of the few debts in her life which she seems to have felt a moral obligation to refund. After this was done, very little was left. It is true that the sale took place at a most unpropitious time in the dead season of the summer and that the prices obtained were unsatisfactory, but it does look as if the money owing to Lazarus must have been a pretty large sum.

Nevertheless, during the first year after Woodward's death, George Anne confessed to having felt "tolerably easy". So far she had received only £59 from Woodward's estate through Mr. Cornish, but she was confident that there would be much more for her when everything had been settled. She was living a quiet life and saw few of her friends, but the lodgings were expensive, and she still kept a manservant and a maid. In order to pay her daily expenses she borrowed money on her plate and disposed of the few jewels that remained to her.

While she was living at Walcot Place, Harry Calcraft, who this year came of age and therefore inherited the £5,000 left to him by his father, returned from his dubious adventures in France, and Captain Metham also got leave of absence from his duties in Jamaica in order to visit his mother. Unfortunately, a quarrel speedily arose between the two brothers about the settlement of the debts for which they had become mutually engaged when George had intervened to extract Harry from his difficulties last time they were in England. Harry declared that that he would not pay one of them, because it was usurious. He would repay only the principal with five per cent interest. Captain Metham, who was the soul of probity, maintained that a high rate of interest was the "usual mode of lending money in such cases of exigence", and that it was necessary to submit to the terms agreed upon, however grating they might be. And, in any case, it was for a man of honour to keep his word. High words passed, and only their mother's tears and entreaties prevented a duel between them.

Harry Calcraft had not yet changed his ways. He gambled heavily, fell into the hands of sharpers, and lost large sums at play. Soon England became too hot to hold him, and he deemed it necessary to go abroad again. Through the interest of a friend he obtained a commission in the service of the East India Company in Bengal, and it is pleasant to record that he afterwards led a distinguished career and ended up as a Lieutenant-General.

Just before he sailed for India, Harry called on his mother at Walcot place and arranged to come again on the following Sunday to meet and become reconciled with George. But to George Anne's great grief he did not come, and the two brothers never met again. She was told afterwards that Harry was jealous because he believed that she had a greater affection for George than for himself. He had been piqued because she had refused to give him some portraits she had already promised to her elder son.

Although George Metham was of a much less erratic character than Harry Calcraft, it is not perhaps surprising that a son of two such parents as his should have been prodigal in his expenses, and before long he too found himself entangled through borrowing money at high rates of interest to pay for his pleasures. He was obliged to return to Jamaica. He had also involved himself in another kind of difficulty. Just before he left a pretty young woman called on George Anne, bringing with her the following letter:

"MY DEAR MADAM,

"Let my situation plead my excuse for this. It is to introduce to you a young woman, whose greatest fault is an attachment to your son. I have no resource left, but to rely upon my father's generosity; a faint but only hope. But though I cannot count upon his protection, I can upon yours; whc are too good, and have too much sense to be offended when I tell you, *that at this time she is entitled to my tenderest rega ds.*

My circumstances are such, that I could not even call on you before I go; but I hope a few years will amply compensate for the misfortunes of this; and that we may both live, till I have proved in numberless instances, with what truth I am

Your most affectionate and dutiful son,

GEORGE MONTGOMERY METHAM."

London, Dec. 22, 1778
    My birth-day.

With her usual impulsive generosity George Anne consented to allow the young woman a weekly pittance, so long as she could afford it. But this proved to be for only a few weeks, for she had a great disappointment and shock coming to her. When she considered that time enough had elapsed for Woodward's estate to be settled, she applied to his executors, only to be told, to her "inexpressible astonishment", that there was no money for her, nor the least room for her to expect any. She must apply to their attorney, Mr. Willet, "as they were determined to be guided wholly by him, and being resolved not to act themselves, they had given their power to him." Cornish, in fact, had left London altogether and retired into the country. And Bromfield refused either to see her or answer her letters, which he referred to Willet. She now perceived what a mistake it had been for her to propose him as executor and not to ask Woodward to appoint somebody who was at least sympathetic towards her. The surgeon may have been an honest man according to his lights, but he had never liked her, he had no sort of interest in promoting her welfare, and he regarded her as the nuisance she undoubtedly must have been, with her extravagance, improvidence, and importunity. She had no alternative but to call on Willet, who treated her with incomparable insolence. When she asked him what had been done to realise the estate, he informed her that he had obtained judgment against a Mr. Crawford, who had married Barry's widow, but that nothing could be obtained from him. George Anne pointed out again that the warrants for the bonds given by Barry were held in Dublin and that it was there that Crawford should be sued. Mr. Willet replied that he did not propose to cross the herring pond. She asked what then she might expect, and he told her rudely that she might expect nothing; the executors had as good a right as herself to the effects, if there were any, as she would squander away anything she obtained. This may have been perfectly true, but it was hardly Willet's province to say so. Moreover, Woodward, aware of this failing of hers, had tried to protect her against herself by leaving her an annuity from capital held by trustees, and it was surely the lawyer's business to see that this beneficent intention should be carried out.

George Anne's situation was now desperate, and she realised at last that something drastic had to be done about it. She was already in arrears with her rent, so she gave up her rooms and went into a small room in the attic storey of the same house. The manservant, who had been with her for some years, was regretfully discharged. She would also have sent away her little maid, but the faithful girl, whose name was Sally, would not leave her and chose rather to share her distress. She did not know where to turn for ready money. She borrowed a little from John Woodward, but that was soon exhausted. Worse still, she had contracted a debt at a neighbouring shop for all necessaries but bread and meat and had given a note for the sum. This was now due; she could not pay it, and the shopkeeper refused to supply her any more. "This," she says, "was a double distress to us, as it deprived us of the greatest part of our subsistence, and reduced us to the utmost extremity of want."

Starvation now stared her in the face, for she had parted with every single thing on which she could raise a shilling. Without money or even the prospect of getting any, oppressed by debt, and without the common necessaries of life, she felt that she was, indeed, a useless member of society, and that it would be a

meritorious action to free herself from being any longer a
burden on the world or herself. Suicide, she tried to persuade
herself, could be no crime in such circumstances, and she
resolved to throw herself into the Thames. The account of this
attempt which she gives in her *Apology* is highly dramatic and
not very credible, though no doubt she may have wandered
forth with some such project in mind, if without the determination to put it into effect. Unbeknown to her little maid,
she left the house between nine and ten o'clock one evening
and roamed about the fields, half hoping that some footpad
would murder her and save her the pains of doing it herself.
When the clock was about to strike eleven, she made her way to
Westminster Bridge, descended the stairs to the river, and
seated herself on the lowest step, where she waited for the tide
to cover her. "My desperation," she candidly admits, "though
resolute, was not of the violent kind as to urge me to take the
fatal plunge."

As she sat there, she suddenly heard the voice of a woman
speaking in a soft, plaintive voice to her child: "How, my
dear, can you cry to me for bread, when you know I have not
even a morsel to carry to your dying father?" Then the same
voice exclaimed: "My God! my God! what wretchedness can
compare to mine. But thy Almighty will be done." On hearing
these piteous words of resignation to the divine will, George
Anne declares that she was struck with horror at the crime she
herself had been contemplating, and burst into tears. As she
put her hand into her pocket to take out her handkerchief, she
felt some halfpence there she had not known that she had, and
she ran up the steps and gave them to the poor woman. Then
she returned to the scene of her intended crime and rendered
thanks to God for the lesson she had just received. For the first
and last time in her life she felt a sensation of happiness from
finding there were persons in the world more wretched than
herself. She prayed for forgiveness for her atrocious attempt
and went home with a tranquillity of spirit she had long been a
stranger to.

She found Sally in tears, lest some misfortune had happened to her beloved mistress. While she had been out, Sally's sister had called and lent her two shillings, which she had spent on getting something she thought her mistress would like for supper and some tea and sugar for the morning. Mistress and maid sat down together to this unhoped for feast, and, says George Anne, "I cannot remember, even in the most elevated situation I was ever in, and when my table was spread with dainties, that I made a more pleasing meal."

Next day, as she was sitting in her attic brooding over her misfortunes, there was a gentle tap on the door, and, on her answering, an unexpected visitor appeared. This was Madame Krudnar, the widow of a Polish baron. She told George Anne that she had accidentally heard of her distress and had taken the first opportunity to come and relieve her. She reproached her for having concealed her situation from her friends and acquaintances, since her present extremity was not due to her own misconduct.

Within the next few days many other people called to offer their assistance. Among them was Harris, who wanted to know why she had not informed the managers of Covent Garden of her distress and gave her five guineas to go on with. Her former dresser, Mrs. Whitfield, came with a message from the actors, Hull and Mattocks, saying that they proposed to raise a sum among the performers to extricate her from the debts which oppressed her. Mrs. Whitfield herself offered to raise a sum among her friends to provide her with a guinea a week. All these offers she gladly accepted. But she was at a loss to account for this sudden access of interest in her affairs, until she discovered that an advertisement had appeared in the journals "That the female Timon was in want of the necessaries of life; and those who had formerly partaken of her prosperity ought to blush at suffering her to be in such a situation." Her name and address had been subjoined. Later she found out that it was Madame Krudnar who had inserted this notice. But if its object had been only to arouse the consciences of those whom her generosity had benefited, it had failed, for according to George Anne, only one person whom she had formerly obliged *did* feel the rebuke. All the others who now came to her aid did so out of generosity, pity, or the goodness of their hearts, for none of them had ever been under any obligation to her.

And now, for the time being at least, her worst anxieties were dispelled. The sum she received from the subscription raised by the actors at the theatre sufficed to pay off all the small debts her necessity had forced her to contract, and the allowance of a guinea a week provided by Mrs. Whitfield and her friends continued for much longer than she had any reason to expect. But to give her any security for the future she would need a larger sum. The solution suggested by Mrs. Abington, a leading actress at Drury Lane, was that she should take a benefit. She herself offered to perform at it, as did also King, of Drury Lane, and her old friend Smith, who was still playing leading roles at Covent Garden. But it was decided that the season was now too far advanced and that it would be advisable to postpone the benefit till next year. Until then she must fend for herself as best she might. She was obliged to leave Walcot Place, as the house had been let, and she moved to Charles Street, St. James's, where she seems to have occupied most of her time in making applications for assistance to anyone who she conceived might help her. The Duke of Montagu aided her several times, but these occasional contributions would not enable her to subsist without contracting debts. And when she wrote to Sir George Metham, all she received was a reproachful letter pointing out the impropriety of requesting pecuniary favours.

Chapter Eighteen

TOWARDS THE END OF THE THEATRICAL SEASON of 1779–80
George Anne ventured to ask Harris to give her a benefit at
Covent Garden, the theatre with which she had been longest
associated. He readily granted her request and showed great
sympathy and generosity, not only placing the house at her
disposal free of all incidental expenses, but also using his
interest with the members of the company to persuade them to
give their services in aid of a retired actress whom many of
them cannot have known. It was arranged that it should take
place on Thursday, June 1st, the very last day of the season.
The weather was exceptionally hot, but George Anne's old
supporters did not fail her; the house was crowded, and the
boxes were filled with people of rank and fashion, headed by
the Duchess of Bolton.

George Anne had chosen one of her favourite plays, *Jane
Shore*, to be followed by *Comus* as after-piece. Although she was
only just recovering from an illness, Mrs. Yates insisted upon
carrying out her promise to play Jane Shore. Very inadvisedly,
George Anne allowed herself to be persuaded by flattering
friends to play her old part of Alicia. Over ten years had passed
since she last appeared on the stage, and she felt so nervous
that, as the day approached, she would have been willing to
forgo all the advantages she could expect from the benefit, if
only she could have been excused performing. And at the very
last moment, when she was about to make her first entrance,
she would have fled if she had not been literally pushed on to
the stage by the warm-hearted actress and singer, Anne Catley,
who hitherto had been a complete stranger to her. Her

performance, on her own admission, was very mediocre. Fear had taken such possession of her that she scarcely knew how she got through her part, and, at the end of the play, she could not trust herself to attempt to speak the address of thanks to the audience that she had prepared.

George Anne justly accounted herself very fortunate that her benefit took place that night, for the very next day the Gordon Riots broke out. Led by that strange fanatic, Lord George Gordon, head of the 'Protestant Association', a mob adorned with blue cockades, carrying blue banners, and shouting: "No Popery," proceeded from St. George's Fields to the House of Commons to present a petition for the repeal of the Catholic Relief Act of 1778, a very moderate measure promoted by Sir George Savile, which had removed certain of the more onerous penalties imposed upon Catholics: the perpetual imprisonment of priests for saying Mass, the forfeiture to the next Protestant heir of the estates of Roman Catholics educated abroad, and the prohibition to Roman Catholics to acquire land by purchase.

In the evening the mob got out of hand and attacked the two privileged chapels frequented by English Catholics in London. The rioters divided their forces; one party marched on the Sardinian Ambassador's chapel in Duke Street, Lincoln's Inn Fields, while the other attacked the Bavarian Ambassador's chapel in Warwick Street, Golden Square, which George Anne herself was in the habit of attending. The mob broke the windows, forced the doors, gutted the interiors, and dragged the altars, ornaments, and furniture out into the street, where they set fire to them. Troops arrived just in time to prevent Count von Haslang's chapel itself from being burnt to the ground, and thirteen persons were arrested. But by some curious mischance—or, perhaps, design—none of these turned out to be responsible for the outrage. Most of them were harmless Catholic bystanders who had merely come to see what was afoot. A proclamation was issued offering £500 reward for the discovery of the persons concerned in destroying the Ambassadors' chapels, but produced no result.

Horace Walpole asserts that the mob also broke into Count von Haslang's private residence and found it filled with tea and a quantity of other contraband articles accumulated by this 'Prince of Smugglers'. But this may have been merely idle and malicious gossip, for Walpole did not like the old Count, who, he says, never paid any rent for his house, and would neither pay nor leave, even when the landlord tried to get him out by offering to forgo the entire amount of the arrears already owing.

To George Anne, at any rate, the old Ambassador was always a kind, generous, and disinterested friend. When all the money she received from her benefit was swallowed up by her own debts and those she was still foolish enough to contract for other people, he promised to assist her "until her affairs were settled"—as if they ever would or could be—by allowing her a small monthly sum, which was punctually paid to her for some time. But then the Count fell seriously ill and was obliged to inform her that the expenses due to his illness were so great that he could not continue her allowance, though he would resume it as soon as he was able.

George Anne herself was confined to bed with rheumatism when she received his letter, and, while still in this state, was seized at the instance of some of her creditors and taken to a sponging-house in Carey Street. Her life was now a constant succession of such vicissitudes, and it would be both melancholy and unprofitable to pursue their monotonous repetition. She raised money when and how she could by borrowing or begging from former friends and patrons. The Duchess of Bolton, for instance, replied to a piteous appeal by sending her a draft on her banker by return of post; an unnamed gentleman opened a subscription for her at Brooks's Club, though owing to the lateness of the season it did not raise as much as he had hoped; and Mr. Harris from time to time gave her free tickets for the theatre to dispose of.

For some time past she had received no answers to the letters she had been writing to Captain Metham in Jamaica, so she wrote to his father, who replied that he had just received the news that their son had died. Not being able to afford to go into mourning, she wrote to Sir George appealing to him to help her at least to do this. He answered that it was not in his power, as his own expenses called for all he had managed to save from the ruin of his fortunes. This was probably no more than the truth, for by this time he had frittered away all the considerable fortune he had inherited from his mother in 1747 and his father in 1763. In 1766 he had given up his seat in the House of Commons in order to take an unimportant office of profit under the Crown, that of Patent Clerk of the Wardrobe. All his estates had been first heavily mortgaged and then sold. He was to subsist for the remainder of his life on a small pension from the Crown and to die in reduced circumstances in Bath in 1793. No doubt his association with Mrs. Bellamy had contributed to his ruin, but he had always been hideously extravagant in his own right.

Fortunately, George Anne's kindly friend, Mr. Stacie, proved willing to come to her aid with a loan on this sorrowful occasion. He also advanced her some money on two portraits which had at last been handed over to her by Woodward's executors, so that she was able after all to array herself in mourning for her son.

As soon as Count von Haslang recovered, he at once promised to renew the little income he had allowed her, but he had a relapse, and the money did not arrive. She was helpless without this regular supply, for whatever other assistance she received was earmarked for the payment of urgent debts even before it came to her hands. Very reluctantly, in May, 1783, she summoned up courage to write to remind the Count of his promise. And the next Sunday she went to the chapel at Golden Square, and found that he had recovered sufficiently to attend mass, which he had not been able to do for some months. He received her afterwards and told her gaily that his health was wholly recovered and he had not been so well for thirty years. He promised that he would visit her soon and told her to send her servant on the following Thursday for an answer to the application she had made to him.

George Anne went home overjoyed. She felt assured now that she would be able to pay her debts and even have a little left over "until her affairs were settled"—the old, familiar phrase. And at twelve o'clock on Thursday her little maid set off as arranged for Golden Square. But she soon returned with the worst possible news. "There is no answer," she said, "you have lost your only friend, the Comte is dead."

After she had left him on Sunday, the Ambassador had ordered his coach and had insisted upon going out to pay calls, in spite of the bleakness of the weather. One of his horses had fallen, the old man, who was well over eighty, had let down the glass window, with an east wind blowing, in order to see what had happened, and had caught cold and died three days later.

For forty-three years Count Franz von Haslang had represented the Elector Palatine and Duke of Bavaria at the Court of St. James and had been a conspicuous and familiar figure in London, arrayed almost always in a tight blue coat, with the star of the Bavarian order of St. George sparkling on his breast. George Anne was horrified to hear that the remains of this distinguished old diplomat had been deposited in the common burial ground at St. Pancras without having the honours paid to him which were due to his dignity and high rank, "and for many months without even a stone or any memorial to point out where he lay." The Ambassador himself, she says, had always disliked this burial ground and had not wanted his old housekeeper to be interred there, although it was by her own wish. He had said that he would pay more respect to a dog that he valued. But George Anne, who was the only Catholic in her family, probably did not appreciate that the St. Pancras burial ground was the most usual place of interment both for priests and for Roman Catholics of the upper classes who died in London.

During the penal times Catholic funerals had to take place in Protestant cemeteries, and the churchyard of St. Pancras was regarded by Catholics with peculiar favour, both because the church was traditionally the last parish church in England in which mass had been said, and because the churchyard had reputedly been the scene of the martyrdom by burning of members of their faith in Elizabethan days. In any event, the Catholic funeral service could only be read in private over the coffin before it left the house, for the public part of the funeral of a Roman Catholic, however illustrious, had to be conducted without ostentation. If the old Count had spoken so disparagingly of St. Pancras churchyard, it may have been because a man who enjoyed life as much as he did strongly objected to the idea of being buried at all anywhere. But if the Ambassador's interment was hasty and unceremonious, the requiem mass was conducted with dignity and solemnity in his own chapel by his own chaplains. George Anne, who attended it, was most favourably impressed and only objected to seeing ladies occupying the Ambassador's old pew, which she thought should have been left empty on this occasion out of respect for his memory.*

On his deathbed Count von Haslang had been prevailed upon to sign a will disinheriting his own son in favour of a relative, who, though by all accounts an amiable young man, weakly allowed himself to be guided by those about him, so that all the old servants who had faithfully served the Count were ousted. The new chaplain, too, who was introduced above the heads of the others and who had formerly been

* Mrs. Bellamy's statement that she attended the chapel on several occasions in 1783 goes to show that it was not totally destroyed in the Gordon Riots, as is commonly supposed, and her evidence is confirmed by other contemporary accounts (e.g. in the *Gentleman's Magazine*). Probably the gutted interior was temporarily repaired and refurnished. A new and larger chapel was later built and opened about 1790. At any rate there appears to have been continuity of worship on the site from about 1730, when the first chapel was built by a Portuguese Ambassador, right through to the present day. Though the chapel lost its Bavarian connection when Bavaria was incorporated in the German Empire in 1871, it continued to be known as the Bavarian Chapel until the 1914–18 war. It is now the Roman Catholic parish church of Our Lady of the Assumption.

dismissed by the Count himself for insulting behaviour, treated his fellow priests with such arrogance that they left, and the chapel would have been deserted by its usual worshippers, had it not been for the timely arrival of "that justly celebrated Irish luminary, Father O'Leary". This wholly worthy and bene-volent Franciscan thus described by George Anne was to become a valued friend of hers for the rest of her life and continued to visit her and dine with her, however squalid the lodgings to which she might be reduced. A man of great charm and simplicity in ordinary life, he was an eloquent preacher and a keen controversialist with a very ready wit. To John Philpot Curran, afterwards an Irish judge, who once said to him: "I wish, Reverend Father, that you were St. Peter, and had the keys of heaven, because then you could let me in," he replied: "By my honour and conscience, it would be better for you that I had the keys of the other place, for then I could let you out." And to a Protestant, who told him that he could not bring himself to believe in purgatory, he slyly remarked: "Ah, my good friend, you may go further, and fare worse."

By the death of her old friend, Count von Haslang, upon whom she had always been able to rely in the last resort, George Anne was left without any regular source of income at all, and was obliged to rely once more on what she could beg or borrow from friends and acquaintances. She did advertise in the journals for a place as housekeeper or attendant to an elderly lady or gentleman, but did not receive a single reply.

About this time she must have started on the composition of her memoirs. Whether they were commissioned from her by Bell, the theatrical publisher, or whether she submitted them to him is immaterial, but, at any rate, he arranged for a pro-fessional writer, one Alexander Bicknell, to help her with them. It appears likely, however, that she herself was mainly responsible for the actual writing of them, and that Bicknell was an editor rather than a 'ghost'. She had always fancied herself as a writer, and her book is full of amusing and racy phrases, thoughts, and flashes of wit very similar in tone, style, and sentiment to the letters she wrote to her old friend, Tate Wilkinson, who later printed them in his book, *The Tablet*, in memory of his intimacy with her "as an acquaintance, friend, and actress". The material for her *Apology* can have come only from her, and it is probable that much of it was printed almost, if not quite, as she wrote it. No doubt Bicknell did re-arrange and join together what she had written, embellishing it—if that is the right word—with most of the trite philosophical and moral reflections that interlard it and probably—since they contain no personal note—introducing the pedestrian guide-book descriptions of various places she visited on her travels abroad.

In her first, and undated, letter to Wilkinson, George Anne tells him that she had been so out of spirits that she had not been able to do anything but correct her *Apology*, which she had just finished. At this time she seems to have contemplated dedicating it to the Duchess of Devonshire, who had honoured her with a pension. She had not felt inclined to resume writing the comedy she had begun at Strand-on-the-Green. "Thalia has not yet visited me, therefore I have laid my comedy in lavender for some favourite of the laughing Muse to finish." And she was feeling very ill. Having broken her ankle, she had ventured forth too soon and had fallen again and fractured the bone of the same leg. She was lame ever afterwards, and often in great pain. "My leg is very bad, my pocket very low, and my spirits quite gone . . . I fear I shall never be able to walk without assistance, and to add to my comforts, I have a cough that tears me to pieces. I have removed to my Doctor's, No. 6, Cleveland Row, St. James's, and am so high-minded as to lodge up two pair of stairs, which really may be compared to Jacob's ladder." She mentioned that the Queen had asked her to wait on her, but that she had been too ill to obey the royal command.

She was, as always, in grave financial trouble and lived in constant fear of being arrested. This must have been because old debts were still hanging like a collar of mill-stones round her neck, for she was not wholly without funds. Besides the Duchess of Devonshire's pension, she was receiving £100 a year from her son, Harry Calcraft, who, although he was beginning to do very well in India, could ill spare it. But he was a good son to her, and, when he returned on leave from India a little later, was ever kind and attentive and did everything he could to help her, so far as his own finances would allow of it. He could not, of course, hope to pay off all her debts. And, if he had, no doubt she would have contracted more. She could never restrain her itch to spend money. Wilkinson relates that about this time a gentleman sent her £50, but always "she wanted ditto, ditto, as the instant it was got, the same instant it was expended".

An Apology, for the Life of George Anne Bellamy, late of Covent Garden Theatre. Written by Herself, was published in five volumes in January, 1785. She received permission to dedicate it to the young Prince of Wales through the good offices of his Governor, the Duke of Montagu, to whom also she addressed an adulatory letter at the beginning of the book. Montagu, who had been created a Duke in 1766, was none other than her earliest patron, the Earl of Cardigan. At the end of the fifth volume she printed a far less amiable epistle, her *Original Letter to John Calcraft Esq. advertized to be published in October*, 1767, *but which was then violently suppressed*. She maintains that she composed it entirely herself, and that nobody had helped her with it or had even read it. The style closely resembles that of the *Apology* itself, though Bicknell had no part in its composition, and this is an additional proof that he merely put together what she had written, a task which he performed rather too adroitly and thoroughly, as will appear hereafter.

Colman's action in persuading her to postpone the publication of this bitter and sustained piece of invective was shown to have been abundantly justified. Had she carried out her intention to publish it during Calcraft's lifetime, he could not have ignored it. He would have been obliged to take action, and his power and influence at that time were very great. Moreover, though George Anne would never have admitted it, there was doubtless much to be said on his side.

The *Apology* itself, which took the form of a series of letters supposed to have been written to an intimate female friend who had asked Mrs. Bellamy for the story of her life, caused an immediate sensation—partly a *succès de scandale*, since so many persons still living, or at least well remembered, were referred to in it. Several more editions were called for at once, the later ones having as frontispiece a charming, if rather misleading, portrait of the authoress, "the face copied after a picture by Coates in the Possession of Sir George Metham, the figure modernised by Ramberg, and the whole engraved by Bartolozzi." The reason why it was misleading was because, although the face was that of the youthful Mrs. Bellamy as painted for her lover by Francis Cotes, who had died in 1770, the young German artist, Johann Heinrich Ramberg, had given her the style of hair-dressing and costume fashionable in 1785, when she was approaching sixty. One, at least, of the later editions was further illustrated with some rather poor little engravings purporting to depict scenes from the heroine's life. The fourth edition contained a few additional letters. Another edition was published in Dublin in the same year.*

Society and the Stage read the book with avidity. Many fashionable people found it extremely convenient to accept Horace Walpole's opinion that it was spun out by a number of names, many falsehoods, and a tolerable quantity of anachronisms. Nor were the professional critics all kind. The first of several reviews in the *Gentleman's Magazine* gave a sneering account of the book itself and concluded: "The Life of this heroine, a continued course, as it seems, of vice, folly, and extravagance, by the distresses in which it involved her, and the remorse which it must now occasion, may afford an useful lesson to the young and giddy of her own sex, especially

---

* In 1822 a French translation, with a most gallant and sentimental preface, was published by a young French historian and politician, M. Adolphe Thiers, later to become first President of the Third Republic.

to those who are so unfortunate as to tread the slippery boards of a theatre; though the candid will make great allowance for such a wretched birth and education (if so it may be called) and the miserable example of such blind guides as her parents." Copious extracts from the book itself then followed, and a number of comparatively unimportant errors were enumerated. Mrs. Bellamy had been wrong, for instance, in asserting that Dr. Francis's translation of Horace was really the work of Mr. Duncombe, since the two translations were quite distinct. But George Anne had more excuse for her undoubted mistake than the reviewer thought, for Dr. Francis *had* been assisted by a gentleman with a somewhat similar name, a Dr. Dunkin.

A later number of the *Gentleman's Magazine* contained an interesting communication from a Dublin correspondent, sighing himself A.T.M. "Some of these things occurred to me upon reading your extracts of Mrs. Bellamy's curious *Apology*. I well remember that lady in Dublin. It seems no great wonder that she should mistake Mr. Francis's translation for one by Mr. Duncombe, when she does not seem perfectly acquainted with her own name. She now, it seems, wishes to hear the masculine denomination of George, but has added Anne, for the sake of softness. Yet, when she was in Dublin, where she was perfectly well known in her feminine quality, she bore the name of Georgiana; by which name she prosecuted, in one of our courts of justice, a certain gentleman (whom I well knew) for a certain dishonour offered to her tea-pot. But when things change by time, why should not names?" Regrettably, George Anne herself omitted to record the tea-pot scandal.

The publication of her *Apology* revived the interest of her former theatrical friends in the unfortunate Mrs. Bellamy, and on May 24th, 1785, she was given a benefit at Drury Lane. She was now so weak and frail that she would have preferred not to attend it herself, but, on being told that it was desirable that she should appear to show her gratitude, she decided that she must steel herself to make the effort. The play was Jephson's *Braganza*. George Anne's old friend, 'Gentleman' Smith, played Velasquez, Braganza was played by Brereton, and the great Mrs. Yates, who by now had herself retired, consented to reappear for one night as the Duchess, and according to George Anne herself, never gave a better performance of the part.

Garbled accounts of the occasion were published, and the *Gentleman's Magazine* even printed a "Farewell Address" said to be intended to have been spoken by Mrs. Bellamy at her benefit and composed by a certain Mr. C. Stuart, author of *Gretna Green*. The address actually spoken by Miss Farren was sent to the magazine later by a correspondent, signing himself C.D., who added: "Why it did not meet with the applause Miss Farren's elegant and pathetic manner of speaking it, and its own merit, entitled it to, was visible to the entire audience." He also sent a copy of the lines Mrs. Bellamy herself would have spoken "had she not chosen to return her thanks to the audience *in her own way*."

This lengthy epilogue, specially written for the occasion by Alexander Bicknell and spoken by Miss Farren, concluded with the lines:

> "But see, oppress'd with gratitude and tears,
>   To pay her duteous tribute, she appears."

The curtain then drew and discovered Mrs. Bellamy, who was to have spoken the following lines:

> "Long absent from these boards, alarm'd, I find
>   Unusual tremors agitate my mind.
>   In vain I strive my feelings to impart,
>   And speak the grateful dictates of my heart.
>   Yet, tho' thus trembling, *something* I would say
>   Fain, fain I would my duteous tribute pay;
>   Tell that your kind indulgence, deep imprest
>   In liveliest tints, is glowing in this breast—
>   But, overwhelm'd by gratitude and fears,
>   Accept th' attempt—accept these speaking tears."

The sentiments put into George Anne's mouth were only too true. She was so overcome by her emotion and herself so touched by the affecting way in which the lovely Miss Farren had spoken the epilogue that she could not even bring herself to utter the lines written for her, but spoke only a few halting words and "left her tears to express her gratitude". Miss Farren came to her side and gently led her from the stage.

Frederick Reynolds, the dramatist, then a young man of twenty, was present at Drury Lane that night, and has recorded his impressions of the scene when the curtain rose before a curious and expectant audience to reveal Mrs. Bellamy. "She was seated in an arm-chair, from which she in vain attempted to rise, so completely was she subdued by her feelings. She however succeeded in muttering a few words, expressive of her gratitude, and then sinking into her seat, the curtain dropped before her; having by those few farewell words, perhaps, more deeply affected her audience, than by her best efforts in Juliet and Cleone."

All the money she received from her *Apology* and the considerable sum she derived from this benefit were speedily swallowed up by her creditors, and she was very soon reduced to the same state as before. "Having thus drained myself of every guinea," she says, "I was unhappily compelled to contract fresh debts to support my wretched existence." Her landlady served a writ on her for the £14 she owed for her lodging, and, when she could not pay, vindictively arranged for her to be arrested at eight o'clock on a Saturday evening, so that she would not be able to obtain her release before the Monday. She was rescued from the sponging-house by Mr. Batten, of Hare Court, Temple, whom she had first met when he was acting for Woodward's brother in the matter of the debt he had owed to the estate and which she had expressed her willingness to cancel. But she was being pressed by other creditors too, and once at least she was committed to prison for contempt of court in ignoring a judgment.

In a letter to Wilkinson, dated from Charles Street on April

12th, 1785, she told him that she was so afflicted with rheumatism in her right arm that it was impeding the sixth volume of her memoirs, on which she was then engaged. She had recollected a number of incidents and anecdotes that had slipped her memory, and, since the original editions had been so successful, this seemed both to her and to her publisher, Bell, an excellent reason for adding another volume. Wilkinson had pointed out to her a number of errors, mostly concerning dates of performances, in the original edition, and she was writing to explain to him why she could not correct them.

The supplementary volume was published in May, 1785. Like its predecessors, it consisted of letters to a fictitious correspondent. The dedication, to an unknown benefactor who had helped her generously, was dated from No. 10, Charles Street, St. James's, April 23rd, 1785—her birthday. Most of the book consisted of additional anecdotes. There were also corrections of a "few unintentioned errors", which she excused by saying that her book was written entirely from memory, "no diary kept or even loose memorandum made," which was no doubt true. But she frankly confessed that it was impossible for her to correct the defects in chronology pointed out to her by Tate Wilkinson and others.

If she did not keep a diary, it would, indeed, have been an extraordinary feat of memory had she managed to recall the exact order in which she played her various parts in the course of her career. She might undertake from fifteen to twenty roles in a season—and it must be remembered also that she played these parts season after season for some twenty-five years. Wilkinson himself remarks upon the difficulty of recalling the exact dates of performances, owing to the fact that the theatrical season began in the autumn of one year and ended in the spring of the next, so that two year-dates were involved in every season. Moreover, there were no official records to which she could easily have recourse to refresh her memory; such records as we now rely upon have been compiled much later with the aid of collections of old play-bills and a collation of allusions to productions in contemporary memoirs and periodicals.

Mrs. Bellamy claimed, however, that the incidents in her book, "though perhaps erroneous in point of time," were all real facts. But she pleaded that to alter dates now would only produce greater mistakes. And in this she was undoubtedly right. Her editor had done his job only too well, and had inextricably woven all the incidents she had given him into a continuous narrative, so that, to make the corrections, the whole book would have had to be resolved into its constituent elements and entirely recast. But does it, after all, matter very much if, for instance, the King of Denmark's visit to London, which took place in 1768, comes after instead of before her own benefit of the following year? Or that Thomson, the poet, should figure in an altogether unimportant capacity in several incidents a few months after his death? Genest, the supreme authority on the theatrical history of this period, remarks that many of her anecdotes were certainly true, even if they did not occur at the times stated in her *Apology*.

The new volume also contained some poems addressed to her by the Scottish poet and actor, John Cunningham, a number of benevolent but not particularly interesting letters from both friends and strangers, and *The Seasons: a dramatic entertainement written by the late Mr Woodward*, who had intended it to be produced at Covent Garden, but had died before this could be done. She now printed it as a tribute to the memory of her benefactor.

A critic in the *European Magazine* had insinuated that she must be some five or six years older than she professed to be, and this indignantly denied. There had been a very slight mistake of one year, but she had not made it on purpose, for "it is a matter of little consequence, when a woman is turned of fifty, what her age may be". And she printed the certificate she had obtained from the Insurance Office when she insured her life at Alderman Cracroft's request in 1764.

The *Gentleman's Magazine* for June, 1785, gave the new volume a rather kinder reception than it had given to its predecessors. No doubt this was partly because sympathy had been aroused for the authoress by the publication of a short book entitled *The Memoirs of George Anne Bellamy, by a Gentleman of Covent Garden*, which was nothing more than a pirated edition of selected passages from the *Apology*. "Such a wretched catch-penny needs only to be known to be universally exploded," said the reviewer, adding that it was "taking a most un-warrantable advantage of a distressed lady." There was at least one more pirated edition. At this time also there appeared another book called *Letters addressed to Mrs. Bellamy, occasioned by her Apology*, in which Edward Willet, solicitor to Wood-ward's executors, repudiated the accusations she had made against him. He maintained that he had settled a regular account on April 15th, 1783, and received the balance. Instead of receiving only £59 from Woodward's estate as she claimed, Mrs. Bellamy had actually received £619 13s. od., and if she had been "distressed, ill-treated, and depressed", it was not by him and his clients, but by "her own duplicity, unprincipled behaviour, and unjustifiable extravagance". He does not explain why this 'regular account' was not settled until six years after the testator's death. His only real defence—and that one calculated to appeal only to members of his own pro-fession—was that practically the whole estate had been absorbed in perfectly lawful legal expenses.

Duplicity and unprincipled behaviour George Anne would have denied indignantly, but to unjustifiable extravagance she was always prepared to plead guilty. She admitted that her "sanguine certainties and sure expectancies" had often led her into many expenses, which, but for the flattering prospects they presented, she would not have incurred. And, un-fortunately, these hopeful daydreams continued almost to the last to alternate with her moods of hopelessness and despair. When she wrote her sixth volume, she announced that she now had "every prospect of being comfortably situated for life". But this expectation, which appears to have been founded on a fantastic hope that a gentleman in Jamaica would send her a large sum of money he was supposed to have owed Captain Metham for a gambling debt, was never fulfilled. Bills and writs were always flowing in, and she was perpetually harried by her creditors.

Time after time she was saved at the last moment by donations from her friends and former patrons. The Dukes of Montagu and Rutland helped her, so did the Duchess of Bolton, the Earl of Mansfield, Sir Francis and Lady Basset, Lady James, Mrs. Hastings, a Mrs. Bull, a stranger to her who had been deeply touched by reading the *Apology*, and various 'generous incognitos.' And she still received the allowances from the Duchess of Devonshire and her son, Harry Calcraft. But she never seemed to be able to get her finances on an even keel, and her continual demands must have made her a nuisance to her friends.

And yet, even during this sordid period of her life, she must have retained something of her old charm, for she never seems to have become entirely friendless and forsaken. Tate Wilkinson, for instance, though he had no illusions whatever about her character, remained always her faithful friend. His assistance to her usually took the judicious form of gifts in kind; after all, it is not so easy to squander a ham as a bank-bill, and at least she would not starve. Her letters to him are the only evidence of what was happening to her in these last years. They make very sad reading. On May 4th, 1786, she informed him that she had parted with her last guinea and even her necessaries, and had anticipated her son's and the Duchess of Devonshire's allowances up to Michaelmas quarter in a vain attempt to avert her "present unpleasing residence". She was then living in Eliot's Row, St. George's Fields, once again within the rules of the King's Bench Prison.

In her description of her surroundings, there is even now a gleam of her old sense of humour. "The impositions are incredible, as the people live by the distresses of others. I am obliged to give sixteen shillings a week for an apartment—a chandler's shop in front, backward a carpenter's; and what with the sawing of boards, the screaming of three ill-natured brats, the sweet voice of the lady of the mansion, who is particularly vociferous with all the gossips who owe her a penny, with a coffee-mill which is often in use, and is as noisy as London-bridge when the tide is coming in, makes such unpleasing sounds, it is impossible to think of any thing; added to this, I have no place for a servant."

Conditions such as these made it impossible for her to work on the book she had just begun, *The Characters of My Own Times*; but if she could only obtain quiet, she would be tolerably easy. If she could only raise sufficient money to furnish an apartment of her own and could borrow thirty or forty pounds a year, she could with certainty repay it, as she was determined to receive no visits and live as frugally as possible. "Indeed for want of exercise I have no appetite, and am reduced to one old cotton gown. Oh, what a falling off is there! But I regret it less as I cannot stir alone without difficulty."

Wilkinson wondered, not for the first time, that she could have contrived to get herself into such appalling difficulties. "How can you ask me how I came to be involved?" she wrote to him plaintively on May 13th, "I told you I paid part of my old debts and renewed securities for the remainder." She had in fact paid out to her creditors all that she had received, and had now been obliged to anticipate her annuity till Christmas, since she had to pay for everything in advance in her present quarters. He had suggested that she should change her lodgings, but this was impossible. "I cannot, without furniture, for the place is over-stocked, and I pay sixteen shillings a week for a dog-kennel and have not even a bed for my maid." She added that she was as lame as ever, and, as the bone could never be set, she would never be able to walk without assistance. In this, and in her succeeding letter of August 11th, she still harped on her craving for a house or apartment of her own, where she could enjoy quiet, which was impossible in her present residence. But nothing but dis-appointment and vexation attended her.

Her last letter, which bears no address, is dated September 23rd. The year is not stated, but from what Wilkinson says it must be 1787. Her replies to his reproaches about her improvidence no longer sound an indignant note. As usual, she had expected to be in a position to pay off all her debts and had indiscreetly not only paid away every guinea she had received from a generous public, but had also given fresh securities. "You need not enforce my error," she wrote contritely, "I am too sensible of it. . . . What I shall do now is a matter of great vexation. But God's Will be done."

A few months after he had received this pathetic letter, says Wilkinson, "the good-natured and unthinking Bellamy, by her death, paid all her debts. I hope she is happy, as she endeavoured to promote to the comforts of others, and never employed either riches or talents, when in affluence and splendour, to render any one miserable." That, surely, is no mean epitaph, written, as it was, by a man who could also call her the "unthinking, pompous, vain, and foolish Bellamy", and who did not extenuate her many faults, but admitted that it was her errors, not fate, that brought on her miseries and dreadful end. He reveals that she ended her days in a prison, but does not say whether she died within the confines of the prison itself or in one or another of the wretched lodgings within the rules in which she had spent the last few sad years of her life. She died on February 16th, 1788.

George Anne Bellamy's morals were, admittedly, not above reproach. But though she loved admiration, she was never promiscuous. Her associations with all three of her lovers verged on the respectable; there would have been much less scandal if they had not, and it was hardly her fault that none of them became so. She would gladly and gratefully have married Metham, Calcraft, or Digges. The blame lay rather with them. There was nothing she would have liked better than to become a respectable married woman; it was always her ambition to achieve a position in society which she could scarcely hope to reach and never to retain unless she did marry.

Hers was a generous heart. She expected much of life, but she gave much, too. John Calcraft was right when he said that she simply did not know the value of money. She did not even know the true meaning of it. To her it was something you inherited, earned, were given, or borrowed, and you, in turn, spent it, lent it, or gave it away. That you could keep it, save it, or invest it, except in jewellery or plate, never occurred to her. Her generosity was lavish, but entirely impulsive and un-discriminating: impulsive, because she gave immediately to anyone who aroused her sympathy or sought her help, taking no account of other circumstances, forgetting often that what she gave so blithely was not morally her own when she was so encumbered with debt herself; undiscriminating, because she trusted everybody, even when they had proved themselves untrustworthy. Worst of all, she trusted herself—and time after time she let herself down.

Her generosity appeared, too, in her praise of other members of her profession. Her *Apology* is full of graceful tributes to the acting of others, even actresses who played the same parts as herself. She may have envied the superior talents of her great rival, Mrs. Cibber, but it was a frank, admiring envy that acknowledged her supremacy, and she lost no opportunity of praising her. She loved Mrs. Cibber, but she also extolled the beauty and the acting ability of Peg Woffington, whom she loathed. It is true, of course, that no excess of modesty ever prevented her from according a liberal meed of admiration to herself.

Mrs. Bellamy was a talented, but not a really great actress. Had she possessed greater gifts, her acting career would have been longer. But she was an actress and not merely a beauty on the stage. Francis Gentleman and other observers of the time always gave serious consideration to her acting and found much to praise in it, quite apart from her looks, and it is not to be thought that she depended upon them alone. Her creation of the part of Cleone, for instance, was a triumph of interpretation, a true actress's triumph. Nevertheless, it must be conceded that the irresistible charm of her appearance in her early youth did form too great an element in her acting equipment, and, when she lost her looks, she lost much of her appeal.

The effect of that appeal can best be gathered from the tribute paid to her Juliet and her Cordelia by 'Sir' John Hill in the chapter entitled "Of an amorous disposition, and its advantage to certain players" in his book, *The Actor, or, a Treatise of the Art of Playing*, published in 1755, when she was at the height of her fame, and her performances with Garrick at Drury Lane were still fresh in the memory. "A thousand," he says, "may rant a Statira, or rave a Hermione, or weep a Belvidera, for one who can sigh a Juliet." And he attributes George Anne Bellamy's touching performance of Juliet to her amorous disposition. He maintains that "illusion can never be well kept up in a love scene unless the persons who perform the characters have hearts naturally susceptible of the passion" and that "only certain persons of those who are qualified for the stage are fit to act love parts; and these can only do it at a certain age. The bloom of youth is required in the woman who is to be courted." According to him, her success as Cordelia was due to the same cause. "In Cordelia we admire Miss Bellamy vastly more than in other characters. People who spoke of her in Cordelia, to those who had only seen her in others, were supposed to go much too far in their praises. It was to the same natural tenderness of heart that she owed this peculiar excellence."

Surely, it was not quite so simple as that. George Anne Bellamy, through her natural tenderness of heart, may indeed have felt her parts deeply, but she had to convince her audience too that those amorous raptures of hers were genuine and heartfelt. Besides the obvious appeal of youth and beauty, she must have possessed some conscious, if indefinable, quality that enabled her to transmit to others the sincerity of her feeling, for there was a grace and an ecstasy in her acting that affected her audiences profoundly, captured their imaginations, and drew them under the spell of her enchantment.

Brief Bibliography

So many sources have been used that I have listed below only those books which I have consulted extensively or which contain facts that are not to be found elsewhere. C.H.H.

An Apology for the Life of George Anne Bellamy, late of Covent Garden Theatre. Written by herself. 6 vols., 1785.

Mémoires de Mistress Bellamy. Edited by Thiers. 1822.

Anon. *Memoirs of George Anne Bellamy, including all her intrigues, with genuine Anecdotes of all her public and private connections. By a Gentleman of Covent Garden Theatre.* 1785.

Barton, Margaret. *Garrick,* 1948.

Boswell, James. *London Journal.* 1950.

Burr, T. B. *A History of Tunbridge Wells.* 1766.

Calcraft, John. *Letter Books.* (MSS. preserved at Rempstone, Dorset.)

Chetwood, W. R. *A General History of the Stage (more particularly the Irish Theatre),* etc. 1749.

Commons Journals. (Tyrawley).

Dibdin, James C. *Annals of the Edinburgh Stage.* 1888.

Doran, John. *Their Majesties' Servants.* 1888.

Dugdale, W. *Visitation of Yorkshire.* (Metham family).

Eyre-Todd, G. *History of Glasgow.*

Fitzgerald, Percy. *Lives of the Sheridans.* 1886.

Fitzgerald, Percy. *Life of David Garrick.* 1899.

Genest, J. *Some Account of the English Stage,* etc. 1832.

Gentleman, Francis. *The Dramatic Censor.* 1770.

Gentleman's Magazine.

Ghosh, J. C. *Otway's Works.* 1932.

Hall, J. G. *History of South Cave.* 1892. (Metham).

Hill, John. *The Actor, or a Treatise of the Art of Playing.* 1755.

Ilchester, Earl of. *Henry Fox, first Lord Holland.* 1920.

Knight, Joseph. *David Garrick.* 1894.

Lawson, Robb. *The Story of the Scots Stage.* 1917.

London Magazine.

Lucey, Janet Camden. *Lovely Peggy, the Life and Times of Margaret Woffington.* 1952.

Molloy, J. Fitzgerald. *The Life and Adventures of Peg Woffington.* 1887.

Molloy, J. Fitzgerald. *History of the Irish Stage.* 1897.

Parry, Edward Abbott. *Charles Macklin.* 1891.

Rae, W. Fraser. *Sheridan.* 1896.

Reynolds, Frederick. *Life and Times.* 1826.

Riker, T. W. *Henry Fox, first Lord Holland.* 1911.

Scots Magazine.

Taylor, Aline Mackenzie. *Next to Shakespeare.* 1950.

Town and Country Magazine.

Transactions of the East Riding Antiquarian Society, Vol. XVI. (Metham).

Victor, Benjamin. *The History of the Theatres of London and Dublin from the year* 1730 *to the present time.* 1761.

Victor, Benjamin. *The History of the Theatres of London from the year* 1760 *to the present time.* 1771.

Walpole, Horace. *Letters.*

Walpole, Horace. *Memoirs of the Reign of George II.*

Ward, Bernard. *Catholic London a Century Ago.* 1905.

Wilkinson, Tate. *Memoirs of his Own Life by Tate Wilkinson, patentee of the Theatres-Royal, York and Hull,* and *The Tablet,* 4 Vols. 1790.

Wilkinson, Tate. *The Wandering Patentee,* 4 Vols. 1795.

Wyndham, Henry Saxe. *Annals of Covent Garden Theatre.*

INDEX OF PLAYS AND PARTS

The titles of plays are printed in italics. All parts played by Mrs. Bellamy during the course of her career are marked with an asterisk.

323

GENERAL INDEX

Willis, 179
Windsor, 177–78
Woffington, Peg, 17–18, 29, 56, 78–81,
83–84, 88, 94–98, 100, 104–8, 120,
156–58, 163–66, 182, 250, 319
Woffington, Polly, 18
Woodifield, wine-merchant, 259
Woodward, Henry, 70–71, 121, 197,
201, 205–6, 247–49, 252–54, 258–59,
264, 270–77, 279–81, 288–93, 295–
96, 303, 314–15
Woodward, John, 288, 290–91, 296,
312
Wordley, Mary, 227–28, 231, 237,
240–42, 244, 248, 251–54, 292

Wycherley, William, 26
Wynn, Sir Watkin Williams, 272

YATES, MRS. MARY ANN, 260, 262–63,
267–70, 300, 310
York, 101–2, 104, 235, 240–41, 252
Yorkshire, 34–35, 101–2, 108–9, 117,
131, 148, 191, 239–40
York Street, 220
Yorke, Charles, 177, 253–54
Yorke, John, 158
Yorke, Mary, 158
Young, Dr. Edward, 83, 125, 134–
36
Younger, Mr., 255